I Always Faint
When I See a Syringe

or

Nurse Student Tales

by

Florence Hardesty, RN, PhD

Janie,

Enjoy,

Florence Hardesty

Silver Tree Books   Silverton, Oregon

OWA '97

Silver Tree Books

Box 707

Silverton, OR 97381

©1996 by Florence Hardesty

Library of Congress Catalog Card Number 95-92850

ISBN 0-9631769-1-9

Cover and illustrations by Sheila Somerville

Book layout and design by DIMI PRESS

Reviews

"*I always faint when I see a syringe* is a warm hearted look at the nursing profession. Hardesty's book captures the humor and poignancy of nursing."

Nancy Jeffries, Senior Editor,
National League for Nursing Press.

"Humor, insight and stories about real people fill the pages of this book. The reader is taken behind the scenes and introduced to a range of people and themes. The stories are woven together by the author's journey through life. Anyone associated with health care will find this book entertaining; they will also find stories that remind them of their own experiences. People not part of the health care workforce will also enjoy this book because it is a tale about very interesting people. I highly recommend it for your 'fun' reading time."

Carol Lindeman, RN, PhD, FAAN
Former Dean, School of Nursing,
Oregon Health Sciences University

"Thank you for the opportunity to review your manuscript. I think every nurse, nursing student and faculty member will see themselves in your stories. Florence, your story deserves to be told."

Fran Hicks, RN, PhD, Professor,
University of Portland School of
Nursing, President, American Nurses
Foundation.

Contents

Saint What's-His-Name, 1962-1964

Western Reserve University, 1964-1966

The Community College, 1966-1969

Kent State University, 1969-1971

The Women's College, 1971-1976

The University, 1976-Present

Introduction and Dedication

This book is about the nursing students I knew during the twenty-six years I was their teacher. It is also about my own teachers, those I met as a mature returning student. The technical aspects of nursing are difficult to learn. The emotional demands are harder. However, in the midst of the pain, death and suffering, one finds courage, camaraderie, humor and hope. Nursing offers many rewards. The opportunity to be close to people and help them at crucial points in their lives is one. I have tried to capture some of those moments in this book.

The book is dedicated to the thousands of nursing students I taught and to the brave patients who allowed my students to learn while giving them care. It is also dedicated to my colleagues, who supported me and taught me the techniques and the art of teaching. Finally, it is dedicated to my own teachers, who taught me as much as our time together allowed and encouraged me to go beyond them.

It is impossible to name everyone. I will name a few in no particular order: Dr. May Wykle; Dr. Mary Kay King; Dr. Helen Burnside; Dr. Fran Hicks; Dr. Carol Lindeman; Francise Bowman RN, MEd; Kay Oliver RN MN; Dan

Kamada RN. MN; Marie Kamada MN; Elizabeth Warner RN MSN; Kay Tanaka RN;MN; Moynell Kilgannon-Schmidt RN BS; Sharon Espersen RN MN; Dr. Lawrence Litwack; Dr. Faye Spring and Dorothy Gregg RN MN.

I wish to express my gratitude to the schools that have shaped me. My basic nursing education occurred at the Hospital of the University of Pennsylvania's diploma nursing school. I was a member of the United States Cadet Nurse Corps which supported that part of my education. The faculty of the Frances Payne Bolton School of Nursing at Western Reserve University (now Case Western Reserve University) never blinked when I, a divorced woman in her early thirties with two small children to support, announced that I hoped one day to have a doctorate and teach nursing. Instead they gave me a full scholarship for my bachelor's degree and helped me obtain a National Institute of Mental Health scholarship for my Master's. Kent State University gave me a scholarship and helped me obtain another NIMH traineeship to complete a PhD. I am profoundly grateful to these schools and to our government who recognized the need for better educated nurses.

A special dedication is reserved to the memory of Dr. Joanne Orr Hall, a wise and compassionate friend who helped me through some dark moments.

Nancy Jeffery, Senior Editor of the National League for Nursing Press, encouraged me to continue efforts to publish this book when I was most discouraged. Thank you.

Sharon Elaine Thompson and Cindy Wall edited the book. Sheila Somerville drew the illustrations. Their help was gratefully accepted.

I also dedicate this book to my daughters, Susan Irvine RN BSN, who joined my profession, and Shevawn

Hardesty, who decided we needed some business sense in the family and became an accountant. (She was right.) My husband, Verl Holden, has supported my writing and is my most ardent fan.

Thank you all. You have given my life purpose and meaning—and given me a lifetime of amusing and inspiring stories.

Saint-What's-His-Name

1962-1964

Chapter 1

"I always faint...."

I was thrilled to finally be a nursing instructor. I had been a diploma nurse for fifteen years and had gone back to school to obtain a degree, a Bachelor of Science in Nursing. Now armed with my new diploma, my cap stiff—its starched peak lined up with my nose, and my shoes polished, I was realizing my dream.

I vowed to be a reasonable, understanding teacher. I had made that vow eighteen years before when, as a Probie (first year probationary student), my instructors performed such silly tasks as checking to see that we slim seventeen-year-olds wore girdles. I hadn't protested then. I knew better than to jeopardize my opportunity to be a nurse, but I had promised myself, that someday I would teach nursing and it would be different.

My title was Assistant Instructor of Fundamentals of Nursing. I was teaching the most basic skills that every nurse needs to know. The laboratory for this endeavor was a hospital ward, and the students learned by practicing their skills on willing and very brave patients, while I stood by observing, coaching and occasionally rescuing one of the participants.

My goal was to teach mental health nursing, but this job had been available, in a three-year hospital school that we will call Saint What's-His-Name* and I needed a paycheck. The University had been very generous in awarding me scholarship money, and my mother had paid the bills and helped with the children. But now I needed to return to work and support myself and my daughters.

In the 1960s there were more diploma schools in hospitals, and they were willing to hire experienced nurses with bachelor's degrees as clinical instructors.

Saint What's-His-Name was a respected hospital and nursing school. The nursing students were young, middle-class-women whose parents had selected this school for their daughters rather than a university school. The expenses for both kinds of nursing education were similar. Perhaps these parents did not want their daughters to be exposed to the attitudes that prevailed in colleges and universities during the sixties. Saint WHN's had fewer archaic practices than the school I had attended eighteen years before, but there were rules that college students of that era would have protested. I kept my more liberal opinions to myself, and resolved to learn what I could about teaching, earn a salary and as soon as possible, go on to graduate school and a job where the prevailing attitudes were similar to mine. I suspect that most of the students had similar plans.

When I began the teaching at Saint What's-His-Name myself the students had already learned how to make beds, give baths, bandage limbs and give enemas. It was time for them to learn how to give medicines, and that included injections.

The students were thrilled with the prospect of gaining this skill. To be able to give a shot would mean that

---

*Asterisks indicate that these are not the real names.

they were really nurses, instead of inept students. We instructors had far different ideas about the definition of nursing but the students were too inexperienced to know that. They had studied the procedure in class, practiced filling and manipulating syringes and even thrusting the needle through the skin of compliant oranges. Now all they had to do was stick a needle in a live human being.

Somewhere in the dark recesses of my memory was the image of myself, a terrified seventeen-year-old, injecting a drug into the arm of an unconscious woman while my instructor stood by murmuring encouragement. But there had been so many subcutaneous and intramuscular injections since. In the late forties and early fifties, penicillin—the wonder drug—was mixed with distilled water and given every three hours. Almost every patient received this drug. I had spent several years as the penicillin, temperature and blood pressure nurse on a seventy-bed ward. I was so skilled at giving shots that later, when I worked in a doctor's office, the patients requested that I be the one to administer injections. I tried to remember that what was now as easy for me as breathing was very difficult for my students.

I carefully selected the patients to whom my students would give their first shots. To begin with, the injection had to be a simple one that didn't burn when injected. It also needed to be a drug that could be drawn into the syringe easily—none of this thick stuff that had to be forced through the needle. Unfortunately for us, there were no unconscious patients on this floor. (They would be almost as compliant as the orange.) I preferred men, who couldn't protest without damaging their masculinity; patients who had enough muscle or fat so there would be no danger of hitting the bone; and persons who received intramuscular injections in their buttocks. These last, because they lay on their abdomen, and couldn't see the terrified face of their student nurse.

The first nine students managed, with support, a few tears and sometimes a hand from their instructor (literally), to give their first shot. The tenth student was a tall red-headed girl (Sorry, fellow feminists. Then we called them girls.) who I will call Miss Faintheart*. She had been sick the first week of this experience and had not yet mastered the procedure. It was Monday morning and I had picked out her patient, a nice young man in his early twenties, well-muscled and willing, who was to receive an injection of penicillin.

When she filled the syringe, I noticed that Miss Faintheart's hands were trembling, but that was not un-usual. She placed the syringe on a small tray and we went into the patient's room.

"Mr. Brave," said my student, "I have an injection for you." She checked the card on the bed and the patient's wrist band. It was Mr. Brave. "Turn over, please. This shot will go in to your buttocks." By this time Mr. Brave was accustomed to baring his buttocks and Miss Faintheart had seen dozens. He flopped over and she carefully fan-folded the covers to expose just one cheek.

She cleansed the upper-outer quarter of his buttocks with alcohol, just as the books described. An injection at this site would avoid the large blood vessels and nerves we have in our seats. I was pleased with Miss Faintheart's performance.

She picked up the syringe. "Mr. Brave, there will be just a little stick." She held the syringe, drew back her right hand to aim it at the insertion point, while holding the skin taut with her left—and froze.

At first I tried to give her rigid hand a little push. It was like a rock. "Here, let me do it," I whispered. She didn't move. Mr. Brave lifted and turned his head. "It will be over in a second," I said.

I pried Miss Faintheart's fingers off the syringe, aimed it like a dart and gave the injection. "There. No more shots until tomorrow," I announced as I pulled his covers up. "Do you need anything before we go?"

He didn't. He was just glad to see us leave.

Out in the hall, I turned my attention to Miss Faintheart.

Her face was absolutely white and bathed in sweat. The back of her uniform was wet with perspiration and her eyes were glazed. I grabbed the empty wheelchair that was standing nearby, shoved my student into it, and forced her head between her knees. When I touched her skin it was like ice. Her pulse was weak.

In a few minutes she sat up and leaned back. Her color had returned to normal. She gasped, "I always faint when I see a syringe."

Student nurses are resilient. In half an hour she was ready to join me in the conference room to talk about our problem.

"Ever since I was a little girl, I always fainted when I saw the syringe the doctor was going to use on me. But I want to be a nurse so bad. My grades are good and the patients like me. Will I ever be able to give a shot?" Then she burst into tears.

I was sympathetic. After all, my daughter Susan had a problem with shots. And my brother, the soldier, always fainted when he saw his own blood. I held her hand until her sobbing ceased.

"You will give a shot," I announced with more confidence than I felt. "You didn't faint this time. You did everything but stick the needle in. Now this is my plan. Every morning I will be here at eight with a patient picked out for you. Each day we will go in with the medication. If you can't push the needle in, I will. We'll do this until you do it. The other students will come at eight-thirty, and we will have finished by then. No one needs to know you've had problems unless you choose to tell them."

"Oh, thank you, Mrs. Hardesty. Do you really think I can do it?"

"I know you can. It doesn't matter how long it takes, it will be done." I was thinking, I hope Mr. Brave doesn't talk. And I hope I can find a patient every day.

We followed the plan. Each day her terror was a little less than the day before. On Friday, a shaking Miss Faintheart, eyes tightly shut and mouth grim, pushed a needle through the skin of an elderly Hungarian lady who graciously said, "You done good, Dear."

The next week Miss Faintheart repeated the procedure with no apparent emotion. And one relieved instructor took a break and bought a candy bar to celebrate.

Chapter 2
Miss Know-it-all

After the students had mastered giving medicines to one patient, they were required to give them to a group of patients. (A group was defined as two or three patients and was far different than what a medication nurse did. She gave medicines to all the patients on the ward.)

However, administering medications to even such a small group as we required of the students was quite a task. The day before they were to do this, they learned which patients would receive their ministrations and took notes from the chart and the doctor's order sheet. That evening they consulted their text books and reference books to learn all they could about the patient's diagnosis and the medicines that had been prescribed. The following morning, their heads full of effects, side effects, interactions and physiology, they again checked the doctor's order sheet. For a nurse, giving medications is not the same as popping a few aspirin into your mouth and washing them down with water. It was a ritual. It was my job to make sure that they had done their homework and that the procedure was properly performed.

One of the first students I supervised in this task was Miss Know-it-all*. She had been a candy striper in a small hospital and was more self assured that most of the students. In fact, it was my distinct impression that Miss KIA thought she knew more than her new instructor. She bustled around the ward and was not above supervising her more timid classmates. Her cap seemed bigger and her apron more starched than those of her peers. I was rather gentle with her, knowing that when she failed to live up to her exalted opinion of herself—and it would surely happen—she would have a difficult time.

Her patients were roommates. Mr. Brown had cardiac problems and Mr. Smith had knee surgery. Miss KIA had studied the pharmacology book thoroughly and was well prepared for the task. She unlocked the medicine closet and spread the medicine cards on the tray. She reached for the medicine bottles, one at time, carefully reading the cards and the labels three times, as she opened each bottle and poured out the prescribed number of pills, without touching the medication. I stood at her elbow, checking each step. Miss KIA was certainly efficient.

Then she locked the cupboard, returned the keys to the staff nurse and bustled down the hall to her patients' room while I hurried behind. She went into the room and approached Mr. Smith's bed. "Mr. Smith?"

"Yes," he replied. She then checked his wrist band and the sign on his bed. This was indeed Mr. Smith.

"I have your medicines for you." She poured water into his glass and handed it to him. She then reached down and picked up the paper cup from the tray and handed him the pills. He tossed them into his mouth and swallowed.

At her elbow, I sputtered, "Wait! Stop!"

It was too late. Mr. Smith had swallowed Mr. Brown's pills. Miss KIA and I had committed a serious error; we had given the wrong medication.

My student looked at me as though I were insane. After all there was nothing wrong with her procedure.

"Please come out into the hall," I said and we moved out of the room. "Now, look at your tray."

Miss Know-it-all studied the tray and then crumbled before my eyes. The starch left her uniform. She was suddenly a frightened eighteen-year-old girl dressed like a nurse. "I gave the wrong medication!"

"Yes. Thank heavens, it was only vitamins." Thank God, the staff nurse had given Mr. Brown his digitalis earlier. "Mr. Smith isn't harmed. But we have problems."

The 'we' was not just a figure of speech. I was in trouble too. We reported the error to the head nurse, nursing supervisor and doctor. Then we made out twin accident reports in triplicate, one of which would be placed in each of our files.

Miss Know-it-all became Miss Careful. And Mrs. Hardesty, the new instructor, learned that teaching the fundamentals of nursing is a very tough job.

Chapter 3
Miss Fumblefingers

C atheterizing a female patient is difficult. Now it is done as little as possible because of the possibility of introducing infection. In the forties and fifties the procedure was done very often. Post operative patients were kept in bed longer and could not urinate in that position. Also the doctors thought it was necessary to catheterize the patient in order to do certain diagnostic tests. Even in the 1960s it was still done often and most students had the opportunity to perform this task.

What makes this procedure difficult is the problem of finding the meatus, the opening through which the urine emerges and into which the catheter must be inserted. It is ususaly hidden in some fold or crevice of a woman's external genitalia. By the time I had arrived at St. WHN's, I had done hundreds and had great respect for the diversity of female anatomy.

Miss Fumblefingers* was a very self-assured student. She must have been a first cousin of Miss Know-it-all. She had spent her summers in high school working in a nursing home and had already mastered many of the skills I was teaching. When the chance to do a catheterization came up, I selected her, feeling that she, of all the students was most likely to do well.

I always felt sorry for the women who had to be catheterized. It is embarrassing to spread your legs and have another woman peer intently at a portion of your anatomy that you can't even see very well yourself. In the physician's office, the doctor glances at one's bottom and then feels it and the abdomen while talking about the weather or stock prices. When one is catheterized, there is always a bright light, and lots of looking.

Miss Fumblefingers was delighted to have the chance to catheterize a patient. She reviewed the procedure in the procedure book while I went in to prepare the patient. The woman had had abdominal surgery the day before and since then every method had been used to help her urinate. Nothing had worked and she had been catheterized during the night, twelve hours before. Now her bladder was full and she was anxious for relief. No, she didn't mind a student doing it, just empty the darn thing. She drifted back into a morphine-induced sleep and I went to get Miss Fumblefingers.

I introduced the student and we drew the curtains. We placed a bath blanket over the woman and folded the covers neatly to the bottom of the bed, tucking the blanket around her legs so that only the perineum was exposed. I positioned a goose neck lamp so it shown directly on her perineum. The student went to the sink and scrubbed her hands. Then she opened the sterile tray and donned the sterile rubber gloves.

She cleansed the area, first with sterile green soap and then with sterile water. I whispered for her to look carefully as she did this. Sometimes a bubble appears and gives you a clue about the site of the meatus. She shook off my suggestion. She was a very confident girl.

There were three catheters on the tray, concrete evidence that this often takes more than one try. She picked up one and poked. "It is supposed to be there. My anatomy book showed it very clearly."

"Yes, but everyone is different. Please be gentle." My fingers actually itched. I wanted to get this over with and let our patient sleep. "There, in that fold."

The student picked up another catheter and tried again in the same place.

"Here," I hissed, "as soon as I get on these gloves, I'll do it."

She thought I was trying to help her. "I want to do it, Mrs. Hardesty." She picked up the last catheter and poked again, to no avail. "I'll get another tray." She disappeared behind the curtain.

I moved to the head of the bed. "Are you all right, Mrs. Patience? We are having a little trouble finding the opening."

"I'm fine. I'll be so glad when I can pee again. That student's a nice kid. I don't mind."

Miss Fumblefingers had returned with another tray. We repeated the procedure. On the third try, she found the opening. Urine began to pour into the waiting pan. "I got it," my student announced gleefully. She let go of the catheter and it came out.

I went to the utility room and got another tray. I scrubbed my hands, put on the gloves and catheterized the patient. Then I removed the equipment, gave her a back rub and settled her comfortably in bed.

Miss Fumblefingers was at the desk telling her classmates that she had successfully catheterized a patient when I came out. She had charted the procedure and was waiting for me to tell her the amount of urine.

My day was over. I went to the office of the head instructor for Fundamentals. Miss Jones was about my age, a very sweet, patient lady who *just loved* beginning students.

"Barbara, I am just not patient enough to teach these students. They are lovely young women, and so eager to learn, but I can hardly bear their ineptness."

"It is tough sometimes. But I have good news for you. The director has just decided that the psych instructor can't handle all twenty students by herself. She asked me to see if you'd like to become her assistant."

I answered, "Yes!" so fast it startled her.

One addendum: Four years later my mother was a patient on the floor where I had taught Fundamentals. When I visited, I found that Miss Fumblefingers was the head nurse. In fact I must change her name to Miss Super-efficient. She was glad to see me and we chatted a while. I mentioned, somewhat obliquely, the she had come a long way since that first catheterization. She had absolutely no memory of the happening. I thought it was amazing that the event that driven me from teaching beginning students was so insignificant to her that she didn't remember.

It makes me wonder, what have I forgotten?

Chapter 4
Sometimes You Have to Teach the Teacher

The day after the conversation with the Fundamentals Instructor, I became the Assistant Psychiatric Nursing Instructor. The school had been sending their senior students to the state hospital for the required psychiatric nursing experience. However, the hospital had recently opened a small psychiatric ward and the school's director decided to use that, instead, to educate Saint WHN students.

The school had hired one of its own graduates, Joan Venable, as the instructor. She had no psychiatric nursing experience beyond what she had gotten in her own basic education, but she did have a BA in psychology and administrative experience at Saint WHN. I had worked at a university hospital's psychiatric unit for two years and been exposed to all the educational opportunities of a teaching hospital. Neither of us had had courses in education. In terms of National League for Nursing accreditation criteria, we were a sorry pair.

In addition to having educational deficits, we had problems. The psychiatric floor had twenty beds and we had almost twenty students. How could we teach so many students on such a small unit without driving the patients and the staff wild? Through my contacts with other nurses in the city, I was aware that the other psychiatric nursing teachers were watching our dilemma with amusement. Their opinion was that it couldn't be done.

We divided the students into two groups and each group had four hours of clinical experience a day, assigned to one patient. We emphasized that they were to be sensitive to the fact that they might be overloading the patients, and we gave them permission to go to the library to study, attend conferences or, if it were permitted and appropriate, take their patients away from the unit. Each patient had only one student nurse.

Joan handled the administrative details of teaching and prepared and gave the lectures. The first time she taught the course, she didn't sleep the night before the lecture but spent the night studying and organizing her notes. I taught the practical clinical portion of the course and was on the ward with the students. I also conducted the daily clinical conferences.

We two novices were too inexperienced to know that it couldn't be done. We did it. When the first group of students finished the course we gave the National League for Nursing standardized test in psychiatric nursing. The mean percentile rank for our first group of students was 97. Joan and I were never again able to equal that. Even with all my later education and experience, my students never made a higher score on that test.

When I began teaching on the ward, I made a decision, hardly consciously, that my focus would be on the students rather than on the patients. Even in my early student days, without the benefit of the techniques pioneered by Dr. Peplau and the other mental heath nursing leaders, patients confided in me and appreciated my interest and support. That is why I became a psychiatric nurse— I was good at it.

This was sometimes a problem. Outside the hospital people also told me their troubles. If I went to a party, the first person I encountered would take me off into the corner and tell me about his surgery or her marital problems. If I am not careful, even now, flight attendants, sales people, and waiters, pour out their lives to me.

With all the people the patients were being exposed to, I felt it was best to let the student be the therapeutic and understanding person. I would pass by and see what was happening, but make an effort not to get into a therapeutic mode. In fact, I would adopt a manner that discouraged confidences.

About a week after the first class began, one of the students came to me and asked to speak in confidence. Her patient was a depressed woman in her thirties, as was the woman who shared her room.

Miss Helpful* (the name fits) told me that both women "couldn't stand that flighty superficial instructor." I knew immediately that I had made an error in judgement. I was heartsick about it and so very grateful that the student had had the courage to give me this feedback . I was also terribly embarrassed.

How could I have been so wrong? I was the teacher. I needed to show the students how to be with the patients. We didn't use the term *role model* in 1962; at least I don't remember it, but that was exactly what I needed to be.

I changed my approach that day. When I made rounds, I focused on the patients and used all my therapeutic skills. The students watched and learned. When I needed to leave, I urged the patients to continue the process with their students.

Two days later, Miss Helpful happily reported that the same patients decided that they had made a mistake in their initial evaluation of me.

I don't remember Miss Helpful's real name but I always will be grateful for the lesson she gave me. Since then I have tried to remain open and non-defensive when students give me feedback. I have had students be totally wrong in their perception of my teaching and a few who have been hateful. But if I didn't listen and consider, I might miss feedback as helpful as this student had offered me.

Chapter 5
Anxiety Plus

The psychiatric ward at Saint What's-His-Name was on the seventh floor of the hospital. There were windows on three sides and patients called it the penthouse. It had been open only a few months when the students and I arrived. All of the patients were private patients of the medical staff. For the most part, they were middle-class depressed people. Occasionally, adding a little spice to our days, there was a hyperactive patient with manic-depressive psychosis. We always had one or two people who were diagnosed with schizophrenia, whose psychosis was quickly controlled with antipsychotic drugs. The doctors who had medical patients who suddenly became psychotic, were happy to be able to transfer them to the psychiatric ward until they were stabilized.

Carol, the head nurse, was an experienced psychiatric nurse who did her job well. The patients received thoughtful, compassionate care, and the administrative aspects of the ward were handled smoothly. The physicians were glad to have a pleasant, protected environment for their patients and were pleased to have student nurses to give the patients support. The students and I were welcomed.

It was an ideal place to teach general nursing students the basics of psychiatric nursing. All state boards of nursing require that students have a psychiatric nursing course during their basic education. Few become psychiatric nurses, but all nurses need to recognize when their patients are experiencing a psychosis. They need to describe and document the symptoms so that an accurate diagnosis can be made. They also need to know how to handle a psychotic patient, often on general hospital ward. Interpersonal skills are important if nurses are to help patients identify feelings and solve the emotional problems associated with illness. It is difficult for students to focus on the emotional aspects of their patient's illness when the students are distracted by blood transfusions and oxygen equipment. On this ward there was the time and freedom to learn the skills so well that they would be practiced automatically in other settings.

The senior students that I was now teaching were far different from the frightened first-year students I had left behind. These women had learned the fundamentals of nursing and practiced them on every ward of the hospital. They had helped deliver babies, cared for tiny premature infants, stood by holding the hands of dying patients and then helped families with their grief. In the intensive care units they had mastered the complicated machinery we use to keep people alive. They were confident, intelligent and very interested in their patients.

I soon was having a wonderful time, sharing all I had learned with these young women, and improving my own skills as I read and learned with them.

But there were problems. At times in faculty meetings and in the school's lounge and office, I felt as though I was walking on eggs. The school at Saint WHN had vestiges of the military and religious orders in which nursing originated. It was more than a institution that taught young women to be nurses— it was also a finishing school.

In my own basic nursing program, I had been required to know how to dance, swim and play bridge because, to quote the director, "One is socially inept if one does not do these things." Students in my class were not permitted to marry. Then the son of the chief of staff, a doctor himself, insisted on marrying his nurse student sweetheart before he left for the Army and World War II—and the rule was changed. Now, almost twenty years later, I was back in a setting where a student was judged not only by her professional activities but by her personal life.

I had close friends among the faculty, many of whom also disagreed with the finishing school aspects of the school. But there was no rebellion. We were under-educated for the jobs we were doing and the leadership of the school was strong. We knew that if we objected to the rules, we would have to leave. I enjoyed the students and was developing as a teacher. I worked eight hours a day, during daylight hours and had weekends free. Staff nursing jobs would require that I work evenings, nights and holidays. I had done that for many years and knew how difficult it was to raise children and find baby sitters when you were forced to work three different shifts during one week.

So I wasn't about to leave. However, my Irish and Scotch-Irish ancestors had instilled in me the belief that when one saw an injustice, one protested. It always seemed strange to me that my dour farmer grandfather, who wouldn't drink or play cards, would defend the right of others to do just that. His best friend, who was cut from the same cloth, sued a school in the early 1920s because they fired his teacher daughter for "bobbing her hair". My other grandfather, an Irish miner, was an early union organizer. I had been raised listening to family myths, in which the heroine or hero defended his own or someone else's freedom. At faculty meetings I found myself biting my tongue shaping my responses in forms palatable to the leaders. I was sure that my dead ancestors were spinning in their graves.

Two women in the first group of students we taught on the psychiatric floor were doing well with the formal class, but they had trouble relating to their patients. One, Mary Whitfield*, was a serious young woman with dark hair and a pale, anxious face. She turned in perfect papers in class, but on the ward and with her patient, a man with chronic paranoid schizophrenia, she looked almost as frightened as Miss Faintheart. During the daily group conference when the students discussed their patients and their care, she was silent. Besides that, she avoided me.

One day her patient was away from the unit, having some medical tests when she arrived. The other bed in the room was vacant. When Miss Whitfield came to the floor to begin her day, I followed her to her patient's room.

"Miss Whitfield, I need to talk with you," I began. I received the blank look that I had so often given my teachers. "You are doing very well in the classwork, but here on the floor you are so painfully anxious. What can I do to help?"

"I hate psychiatric nursing."

"Yes, I can see that. You don't have to like it, but you do have to get through it. After you graduate, you only have to come near a psychiatric patient long enough to refer him to someone else. But you are here now and you have two months left to go. For the past month, you've looked as though you would give anything to be anywhere else."

"I didn't know that it showed."

"Is there any patient on the ward that you feel you could work with?"

"Yes, that new one, the one with cancer who is so anxious."

Now this patient was an elderly woman, who was so anxious, that she had picked off one of her fingers. (Honest.) Anxiety communicates itself. For most of us this would be the most difficult patient on the floor. Yet the student preferred her to the shy, mildly delusional, middle-aged man to whom she was assigned.

"She will be a tough patient, but if you want to try, I'll assign you. Mr. Shy will be going home in a day or so. We can just tell him that we need you with the new patient." Frankly, I was sure Mr. Shy would be relieved.

"But won't he feel as though I am abandoning him?" Her eyes filled with tears. Something more was going on here.

"No, I don't think so. You can drop in and chat a bit with him. He has been busy with activities." We sat in silence for a while, a sure way to elicit confidences. "Miss Whitfield, I realize that you are reluctant to tell me what has been happening with you, but if you feel you can, I would like to help." More silence.

Finally she said, "My father has paranoid schizophrenia. He developed it when my mother was pregnant with me. He has been in the state hospital ever since. I wanted to be a nurse, but I've been dreading this part of the education every since I started."

"And as luck would have it, I assigned you to a man with the same diagnosis. You've had a terrible month. I'll do my best to help you finish out the term."

"O. K., but I don't want to talk about it. If I need to, I'll go to the psychiatrist in the health service."

"There's no need for you to tell me more unless you decide to. We will confine our discussion to what goes on between you and your patients."

She did finish, hating every minute. She bade Mr. Shy good-by when he was discharged, and gave loving thoughtful care to the anxious woman, making her last days more bearable. She ended the term with a B in the clinical portion of the class, still vowing that she would never work on a psychiatric floor.

Miss Whitfield graduated at the end of that year and began work on the medical floor. Her head nurse stopped me one day in the cafeteria to tell me how well she was doing. "Of all the new graduates I've ever had, she is the best with anxious patients. She is just great. You and Joan are doing a good job."

I thanked her. And spent the rest of the day thinking that every student has her own goals, and they aren't necessarily the same ones that the teacher has. It is nice when it turns out that both the student and teacher are satisfied.

Chapter 6
Anna Mae Kovach*

Anna Mae Kovach was the other student who did not do well on the psychiatric ward. It was almost as though she were behind a glass shield that separated her from the strong emotions her patients were feeling. She did well in class, came to the ward on time and left when required. She even talked a little in conference—about other students' patients. But there was no warmth, and only perfunctory interaction, between Anna Mae and her patient.

Anna Mae was a tall, attractive young woman with a thick mane of red hair. She was a few years older than her classmates. I learned from the other students that she had begun school at Saint WHN in a class that had already graduated. She had been on leave of absence for a year and had just returned.

With me, she was guarded. She was polite, noncommital and offered no information. The students and I had evolved a pattern of naming. When we were with patients, their families or doctors we were Miss Whatever and Mrs. Hardesty. But in the daily conferences or in the ward's office with the staff nurses we used first names. Miss Kovach always called me Mrs. Hardesty. She was cordial with her fellow students, but always left the ward alone, never in the chattering happy gang that crowded the elevator at the end of the day.

I tried all the techniques I knew to find out what the barriers were that locked her away from her patient. Joan was new and didn't know anything more than I did about the student. When I asked faculty who had had her as a student in the earlier courses, they seemed uncomfortable and offered nothing.

The end of the term came and I gave her a C, a passing grade, but for a senior nursing student, a partial failure. At our final conference when I gave her the evaluation, her eyes filled with tears but she made no objection. She made an A in the class work portion of the course. When the National League for Nursing test scores came back, she had scored in the 99 percentile.

Since the students were then in other classes, I wrote them little notes telling them their NLN test scores and took them to the office to put them into their mail boxes. Miss Kovach's box was not there. When I asked the grey-haired secretary where it was, she told me that the student had left school.

"She had done something and was on leave of absence for a year. She was supposed to make B's when she came back and she didn't. So she had to leave the school."

I felt sick. My C had forced an otherwise good student out of the school. "What did she fail? She was so good in the class part."

"Oh, it wasn't her work that was the problem." Mrs. Secretary had been there since the Saint's time. She knew everything.

"What was it?" I asked.

"I really can't say," answered the secretary and began typing.

"May I see her file, please?" I asked through clenched teeth.

"It's being used. The director has it."

So I went asking in earnest. Everyone was uncomfortable and vague. Anna Mae's problem had something to do with a certain medical resident, a low-cut dress and a flirtatious event one evening in the hospital cafeteria. The details were vague or nonexistent.

When I asked the director why Joan and I hadn't been informed, she said that it was felt that we'd be more objective in our evaluation if we didn't know the student was on probation.

I wrote the student a note. Included with the NLN score, I told her that I hadn't known what a precarious position she had been in and that I was sorry I hadn't helped her do better in the course. I pried her home address from the reluctant secretary and mailed the note with a heavy heart.

I was angry that I had been placed in such a position, and angry that I hadn't been trusted with the facts. I was having a wonderful time teaching the students and I was fond of my partner, Joan. But this incident convinced me that as soon as Western Reserve began its program leading to a master's degree in psychiatric nursing, I would leave. I had to prepare myself so that I could teach in an institution that had the same philosophy I had. I also had to have the educational credentials and experience so that I could speak up in faculty meeting and successfully challenge policies.

I taught at Saint What's-His-Name for two years and then entered the master's program at Western Reserve.

Three years later, I met Anna Mae at a nursing association meeting. She had transferred to another hospital school in the city and had finished. She told me that she was grateful for my note. Her crime? It seems she began dating one of the residents before his divorce was final and the affection they felt for each other was noticed. His chief had talked to him about it, but Anna Mae was more severely punished. She was now married to another doctor and was pregnant. She told me that she had been unable to trust anyone at Saint WHN, but she did appreciate my trying to help her.

It is strange, isn't it, the way chance events alter the course of one's life? Anna Mae and the events surrounding her propelled me from a comfortable situation into situations in which I would have more power and could prevent such things from happening.

Chapter 7
Sarah Rosenbaum*

When people ask me why I chose psychiatric nursing and I reply that the psychiatric patients are my favorites, I am usually thinking of Sarah Rosenbaum.

I first met Sarah at University Hospital. I was working evening shift when the hospital receptionist called to say the police were bringing up a new patient. I went to the elevator to greet the new arrival. The elevator opened and two smiling policemen and a full-figured woman in her late thirties emerged. She was wearing a bright red dress with many strings of beads. She extended her hand and, looking at my name tag, said, "Good evening, Mrs. Hardesty. I'm Sarah Rosenbaum and this is Patrolman Russo* and Sergeant Brown*."

I settled the policemen in the lounge and unlocked the ward door for my new patient. The harried psychiatric resident arrived a few minutes later with the paperwork. The resident was new, but the patient's history was clear. She had been hospitalized for mania and depression periodically for the last fifteen years.

It seemed that Sarah had decided to visit all her old college friends and had charged thousands of dollars worth of plane tickets to do this. She also had ordered two grand pianos delivered to her home, so she and her daughter could play duets. Her husband, who had a modest job and lived in a middle class neighborhood—my neighborhood— concluded that Sarah was high (in a manic state) again and was able to get the paperwork through to bring her home and have her admitted to the hospital.

Sarah didn't think she needed to be hospitalized, but she did admit she was a little high and signed the papers for voluntary commitment. A short time later, Mr. Rosenbaum arrived, carrying a typewriter and two suitcases. One held clothes and the other contained a manuscript. He was a small, worried man. The pair greeted each other affectionately. The manuscript was Sarah's unfinished autobiography, The Rabbi's Daughter. She worked on the book only when she was in a manic state.

She endured the admission procedures, blood pressure, etc.— and then set out to tour the ward to see if any of her old friends were there. She paused in the dayroom and began to play the piano, ignoring the irritated group who were watching television.

"I'll play softly," she said, and then proceeded to launch into "If You Knew Suzy," fortissimo, embellished with trills and runs.

The group watching TV stirred, and I said politely, "Please stop. You can play when the program is over." I didn't want to set limits on the woman in the first half hour.

I was rescued by a wise older man, a veteran of many stays on the ward, "Never mind. She's too busy to stick to one thing. She'll quit in a minute."

In a minute she was in the kitchen looking in the refrigerator and planning to cook blintzes for the patients the next day. Five minutes later, during the commercial, she was back in the day room, planning a bridge tournament with the television group. The resident intervened and ordered heavy sedation. In half an hour Sarah was asleep for the first time in forty-eight hours.

Her chart was heavy, even though the early years had been summarized. The diagnosis was of course, manic-depressive psychosis (Now called bipolar disorder). Sarah had been high once a year since she was fifteen, and once a year she spent an agonizing month in deep depression. Her illness had not been severe enough to be diagnosed until she was in her twenties when she was first hospitalized. The rest of the time she was well. She was the mother of three daughters and served as a girl scout leader and room mother at school. Her address was three blocks from mine and she had a daughter the same age as my older daughter.

The next day, I followed her around the ward and between activities and witty comments she told me her history. Before psychotropic drugs, electric shock was the only treatment for mania, and although it worked to shorten her depression it did not affect her mania. She told me of being locked in a room, tearing her clothes to shreds, and dancing and singing all night. "They gave me a blanket, and I tore it to shreds and decorated myself with the scraps. In the morning they sent the orderlies in and forced me into the tubs—hydrotherapy—and I rested a little. Those places were really snake-pits then."

She told me that she was often depressed but didn't want to think about it.

After a few weeks of psychotropic drugs, she was calm. She packed up her typewriter and manuscript and left the hospital.

Six months later, Sarah was again admitted. She looked twenty years older and was thin, disheveled, and smelled of body odor. When she could bring herself to speak she slowly uttered only morbid thoughts—fears that her children were suffering from some horrible disease, as punishment for their mother's sins—and the strong wish to die. After a few electric shock treatments she was a gracious, intelligent woman and returned to her family.

Sarah possessed a curious talent, not uncommon among psychotic patients. She had the uncanny ability to pick up cues about people's lives. When she was in the manic state, she loudly announced them to all who would listen. One very prim staff nurse, who rigidly followed the rules, was shocked one day in the dayroom when Sarah said to the resident, "Miss Prim has the hots for you. There is a lot of fire behind that starched uniform. Ask her out." The resident's face flamed. He'd had a date with Miss Prim the night before.

Another time, she asked one of the instructors, who'd had her nose injured in an accident, "When are you going to have enough money to get that plastic surgery? You are too attractive to let that nose spoil your face." This young woman was sure someone had discussed her appearance with Sarah and revealed the date for her surgery. I was aware that our patient was acutely sensitive to nonverbal and verbal cues.

The resident who had been Sarah's doctor finished his training and began practice. He had hospital privileges at Saint WHN and Sarah's husband had new hospital insurance. And so my favorite patient arrived on the ward where I was now teaching.

When she was high, she led the students a merry chase, trying to keep her out of other patients' rooms and preventing her from charging everything at the hospital gift shop. Sometimes it was only chance that prevented her bridge games from turning into brawls. We all were busy "setting limits, avoiding confrontations, and reducing stimulation." It was all hard work, but it was done willingly.

One of the hardest things for me was not becoming hyperactive with this patient. She was fun and her mood was contagious. It was difficult to maintain a wet blanket stance when she was so entertaining. I constantly told the students, "Remember you have to be a drag."

But even in her high moods, there was a hint of sadness. One day at the height of her mania she threw her towel at me and said, "J___C___, Hardesty, don't be so sympathetic." Then she began to cry.

The students didn't see her during her full cycle because their experience was only three months. But they did tell each other about their patients since they lived together in the same dormitory. It was hard for them to believe that the Sarah they knew was the same person their roommate was describing. They said, "She seems like two persons."

But I saw Sarah as one wonderful, strong woman, who struggled with a horrible illness that cost her and her family an enormous amount of emotional energy and money. When she was well, everyone close to her was constantly monitoring her behavior for signs of highs and lows. I once met her at a Fourth of July parade and remarked on how well she looked. She told me that she had tinted her hair and sent the family into a panic because they saw it as a sign that she was getting high.

Her daughter became friends with mine and knowing that I was her mother's nurse, she told Susan how distressed she was when her mother was depressed. Mr. Rosenbaum confided to me one day that when his wife was stable, she was not nearly as pleasant to live with as when she was just a little high.

After antidepressants were developed, Sarah no longer had to submit to electric shock. By the time I left Cleveland, lithium was being tried and apparently my favorite patient responded well to it because her cycle leveled out and she was stable all of the time.

Years passed. I acquired more education and moved on to other jobs. But for the next quarter century, when I lectured about manic-depressive psychosis, or bipolar disorder, as it was later called, I was talking about my favorite patient, Sarah Rosenbaum.

Chapter 8
Ernie

The Physicians who brought their patients to Saint What's-His-Name's psychiatric ward were a decent group of experienced psychiatrists. After years of listening to the dreams, pain and folly of thousands of humans, most wore an air of patient acceptance. They were comfortable to be with and easy to talk to.

Much has been written about the nurse-doctor conflict. It exists, particularly on an organizational level. Medical associations and physician-run hospital boards have put forth policies that limit nurses' practice. Nursing and medical organizations battle each other and compete for the support of legislators. It is true that young doctors, particularly residents and interns, are sometimes hard to deal with. They haven't yet learned to respect the expertise and judgment of the nurses who spend long periods of time with their patients. And yet I have always had warm collegial relationships with the physicians with whom I have worked. It was to both our and the patients' advantage that we work harmoniously and cooperatively, and we did.

The chief of staff at Saint WHN was a silver-haired patrician who had studied in Vienna. His clients were from the group whose name appeared on the society page of the city. Although he was handsome and dignified, he was so easy to be with that the students called him Dr. Teddy Bear*.

Dr. Hotshot* was a young psychiatrist who loved to spout far-out theories, just to shock the older doctors and staff. Fortunately they didn't shock easily. He did stir up some interest among the students and I spent more than one conference pointing out that his treatment of patients was very conventional and he only talked about his wild theories. He was tall and good looking, in his forties and wore cowboy boots. He was married to a beautiful society woman. He had the desk chair in his office engineered so that if he pressed a button, he would be dropped into a trapdoor and away from any murderous paranoid patient. Psychiatrists have been killed by patients, but it is a rare event. I concluded that Dr. Hotshot had chosen the wrong profession. He should have been a surgeon, a stunt man or an astronaut—something with more excitement. He enjoyed preening and strutting for the students. An audience of lovely twenty-year-old women is exciting for a man who craves adventure.

Dr. Ernie Mihilovich* was a bald energetic man in his late forties. His patients were working-class people from the dozen or so ethnic neighborhoods that made up a large part of Cleveland. He wore tailor-made suits, a little too fashionable, and a large diamond on his little finger. He was a neurologist as well as a psychiatrist and gave electric shock to his depressed patients more often than the other psychiatrists.

One day he explained why. His patients did not have the resources to be sick for any length of time. The women sometimes had young children and there was no one to be with them. A steel worker with a mortgage could not afford to be away from work for two months while he worked through his depression psychotherapeutically. "I shock them a few times. Get them past the danger of suicide and back where they can function and send them home. Then I follow them up carefully in the office." It made good sense.

The chief of staff's patients returned to the ward frequently and stayed for long times. We seldom saw Ernie's twice.

I was impressed that he knew the neighborhoods of the city so well. He knew the priests in all the parishes. He was a musician and had played in bands in most of the parish halls, at weddings and dances. Ernie spoke many of the Eastern European languages. He had picked them up along with Latin at the Catholic high school he had attended. I had always loved language and was very impressed with someone who could quote Cicero at length and tell off-color jokes in Latin.

I gradually grew to have a great deal of respect for his therapeutic skills. He was more direct than the other psychiatrists, and he seemed to have excellent results. But it wasn't until Mrs. Burns* was admitted that I realized the depth of his healing power.

Mrs. Burns was a mousy little woman in her middle forties. I didn't know her well, but since the student assigned to her reported to me daily, I learned that she was depressed. She came to the hospital every year near the aniversary of the day twenty-five years before when her three children had been killed in an accident. Day by day, she told the student a little more, until finally we learned the whole story.

She had experienced an acute psychosis. The voices in her head told her that she and the children were possessed with demons. The only way to rid them all of these monsters was for them all to die. Following the instructions of the voices, she cut the throats of her three young children and dropped them into a bathtub of scalding water. Then she cut her own throat and dropped in on top of them. When her husband found them she was still alive.

She was not charged with a crime. Instead she was sent to the state hospital, a tomb-like fortress, and confined to a back ward, beyond the sight of anyone who could help her—and beyond hope. Her husband divorced her. She recovered from the psychosis, and then, remembering what she had done, she relapsed. This had happened again and again.

Five years before, a family member had hired Ernie to see if anything could be done to help her. He had gone into the state hospital, daily at first, and offered her forgiveness and understanding. The strength of his resolve to help enabled her to forgive herself, and she was able to face what she had done without fleeing back into psychosis. When she was ready, he arranged for her to be discharged and helped her adjust to the world she had left twenty years before. Her former husband contacted her; they dated a while and then remarried. She finished the year of college she needed and was teaching in a city school. The anniversary of "the horrible accident" was a difficult time and some years Ernie admitted her to the hospital so she could have help living through it.

Knowing this patient and the others with less dramatic stories, and seeing the changes that Ernie had made in their lives, convinced me that this man was one of the best psychiatrists I had ever known. This fast moving man who resembled a musician or a gambler was able to heal patients that others had pronounced hopeless.

Chapter 9
The Retirement Home

The faculty at Saint WHN decided to offer the students experience with geriatric patients. Joan and I volunteered to include it as part of the psychiatric nursing experience. Several groups of students had finished the class on the psychiatric unit at the hospital, and Joan now felt comfortable doing the clinical supervision. If I were to take the students to another site for part of the time, the unit would be less crowded. Besides it was a wonderful idea and I looked forward to teaching in a new setting.

We selected the Mildred Jones Home* as our new clinical area. This facility was a retirement center in which each woman (there were only one or two men) had her own room, bath and furniture. Meals were served in a dining room, and recreation and medical supervision were provided. A portion of the home was a nursing home and was available to any of the residents who needed it. The women paid a fee for their lifetime care or signed over their remaining assets to the home.

It was a pleasant environment. The living room had the largest and most beautiful oriental rug I have ever seen; it was furnished with rare antiques and an ebony grand piano. But even more important was the staff. The home was run by an enlightened social worker. A geriatric psychiatrist consulted there weekly and conducted conferences for the staff. The physical therapy department was fully staffed and a varied and interesting recreational program was in place. Our students would be seeing the best care that was available.

The students were assigned to spend time with three or four of the women and to help them with any problems that were presented. They also were free to choose any other woman that interested them to work with.

We soon discovered a paradox. There were more people suffering from organic brain disease in the home than in the general population. This was expected because of their age. But there were also more acute psychological problems, even acute psychosis, brought on by psychological stress, than I had ever seen. The students had the opportunity to intervene and treat these problems using purely psychological means. They were thrilled with the results of their care, and many decided to become geriatric nurses.

Miss Priscilla Wilson* was one of our most gratifying cases. Miss Wilson was a ninety-four year old retired school principal who had been a resident at the home for twenty years. She had broken her hip five years before and it hadn't healed. She was deaf, almost blind, and had an aortic aneurysm that could burst at any moment and end her life.

We didn't discover Miss Wilson until two weeks before the students were to leave the home. She was hidden away in the nursing home section. One of the healthy residents told her student that it was a terrible shame what had happened to Miss Wilson, and the curious student had gone searching for her.

Miss Wilson had been the leader of the Mildred Jones community the first fifteen years she had lived there, and she'd had many friends. But after she had broken her hip, and was confined to a room in the nursing home section, the ladies stopped visiting. "I couldn't stand to see her that way," her old friend said.

When we met Miss Wilson she was alternately mute and very hostile, lying in bed with her eyes closed and a frown creasing her face. Her skin was intact, which was evidence of the good physical care this bitter bed-ridden old woman had received. Although the nursing home aides cared for her physical needs, they hated her.

We listened to their stories. "I just finished cleaning her all up; the bed was changed with all new fresh linen, and then that mean old girl grunted and shit all over it." And "I got a new uniform. Milly said how nice it was when we was doing up the old bitch. I was holding her over so Milly could change the sheets, and she reaches back, gets a hand full of poop, and smears it on my uniform." The aides drew lots to see who would be responsible for her care each day.

It was obvious that Miss Wilson was angry. It also seemed that she was using the last weapon she controlled—her bowels—to express her unhappiness. Cynthia Holden*, a tall attractive twenty-year-old, said, "Mrs. Hardesty, I'd love to try to see what I could do with her."

I agreed. The students and I decided that the reason Miss Wilson was angry was because she had absolutely no control over her life. She was also reacting to the way she was being treated. The plan was to try to give her as much opportunity to control the details of her life as possible. In addition she was to be treated with exaggerated respect.

Cynthia asked Miss Wilson if she cared to be bathed, and then, at what time. Rather than giving her a bed bath, Cynthia brought the basin and handed the old lady a wash cloth. She stood by to help, and did what ever was asked, but Miss Wilson was the one who was in charge.

Then the student, with Miss Wilson's permission, sat beside the bed and read aloud from the worn poem book she had found on the dresser. After a few pages, Miss Wilson was requesting her favorite verses. Half an hour later, the old woman was pouring out her feelings of powerlessness and humiliation.

In less than two weeks, Miss Wilson was bathing herself, sitting up in a wheel chair, using the toilet chair which was placed beside the bed, and entertaining old friends who had been told of Miss Wilson's miraculous improvement. And we were struggling with guilt. How could we leave her?

It was decided that Cynthia should be the one to work with the aides in the few remaining days. She patiently explained what she had done and why. She also wrote a simple but detailed nursing care plan and placed it in a prominent place in the nurse's station. Then she fought back tears as she said goodby to the dignified old woman.

Six months later when I returned with a new group of students, we attended an in-service conference conducted by the consulting psychiatrist. The aides were presenting a case. It was Miss Wilson's story. They described her earlier behavior in graphic terms and then told of the changes in the way they cared for the old woman and the happy results.

I was delighted that they had followed Cynthia's plan and Miss Wilson was continuing to do well. The psychiatrist asked, "What happened that you decided to change the way you dealt with Miss Wilson?" He knew of course, because we had told him what we were doing.

"I don't know," the aide who made the presentation replied, "I guess we just got tired of doing it the old way."

This was no time, I decided, to challenge a staff member's denial. I would always know that it was Cynthia who began the change. Cynthia was then in a bachelor's program with plans for a Master's in geriatric nursing. She didn't need any acknowledgment.

A few years later, I read Miss Wilson's obituary. It spoke of her years of service as a teacher and principal, and the honors she had garnered. I felt grateful that one of my students had made her last years bearable.

Western Reserve University

1964-1966

Chapter 10
A Student Again

I had been taking graduate courses at Western Reserve and waiting for the psychiatric nursing program to be developed. I had always been a good student in any of the educational endeavors I had attempted, but I was seldom the best. In part this was because of an independent streak that sent me off in different directions to fulfill my objectives rather than meet the teacher's. Then there were the few occasions when my grade school and high school habit of skipping school in order to pursue my reading caught up with me, and I discovered omissions in my basic education. But in general, I had seldom doubted that I could learn whatever I chose.

The faculty of the new program scheduled interviews for prospective students. When I arrived, I found that all four of the professors were gathered in a room to interview me. It was one of those stress interviews that are supposed to screen out the weak. They asked questions like. "What was your most frustrating experience last week?," and "What have you done in the last month that you are proud of?" When I answered the question, these skilled interviewers probed and searched my answers for clues to my personality. I kept my composure, but I was mad. I felt as though I were in a lion's cage, with no chair for protection.

I passed muster, however, and was accepted. For several months, I wondered how I would be able to work with the women who had subjected me to such a traumatic experience.

During the time I waited to begin the program, I battled my own doubts. I had done well in school because I was in a group of average people. Now I would be with the best. If I were lucky and worked very hard, I would pass the courses. What would happen if I could not meet the standards? How could I ever adjust to the fact that I didn't have the intellectual capacity to do what I wanted? I had been an ordinary looking-teenager who thought she was a dog.I had always been a klutz when it came to athletics, and I was slow to learn physical skills, but I had always consoled myself with the knowledge that I was smart. Now how would I deal with the blow to my self-concept if I discovered in this new important endeavor that I wasn't as smart as I thought I was? I was so concerned that I developed some obsessive symptoms. I knew that they were the result of anxiety and did not respond to them. But they did serve as a gauge to let me know the severity of my own doubts.

The teachers who had interviewed me soon became my mentors. Dorothy Greg who was head of the program gave a little speech at the beginning of the term stating that the faculty would pass on to us all the knowledge they possessed, but they expected to have us stand on their shoulders as our careers advanced and go far beyond them. It was soon apparent that they meant it.

When the program began, there were four faculty and ten graduate students. A student faculty ratio like this was unbelievably rich. It was even higher as the year progressed and the ten students had become six. I don't remember the drop-outs well. Their faces were lost in the anxious rush to learn everything. I do remember that one woman had a psychotic break the second week of school. I guess I wasn't the only one who was anxious.

We students chose patients—some from the psychiatric unit of the hospital, others from other sites around the city—and began to see them daily or several times a week for psychotherapeutic interviews. We made verbatim records of every word that was said. We had the option of using a tape recorder, but soon discovered that transcribing an hour-long interview took eight hours. It was easier to take notes during the interviews. For me, who always speeded up and became tangential when I was anxious, the writing slowed me down and gave me time to think before I spoke. I developed my own shorthand methods and ruined my formerly graceful handwriting. Each evening we students would analyze what had occurred, line by line, and document our conclusions from the literature. The following day, we gave the transcripts to our particular supervisor to read, and then we would meet with her for an hour's supervision. This is a very expensive method of teaching psychotherapeutic skills, but it is also the most effective.

The faculty was doing research on the therapeutic process itself, and they requested that we give them typed transcripts of our interactions with patients. I didn't type and had to hire it done. My budget was stretched to the limit, but I did what was required without protest. Later a copy of one of those transcripts helped me get a job as a psychotherapist.

I can't say enough about the wonderful education I received in the master's program at Western Reserve. Dr. Anita Werner, now O'Toole, was my first supervisor. She was ten years younger than I, in her middle twenties, extremely intelligent, new to teaching and very quiet. I suspect that I was a handful for her. I was more socially confident (translation: manipulative or seductive) and argumentative than she. But slowly and patiently, using the indisputable black and white of the transcripts as evidence, she cured me of my bad habits.

I cheated a little with Anita. If I really wanted to say something to a patient that she wouldn't agree with, I did it in the hallway, before the transcribing began. What things? I remember telling my patient, a black, single mother who was diagnosed schizophrenia, that I hoped she and her children had a pleasant Christmas. This was taboo, at that time, for a number of therapeutic reasons which I seem to have forgotten. Why didn't I just do it in the session and forget to record it? Well, I had tried that. Every time I tried to doctor the transcript to make myself appear to be a better therapist, my teacher would ask why I hadn't said what I had actually said. I couldn't very well say, "I did say that and lied to you on the transcript."

We remaining students had become a close knit group. As we conferred, we concluded that it was easier to tell the truth and face our mistakes than try to hide them from our supervisors.

Some people think therapy is a dramatic occasion, when the patient reveals his deep unconscious secrets and the wise therapist makes insightful connections. The patient then has an insight and his whole life is changed. That only happens on television.

The actual process is slow and painstaking. The patient tells you what he is experiencing, and you slowly broaden and deepen his perspective of the situation by the questions you ask. Then when both of you see the situation more clearly, you lead him to a new perspective and help him choose new solutions. Over time, feelings change also.

The typist who typed my transcripts told me she was almost driven wild by the constant repetitions that the patients produced, and by my patient responses. However boring the typing may be, the actual process of therapy is extremely interesting. Nothing is more exciting than when, for instance, a depressed man, who always began the sessions by stating—"No one likes me,"— begins by saying, "I must be getting a little more depressed. I'm beginning to get that feeling again, you know the one, that no one likes me." This meant he was connecting his symptoms to his mood, and now we could really begin to work on his actual situation.

During the second year of the program, Dr. Fay Spring was my supervisor. Since Anita had cured as many of my bad therapeutic habits as possible, Fay was able to help me develop my own therapeutic style. She helped me see how to use humor effectively. When I had been a staff nurse on the psychiatric ward at University Hospital, I had been reprimanded for joking with patients. The rule was, "Never joke with patients. They will misinterpret it." I was tempted, when I analyzed the transcripts of my interviews which Fay would see, to leave out my funny remarks. But I included them. Her response was, "What a clever way to defuse a bad situation and help put it into perspective."

I also learned to use humor the way some therapists use paradoxical instructions. This is a technique in which the therapist instructs the patient to do exactly the opposite of what is desired. The patient then responds the way you wish. Parents frequently use this device with children— "So you want to run away? Here let me pack your bag." I never could do this. It seemed dishonest. However, I did learn to present the opposite idea in a satirical or patently exaggerated way. The patient and I would laugh about it, and then he would decide to take the more reasonable course.

At the beginning of the program we were given reading lists with hundreds of references. The idea was that we were to choose from among the readings those that directly applied to our patient, or those that particularly interested us, rather than read the entire list. One classmate, Elizabeth Warner, began reading the books on the list starting with the A's. It took her longer to graduate, but we called her our walking library. If you wanted to know where to find a discussion of a certain topic or a particular type of research tool, you just asked Elizabeth.

Our classes were conducted as conferences. In these conferences we shared what we had gained from the readings and in working with our patients. It was a rich learning environment. The four experienced psychiatric nurses and six interested novices produced a heady mix. Sometimes the stimulation was so much that I talked more than was helpful or became tangential. My teachers were concerned about these symptoms of anxiety and suggested therapy. I knew that therapy would not help.

At that time, I was dealing with an adored daughter who had become a rebellious teenager, serious financial problems and a demanding educational program. But even more troubling was my marriage.

My first husband and I had divorced after 11 years of marriage. Struggling with the heartbreak and betrayal, I had determined never to be dependent on another person for income or status. That is one of the reasons I was driven to get more education. But I was hungry for affection too, and five years after the divorce, when I was working at Saint WHN, I had remarried.

My new husband was a former Hungarian freedom fighter, a charming, intelligent fellow, but a poor choice for me. He was studying for a doctorate in chemistry and we were both under stress, but the major problem was his ineptness as a step father. The marriage was doomed from the beginning.

My goal was to keep my personal problems in check and use the energy created by my situation to finish the program. Then when I was finished, I would deal with the other problems. By then, my earlier doubts had vanished. I knew that I was all right and that I would earn my master's degree. Six months after I graduated I filed for divorce. I was embarrassed rather than heartbroken and I suspect that he was relieved to be out of a situation he couldn't handle.

During the program, we also had classes with psychiatrists. It was easier to sit and be lectured to than to struggle with group-problem solving and learning from each other. We didn't always agree with the psychiatrist's masculine and Freudian point of view, but we were too tired or indifferent to protest. We also knew that he interpreted protest as penis envy. We just raised our eyebrows and nonverbally agreed to disagree as he droned on.

One time, however, we did react. This was in the middle sixties and women had begun to wear heavy eye make-up, the sort of eye dressing that had, until then, been seen only on stage. If you've forgotten, look at some of the old movies, and see the eyeliner, artificial lashes and blue eye shadow. It was also *in* to wear fishnet stockings. I had found that they didn't run the way more conventional nylons did and they were warmer. (Graduate students who were seeing patients didn't wear slacks or jeans then.) When our professor discussed the symptoms of hysteria, he talked about the physical cues that let you know you are dealing with a woman with this diagnosis. He read from his notes that these signs include, heavy eye make-up, blue shadow, and fishnet stockings. The six of us batted our mascara-laden eyes, planted our fishnet covered legs on the floor and hissed at the gentlemen. I don't think he got the message that appropriateness of dress must be judged in context, but this experience certainly pointed it out to us.

I am so grateful for all I learned from my teachers, but I also was learning, day by day, from the patients who permitted me to be part of their experience with mental illness. There were so many and I can only mention a few, but they made profound changes in my practice. I hoped I helped them with their lives.

Chapter 11
Mary Carter*

I met Mary Carter on the female ward of the short-term state hospital, the hospital where patients stayed for a short time and then, it was hoped, returned to the community. We students were studying groups and I was observing the informal social structure of the ward. I sat in the corner of the ward dining room, trying to be unobtrusive and watched.

Mary was a twenty-one-year-old black woman who had been diagnosed schizophrenic, although there was some question as to the type. She was mute most of the time, but she had told her doctor that, before she was admitted, she had heard the voices of men calling to her from the street below the apartment where she lived with her mother, brother and two small children.

We were permitted to pick any patient we chose to work with intensively. I was already seeing a patient at the psychiatric unit of the hospital and did not particularly need another to meet the requirements of the course. Mary was not the sort of patient that interested students. We liked verbal patients, preferably educated, who had fascinating things to tells us and would benefit from talking about their lives. Frankly, these patients made us look good to our supervisors.

The patients were sitting on the hard straight chairs in this gloomy room waiting anxiously for visiting hour and the arrival of their relatives. I looked across the room at Mary. She was looking toward the door and her face was luminous with hope. This dull, quiet woman was suddenly beautiful.

Visitors began spilling through the door. There were hugs for relatives and greetings for other patients. Some of these people had been coming here for three months and friendships had been made among the visitors and patients. A full-figured black woman with a pleasant round face came through the door. She called, "Hello," to a patient and her visitor and exchanged a few words. Then she moved toward Mary and handed her some food as she greeted another family group.

Mary's mother never looked at her daughter. They sat together, shared the food, and spoke a little about Mary's children, but the woman's smiles and warmth were all directed toward the acquaintances she had made in this room. Mary's face changed from one that radiated hope, to a mask of disappointment, then to a dull withdrawn expression.

I felt tears form in my eyes. My incontinent eyes, as I called them, had been a source of embarrassment for me all of my professional life. I opened them wider and hoped the tears wouldn't spill. Mary looked across the room and our eyes met. I knew then that I would work with her and perhaps make a small difference.

My supervisor and Mary's doctor discouraged me. Mary had been at the hospital several months and shown no improvement. They felt I would be wasting my time. She was soon to be sent to the long-term state hospital to become one of the the hundreds of forgotten people for whom there was little hope. But I persisted and they finally agreed.

I told Mary I would come to see her for an hour, three times a week. For that hour she could tell me whatever she wished about her life. I also explained that I would be writing down everything we said so that I could show it to my teacher. She agreed and we began meeting in a windowless office the size of a closet.

At first I didn't know if what she told me was fantasy, hallucinations or facts. I listened intently, took notes and offered responses that encouraged exploration. The old standard was, "Tell me...," alternating with, "I'd like to hear more about..." and an occasional, "I'm having trouble understanding. Would you please explain more?"

Mary would wait until I had finished a note before she offered more. She took breaks to go to the bathroom or get a drink. I patiently waited and soon she would be back to tell me more. Occasionally she used slang or terms that I now know are part of the Black English vocabulary, and I would ask her to define them.

She was a minister's daughter. The family had moved from a small Indiana town to Cleveland when she was sixteen. Shortly after, her father died leaving the family in a strange city. The mother worked as a cleaning lady. Mary had a hard time fitting into her new school and she dropped out. Before long she was pregnant. She thought the fellow would marry her but he disappeared. A new man arrived on the scene. When she became pregnant again, he said they would marry. She bought a wedding dress and made preparations. Then she learned that he already had a wife.

Her youngest child had asthma, and there were frequent frantic trips to the emergency room. Her brother worked as a landscape maintenance man during the summer. He was an artist, she said, and painted most of the winter.

I had seen the mother, a woman who couldn't look at her daughter. I never met the brother, but he seemed to be the one satisfying figure in her life. He was caring for the children while she was in the hospital and diligently followed the doctor's instructions about the sick little boy. Mary had a few women friends, she said, but I noted that no one other than her mother visited her in the hospital.

I had no solutions to offer this young woman. As I listened to her tell of her life, I felt profound gratitude for the circumstances of my own life. What would it be like to be trapped in two small rooms, with the responsibility for young children, one chronically ill? Her mother was rejecting her and she feared that her brother would leave. All I really could give her was deep interest and some of my time.

She began to improve. She talked with the other women on the ward and began to sing when one of them played the piano. Her voice was lovely, and she told me that she had sung in the church at home in Indiana. Her doctor postponed the planned transfer to the long term-hospital. When I spoke with the doctor, I emphasized the depressive aspects of her illness. The hallucinatory experiences had not reoccurred.

Two months after I met her, Mary was discharged and came to see me in the clinic, once a week on Tuesday afternoon. She had to take two buses to get there, and if she didn't have the money, she didn't come. I accepted her explanation without reproach and told her I'd be there.

She began to attend church and to sing in the choir. She and her brother took the children to the zoo. She began to wonder if she could get a job cleaning houses. She recognized that when she was very lonely she began to listen for the voices from the street. She decided that that was a good time to take the children and go to visit a friend.

One Tuesday, I made a presentation in class. I had been worried about how it would go and was very relieved when it was finished. Following that, I met with Susan's teacher to discuss her progress. I picked up groceries and arrived home about one. The house was empty and I reveled in the serenity and stillness of its pleasant rooms. It was so good to have the presentation finished. Thank God, Susan was doing better in school. Gosh, it was nice to have a moment to myself.

And then I remembered my appointment with Mary! I raced through the streets to the clinic and ran from the parking lot. She had waited forty minutes. I said, "I 'm so sorry, I just forgot." She looked as though I had struck her, and I felt sick.

The next day in class, Dr. Hildegard Peplau, whose work made psychiatric nursing a respectable specialty, gave a presentation. At break, I told her what had happened and asked her advice about how to repair my mistake. She told me what I already knew, that it would have been better to make some excuse rather than tell her I had forgotten her. Then she said, "You must have been overloaded with responsibilities and desperately needed some relief."

Bless Dr. Peplau.

Mary was there the following week and we continued as before for the two years I was in school. She made slow but steady progress toward building a more satisfactory life for herself.

When I wrote a paper about this patient my teachers gave me a B. It was a B, they said, rather than an A,

because it read more like a novel, and less like a professional paper. I was flattered.

I have also learned that when I get that serene, tran-
quil feeling, in the midst of a harried time, to check my
appointment book and see what obligations I am shirking.

Chapter 12
The Group

The class was doing well with their individual patients. Now it was time to learn to be group therapists. We formed into pairs and began the difficult task of deciding what sort of a group we wanted to run and where.

My partner was Holly Skodol. Holly was the class baby, a brilliant baby. She was twenty-one. Elizabeth Warner and I were in our late thirties, and the other three classmates were in their early thirties. All of us, except Holly, were experienced nurses, and had been administrators or teachers. Holly arrived fresh from a bachelor's program.

Holly had known when she entered nursing school that she wanted to be a psychiatric nurse, and she headed straight for that goal. Her teachers provided her with special experiences so that by the time she arrived in graduate school she was already an experienced therapist. She shocked us staid old nurses with her stories of how she had managed to get her long suffering friend, Sally, to do the tasks she found distasteful, things like giving enemas. But at the same time we admired her clear devotion to her goals.

My daughter Susan was a teenager and Shevawn, her younger sister, was a wannabe. Holly was their idol. She was a lovely young woman with long dark hair and blue eyes. She dressed in the fashion of the sixties, danced the frug and monkey with abandon, and was a Beatles fan. Yet, she was also their mother's peer.

Holly and I decided to select our group of patients from among the patients at the short-term state hospital. We would hold the sessions twice a week for ten weeks, and the focus would primarily be on plans for discharge and return to life outside the hospital. We would tape all the sessions and then analyze the tapes from the view point of a number of different theorists. We wanted to see which theory offered the best guidance for the therapist in this kind of a group.

Holly insisted that we have intelligent, verbal people for our group. I agreed, thinking, why not? It would be easier. We talked with all the doctors on the staff and they made referrals. On the appointed day we collected our ten patients in a conference room, made introductions and began.

The group launched immediately into the process of making a disparate collection of persons into a cohesive group. We had no problem getting them to talk; the problem was to keep them from bounding off the walls.

There was one exception. Magda was a mousy fifty-year-old single woman who lived with her sister in the nearby Hungarian neighborhood where she had been born. She had dropped out of high school to go to work in a factory. Her only recreation was attending mass and playing bingo. The diagnosis was depression, but the head nurse later confided that the physician suspected organic involvement. It was possible that he had played a trick on us, or perhaps was teaching us a lesson, when he referred Magda to our group. Physicians have been known to do that to uppity nurses, ones that aspire to more education.

Magda said nothing during the first nine weeks of the group. She always came early and sat primly in the same chair. The group was lively and she looked as though she listened intently. A black woman, who learned her living by modeling nude for students at the art institute, was our most colorful patient. This lady had had several other interesting occupations and she openly shared details of her experiences. Magda sat across from her, with wide eyes and occasionally a wide open mouth, in shock.

Another group member was a good-looking young man in his early twenties. He had dropped out of college in his junior year and joined the group of former students who hung around the colleges, doing drugs and experimenting with alternative lifestyles. His speech was liberally sprinkled with the F word. Magda's face registered alarm every time he uttered it.

When I realized that I could not get Magda to say what she was feeling or to add to the group discussion, I began giving her nonverbal support. When the artist model talked about her torrid affair with the professor, I would meet Magda's eyes, smile a little and shrug. Her mouth would close, her expression would fade and she would settle back in her chair—until the next scandalous story spewed forth.

The tape ground on, and every day after group, Holly and I would transcribe and analyze it. We found that, for us, it didn't much matter what theory you used they all provided some structure and guidance to the therapist.

The end of the semester was drawing near and we began reminding our group that it would end soon. They handled the separation the way many people do—they left us first. All except Magda.

The last day we met, Magda was our only patient, and she spoke for the first time. She told us that she had really enjoyed the group. She said it made her realize what a sheltered life she'd had. She had decided that she wanted to bring a little more excitement into her days. So she had selected a romance novel from the library cart and read a book for the first time since high school. She had also talked with her priest and made plans to volunteer at a nearby nursing home when she was discharged. Then she shook our hands, thanked us again, and left.

Magda taught me a valuable lesson. You try to help your patients deal with their problems and have better lives, but you frequently are not aware of what effect you have had. The patient who talks may not be affected while quiet ones, like Magda, may be making positive changes.

What happened to Holly? Holly Skodol Wilson is a well-known psychiatric nurse. She moved to the west coast and earned a doctorate in sociology with a brilliant dissertation. Her psychiatric nursing text is a best-selling text book and she is sought after as a keynote speaker. In addition to living up to all the promise she showed as a student, she has raised three very nice children.

There has been a general belief in nursing that it is better to work a few years after a bachelor's program to gain some general experience before entering graduate school. Knowing Holly caused me to question this idea. Since women frequently take some time out from their careers when they have children, their career trajectory is already delayed. It seems foolish to delay it even longer while practicing a type of nursing that is different from your goal. Experience can be gained more easily than graduate education. Then, too, the longer you have a position the more valuable you become, and the more encumbered you are with responsibilities and monthly payments. I now urge nurses whose career goals require graduate school to go as soon as possible.

Gosh, I learned a great deal from the group that Holly and I managed.

Chapter 13
Statistics, or How I Made It

When I was in fifth grade, I discovered Dickens, Dumas, and all the other wonderful writers on my parents' bookshelves. Sometimes I was so busy reading that I didn't go to school. My mother was a very modern teacher, with radical ideas about readiness, interest, etc. She let me stay at home and read. Besides, she was busy trying to earn a living and support my father's expensive tastes. My report cards were satisfactory; in fact, I was listed as first in the class ranking.

But as the result of this, I have omissions in my basic education, particularly in math. I have always been slow in computations and possess a high degree of anxiety about mathematics. I made Bs in algebra and As in geometry, which I thought was fun. That was all the math formally offered in my high school. When the math teacher organized a lunch-time trigonometry class, no one thought to tell me. This was strange because I was in the physics class—the only girl and the person with the highest grades.

In my bachelor's program, I entered the last semester needing one four hour science course. Somehow I found myself in chemical calculations—and I almost drowned. I approached the teacher, male and middle aged, and told him that I was having trouble and that since my plans included graduate school, I dared not fail.

His response was, "Some people have it and some people don't."

I got a tutor, a high school chemistry teacher. He couldn't work the problems using the method the professor required. I was dating a chemist who was working on his Ph. D. (Why have there been so many chemists in my romantic history?) At first he couldn't fathom the teacher's method. Then suddenly just before the final, the light dawned and he understood.

He said, "That's why all those young guys at school could work the problems faster than I could!"

He was delighted to learn the new method and his help enabled me to get a high enough grade in the final to bring my class grade up to a C.

Now I was in graduate school, facing statistics with fear and trembling.

The class was a large one, with eighty students from all the programs in the university. It was taught by a middle-aged, flamboyant professor and two graduate assistants. The professor wrote the formulas on the board with a flourish, and I looked at them uncomprehendingly.

My classmate, Elizabeth Warner, was doing well. She tried to help me, but we didn't have much time to study together. My husband was working for a Ph. D.; surely he could help. He tried and went off into lengthy explanations, punctuated by words in Hungarian. It reminded me of when my first husband had tried unsuccessfully to teach me to drive.

I was desperate. Then help arrived. My daughter, Susan, was thirteen and was good at math. "Let me look at your book and see if I can figure it out," she said.

She did, and patiently explained it to me, in English, rather than symbols. Suddenly I understood. It was absurdly simple. Why had my teacher made it so obtuse? In fact, there were times that I had a wonderful feeling that the concepts were beautiful, the same feeling I had when looking at art.

I was getting better but my teacher was getting worse. The flamboyance increased to mania. The graduate assistants just laughed at his behavior in class. One day he wandered into class, ten minutes late, smelling of alcohol and carrying a dozen ties. He asked us to decide which one was the most attractive and tried to connect our answers to statistics. Then he wandered out and the graduate assistant finished the class. The man was sick and no one was doing anything about it.

My classmates and I had been complaining about the class to the teachers in the psychiatric nursing program. In the seminar that afternoon we insisted that something be done. Not only were we being shortchanged, but the man was going to ruin his reputation and possibly his career. They listened to our concerns and then told us, "It has been taken care of. He was just admitted downstairs." He was now a patient in the university's psychiatric hospital.

The Statistics class proceeded with the graduate assistants working hard to make up for the material we might have missed. The time for the final approached. I sat near an apple-cheeked nun named Sister Mary Joseph*. She said she wasn't worried about the final because she was going home that weekend and would ask her mother to pray for her. She said her mother's prayers had always brought her good grades. I asked if she could please ask her mother to pray for me. She patiently wrote my name in her notebook and promised that she would.

The day arrived. I entered the class with sharpened pencils and my own prayers. The test consisted of one hundred multiple choice questions. We were supposed to work the problems on scrap paper and then choose the correct answer from the four alternatives.

I started out, calculating at my own slow speed. An hour into the test, I glanced around me. I had succeeded in working ten problems. My adjacent classmates were working on their thirtieth question. I'd never make it.

Then I thought, if I guess, the probabilities are that I will get twenty-five correct. If I read carefully and give an informed guess it will be higher. If I work the problems, I will get thirty finished. Conclusion: I'd do better to guess and avoid all the trauma of two more frantic hours.

So I went through the test, reading carefully and choosing the most probable answer. I kept thinking I was crazy. I hoped that Sister Mary Joseph had remembered to ask her mother to pray.

Three nervous days passed. Elizabeth went to the building where the class was held to see if the grades were posted. The rest of us were afraid to look. She came back with a shocked expression on her face. She made a solid B as we all expected. And I, who had moaned and sweated about the class, had made a grade in the final exam two standard deviations higher than the next highest grade.

Susan, Sister Mary Joseph's mother, and I, perhaps with the help of a higher power, had made an A in statistics.

When I entered the doctoral program, I suggested that I might want to take the first statistics course again. I guess I didn't trust my A. But my adviser said, "Oh, no, anyone who made an A in a master's program, especially from Dr. Flash* doesn't need to take that course. We'll put you right into the advanced courses."

The math anxiety returned. I struggled. But I had a new ally, my younger daughter, Shevawn. Shevawn was now thirteen and was a whiz in math. One of her early grade school teachers had helped develop the new math program, and Shevawn had helped her later teachers understand it. She tutored me through two advanced statistics classes. I never repeated my brilliant coup. I chose to work the problems and my grades were mediocre.

Occasionally Susan and Shevawn have slipped and said something like, "When we were in graduate school....," They then correct themselves and say, "I mean when Mom was in school."

The earlier version was correct. I never would have made it without their help.

Chapter 14
The G. I. Ward at the Veteran's Hospital

I had a sociology class with Dr. Leo Simmons, a visiting professor from Yale. Yale nurses were highly respected by the general faculty of that university and, indeed, by all the academic nurses in the country. It was a pleasure to be part of this class because Dr. Simmons treated graduate students as fellow professionals. He introduced me to a young (translation: my age) professor, Dr. Richard O'Toole, who was doing research at the Veteran's Hospital.

Dr. O'Toole had several projects going but the chief of the gastrointestinal service had suggested another to him. It seemed that the VA patients weren't following their doctors' instructions. He suspected that a culture existed among the patients, the norms of which were not in line with good health practices. He guessed that the patients operated with a different sent of rules from the physicians. It is difficult to study group norms without becoming a part of the group. However Dr. O'Toole thought that the nurse, working as a regular staff nurse, might be able to gather data. Nurses are sometimes invisible—like the furniture and the beds—so much a part of the environment that no one notices them anymore.

I needed a job for the summer, and the VA paid better than other hospitals. I would have preferred to work on a psychiatric ward, since it had been six years since I had done medical nursing, but there were advantages to this situation. It seemed a good way to gain research skills and earn money at the same time. At that time I thought that I might want to obtain a doctorate in sociology.

I got a job at the Veteran's Hospital and was assigned to the GI Ward. The chairman of the sociology department, who didn't share Dr. Simmon's and Dr. O' Toole's respect for nurses, at first decreed that I couldn't be paid for the extra work involved in recording my findings because I would be getting two federal checks. Dr. O'Toole interceded and fought hard for the modest amount I would get. I concluded that besides being an excellent sociologist, he was a very fair man. I reported this to my teachers. A few years later he married one of them, Dr. Anita Werner.

The summer I spent at the Veteran's Hospital, functioning as a staff nurse and as a secret data gatherer was a wild one.

The Veteran's Hospital was new. The G I Ward had forty patients. The layout of the ward was such that two forty-bed wards were close together with a door between the two nurses' stations. It was planned this way so that if there were a staff shortage, the nurse from one ward could take responsibility for the second ward. This tells you something of the VA's ideas about staffing.

Most of the patients on the ward were suffering from the effects of alcoholism. They had cirrhosis of the liver, chronic hepatitis, peptic ulcers, and esophageal varicosities. Although these conditions can be found in persons other than alcoholics, there were very few of those people on this ward. We had a few patients with cancer. For some reason, several men with renal disease were also located there.

Most of the men were ambulatory and able to take care of their personal needs. Most of the time, the pace of the work was slow. I worked the evening shift with one aide to help me and we were able to do what needed to be done without much stress. However there were crises when more people were needed. Mr. Risso's* bleed was one of them.

Mr. Risso had been taking a nap when I made rounds at three. His wife arrived about four, bringing a basket of Italian goodies. He sat up in bed and vomited a quart of blood. Mrs. Risso screamed and the three other men in the room yelled. I ran to the door, took one look and dashed for the phone. Suddenly a quiet ward was chaotic. Three residents and as many interns were pounding down the hall by the time I got back to the room after calling the lab for a type, crossmatch, and blood. I ushered Mrs. Risso to the waiting room and left her in the capable hands of another visitor. Then I returned to help start the intravenous. I took the patient's vital signs and reported the frightening results to the resident. Blood arrived from the lab and our patient began to look a little better.

The floor around the bed was slippery with blood and care was needed to keep from falling. After assuring a terrified Mr. Risso that we would not let him bleed to death, and adding more blood to the transfusion, I shooed the gaping interns out of the way. I hurried down the hall to the broom closet and got a mop and a bucket to take care of the dangerously bloody floor. The phone rang constantly, and there was a parade of laboratory technicians in and out of the room. Thirty-nine patients accepted the ministrations of the aide and waited until I could attend to their needs.

The patients stood in the hall and watched. As I rushed by, I told them to go to their own beds or into the day room. The group stirred a little as though to obey my instructions, and moved a few feet. On the periphery of my consciousness, I noticed things.

Mr. Dixon*, a tall black man, was instructing the other patients about what was happening. "They're gonna give him lots of blood. That usually stops the bleeding. Something in the fresh blood helps it clot. If it don't, then he'll go to the operating room. But the blood usually does it."

This overheard conversation was a crucial bit of data. It was also reassuring to me. I had taken care of a few patients who bleed from their GI tract in my fifteen years of nursing, but Mr. Dixon had spent years on these wards. His chart was inches thick—he was an expert.

Several hours later, the ward was deserted. Even Mrs. Risso had gone. The aide stayed with Mr. Risso who stated before he drifted off to sleep that he was never going to take another drink. I dashed around trying to pass the medicines and catch up on my work.

That was the only serious GI bleed that summer. Thank heavens no one bled from the esophagus. I examined the balloons that are inserted to stop that kind of bleeding and hoped that I'd never have to use them.

Evan Jones* was a dear old man, a World War I veteran, who had cancer. We knew that he was dying and so did he. We gave him the best care we could and kept him as comfortable as possible with massive doses of narcotics.

I had been a nurse for almost twenty years and had often worked on wards where we lost three patients a week. In the fifties and sixties, hospitals were not so expensive and there were fewer nursing homes and no hospices. Patients stayed with us until the ends of their lives. When Mr. Jones died, grief and sorrow hit me like a sharp blow. In the six years that I had been a psychiatric nurse, not one of my patients had died.

The aide was a man in his fifties. He looked at me curiously when he saw how moved I was. But when I explained apologetically that I hadn't had a death in six years, he patted my shoulder, and suggested that I go to the medicine room, close the door, and cry. He watched the ward and I disappeared with a box of Kleenex to weep for a dear old man. Then I composed myself, repaired my face and went back to work.

Another typical crisis occurred three days after a new man, Clayton Williams*, was admitted. He arrived with his suitcase and a worried family. I'd shown him to a bed in a cubicle of the main ward and told him the routine. When I went to get the blood pressure apparatus, Mr. Dixon and the other patients moved close as soon as I was out of sight. They didn't know I had paused behind the cubicle to collect equipment that the intern had left. I heard Mr. Dixon say, "The nurses are O. K., but ya best not to tell them too much 'cause they do put things on the chart and the doctor will see." Then, "Be careful what you tell the docs. They're up tight and don't understand us veterans." (More data for Dr. O'Toole.)

Mr. Williams settled into the routine, had his history taken and a physical done by the third-year resident, again by the second-year resident, a third-time by the first-year resident. Then came the intern and finally a very nervous medical student. (Of course I had taken a history also.) Most men enjoyed all the attention. Besides that they were veterans, and used to saying, "Yes, Sir." Mr. Williams was X-rayed and poked and prodded by the laboratory technicians. The chief reviewed his case when he made rounds, and all of the above-mentioned doctors nodded their heads, affirmatively endorsing every pronouncement of that mighty man, the chief of the G I Service. Everyone asked Mr. Williams how much he drank, and he said, "Doc, I used to go at it pretty heavy, you know that. But since the last time I've been here, I quit. That time scared me."

Three days later, when I made rounds, I noticed that Mr. William's hands trembled and he looked pale. His face was glossy with moisture and his pulse rapid. All evening he kept coming to the desk and saying how nervous he felt.

The aide and I moved a patient, who was in a private room that had a lock on the door, put him in another room, and pushed in Mr. William's bed. I called the resident and told him that Mr. Williams looked as though he was about to go into DTs. The resident was surprised and doubtful. But I insisted and obtained an *as necessary* order for medication. Then Mr. Williams admitted rather sheepishly that, yes, he still was drinking, right up to the time when he was admitted.

I told the aide to hurry up with his work, because he might have to stay with the patient. He, of course, was all ready doing that. He had worked on this ward ten years and knew the signs of impending DTs much better than I did. I prepared all the night time medicines ahead of time and locked them in the cupboard. We knew that Mr. Williams might be just a little nervous, or he might be into a full organic psychosis before the evening was over.

He did go into DTs. Fortunately the medication helped and the resident came quickly to check on him. The aide was the best medicine, however. He turned the overhead lights on as high as possible, driving away the goblins that lurked in the corners and elsewhere. He offered reassurance with the conviction of years of experience. In a few days, Mr. Williams was back on the ward, vowing that he would never drink again.

Rules were strictly enforced at the VA. Much to my embarrassment, it took me a while to learn this. For instance, the television was to be turned off at ten o'clock no matter what happened. I had some problems with the rules. Indeed, I have always had problems with rules that are enforced without regard to special circumstances.

One evening a no-score extra-inning baseball game was on the TV. The men crowded the lounge enjoying every second, cheering their particular team and booing the opponents. Ten o'clock came and the game was still in progress and still tied. Tension was high. I closed the door and told the men to dampen their enthusiasm and turn the volume down. Then I went back to the medicine room to finish preparing my night time medications.

A very angry nurse, who was in charge of the ward backing mine, marched in and closed the medicine room door behind her. "I turned off your TV," she announced. "You were breaking the rules."

Now I had been told that she was to be my mentor and that if I had questions I was to refer them to her. So in a sense she outranked me. She also told me that she had scolded the men. I felt more sad than angry. It seemed such a shame to end the patients' pleasure just for the sake of conforming to an arbitrary rule. That was when I decided that I would never work at the VA again.

When I made rounds, I told the men I was sorry I had exposed them to a scolding. Mr. Dixon said, "Ms Hardesty, I should have told you television is supposed to be off at ten."

A few days before my final day on the unit, I played *Who's got the bottle?* with the men. Two of the fellows had been away from the ward taking care of personal business. They returned about six and the evening progressed in its usual quiet way for several hours. Then I noticed that the ward was more noisy than usual and went to investigate.

When I walked into the large ward, my nose was assailed with the odor of alcohol. Most of the men were happily inebriated. Now in ordinary circumstances that would not be such a crime, but almost all of these fellows were suffering the complications of alcoholism. Joe Mitchell* was in a side room, in liver coma, close to death. Yet here was his roommate, jaundiced and with the large abdomen that goes with severe liver disease, damaging his own liver further.

The men laughed when I asked who had brought in a bottle. But no one would tell me. I called the resident and the supervisor and was instructed to find the evidence.

The Aide and I looked everywhere—in the patients' stands, in the laundry basket, in the closets, the toilets, the showers—everywhere! I asked everyone on the ward. We never found the bottle.

The last night I worked at the VA when I went to say good-bye to Mr. Erickson*, a man who was on renal dialysis, he said he had something to tell me. It seemed that the bottle had been hidden in his night stand. We hadn't checked there because he was such a sober upright man. He had objected to being part of the game but was afraid to refuse the others because they might retaliate. "Mr. Dixon brought it in and told me I'd better keep quiet, "he said.

I finished my time at the VA and wrote up a summary of my observations for Richard O'Toole. I had concluded that Mr. Dixon was the leader of the patient population on the GI ward. His power resided in the knowledge he had of the system. He introduced new patients to the rules, and even at times did the same for new staff. There were several ways a person might deal with this. One would be to use his position to promulgate the norms of the medical staff. I was sure Mr. Dixon could be corrupted with privilege and recognition. The other would be to provide the information directly to the patients, and bypass Mr. Dixon.

Then I added several other observations. One was a description of the behavior of the residents, interns and students during rounds, when all heads nodded in unison, and the gestures of the chief were unconsciously mimicked.

The other observation was about the "functional blindness" the medical staff experienced toward nurses during rounds and when in the presence of the chief. I would push my medicine cart down the hall which was blocked with white-clad male bodies, intent on the wisdom they were hearing. Although the men looked my way and surely could see that I needed to pass through the spot where they stood, no one moved. Finally after I said, "Excuse me," half a dozen times, they moved aside and I passed through.

The chief didn't receive my two extra observations with good humor. He denied that they ever happened. When he was told that Mr. Dixon was the leader of the patients' group and had a great deal of influence, he said, "That can't be right. He's just a bum!"

My wild summer was over. Richard O'Toole paid me and I left and returned gratefully to the university to begin my second year in graduate school.

Chapter 15
A Family with Problems

Our class was the first one passing through a new program. It was wonderfully rich in the amount of supervision we received and the interest the faculty had in all aspects of the program itself. But there were a few great ideas that in practice turned out not to be workable. Since the faculty viewed the structure as tentative, and were flexible, students were not allowed to suffer from the faculty's miscalculations—for long.

We each were assigned to a problem family in the community. These families had been suggested by a visiting nurse agency and approved by our faculty. We psychiatric nursing students were to present ourselves as public health nurses from the agency. It was decided that we shouldn't mention that we were graduate students in psychiatric nursing. In our undergraduate program, we had had didactic classes in public health nursing and had practiced for six months, so presenting ourselves in this new role would not be difficult.

The family I was assigned to consisted of a twenty-nine-year-old white woman, of Italian descent, who had six sons, ranging in age from two to eleven. Her husband was in the state hospital with a diagnosis of paranoid schizophrenia. She was on welfare and lived in a small dilapidated house on the west side of Cleveland. She had some serious gynecological problems and some time in the near future would need to have a hysterectomy. She also had chronic urinary difficulties.

My supervisor was Dr. June Watt, a woman for whom I had a great deal of respect and liked personally. She and the rest of the faculty felt that this woman, who evidently had gained so much from mothering, would have emotional difficulties when she had the surgery, and that I should help her explore and prepare for it.

On a rainy fall day, I made my first visit. The house was built in the backyard of a large house that faced the street. I carefully made my way back over the broken sidewalk, through a collection of rusty tricycles and bikes, and knocked on the door of a house with peeling yellow paint. I was admitted to the kitchen by a thin young woman with a mass of curly black hair; Her name was Yolanda Izzo*.

Yolanda invited me to sit in one of the two chairs in the kitchen. She offered me coffee, which we drank black because she was out of milk. From the kitchen I could see into the living room which contained one well worn-couch with an amputated front leg and a small television. Three wiggly little boys were snuggled on the couch, eyes glued on the TV. Yolonda said she was glad to see me because she had a problem.

Her feelings about the impending hysterectomy? No, she was upset about the way the clinic scheduled her to see the doctors. She took two buses to get to the free clinic, with her three preschool kids in tow. There were no definite appointments. Everyone just showed up at eight o'clock, and the residents started working through the crowd. I was very sympathetic with this because I had had the same experience at the University Hospital's orthopedic clinic when Susan broke her arm. But Yolonda's problem was worse. One day she saw the gyn doctor and the next the urology resident. Could I help?

I said that I'd try. I spent several hours on the phone with the residents, nurses and department head, explaining, coercing and pleading. When I went back the next week, I was able to tell Yolanda that arrangements had been made for her to be seen by one doctor who would handle both her problems. In addition they would plan to see her first.

She was grateful. Then I said, "How do you feel about your upcoming surgery?"

"O.K.," she replied, "but I need you to take a look at little Jimmy's hand. He got it cut two weeks ago and I took him for stitches. I don't have bus money to take him back to take them out. I think they have been in too long."

I looked at Jimmy's hand. The wound was healed but the stitches did need to come out.

"Where do I cut," she asked, "I will take them out myself. Jimmy go get the scissors."

Now, I had worked for surgeons and on surgical floors. I had removed thousands of stitches. I knew I was breaking the rules of the public health agency that I represented, but the rules seemed so foolish in this situation. I said, "I'll do it." and I unwrapped my sterile scissors.

A few snips and the deed was done. My mistake was tht I recorded it. The agency was upset that I had done something that was medical practice and June was concerned. "You really must have wanted to do something to help," she said. "Why are you having so much trouble getting her to talk about the loss of her uterus?"

The next week when I arrived, Yolanda was ecstatic. He husband had been given a leave for the weekend and they had gone to a furniture store. They bought a breakfast set—so almost everyone could sit at the table together for a meal. There was a new couch to replace the one without a leg, and a second bed had been added to the one where all the children slept. Yolanda had been sleeping on the couch. She didn't have any idea how the payments could be made, but she doubted if the store would repossess the furniture. I looked through the doorway into the living room where six boys sat in front of the TV and agreed that it would soon show signs of wear.

Now each visit I explored some aspect of her life. I asked about nutrition and found that she knew more about food than most middle-class mothers, although she was often frustrated by the lack of money. The boys were immunized and their general development was at the expected level for their age. The genuine public health nurse who I was replacing had been doing a good job.

When I asked, she said, yes, she was doing well at the clinic but there was another problem. "The oldest boy, Tony, doesn't want to go to school. He says the teacher doesn't like him." Then she showed me a note from the teacher that said Tony was disinterested and disruptive.

I suggested that she make an appointment with the teacher and discuss the problem with him. She presented so many excuses that I knew, even if I worked through them all, she would be unlikely to go and my semester would end before anything was done.

After receiving her permission to discuss Tony with the teacher, I made the appointment. I met with Mr. Green* in his classroom one dark fall afternoon. He was a good-looking young man in his late twenties. I told him that I was working with the family who had many problems, and I wanted to hear about Tony.

He told me what I had already read in the note. Then

he said, "I bet there aren't many books in that house."

"Books? I've never seen any." Then I went on to describe the sleeping arrangements, the father's illness, etc.

Mr. Green said, "I had no idea that Tony was living like that. Listen, I work out at the Y a couple times a week. I'll see if I can get Tony a membership."

The next week, Yolanda was thrilled. Mr. Green had stopped twice to pick up Tony and take him to the Y. She wondered if he could get a membership for the next boy, and said, she'd ask him.

Her surgery? No problem. Her infection was clearing up and the hysterectomy would be scheduled soon. But she did have a problem with the phone bill. The neighbor used the phone to call her boyfriend in Alaska, and now she had a $200 dollar phone bill. She was going to lose her phone. I had no solution for that problem.

All this time I was reading about the values of low-income families, the culture of poverty and mental health work among the poor. I kept telling June that the difficulties I was having in doing psychotherapeutic intervention with this woman were to be expected. Poor people focus on their most immediate problem and look for concrete help from their caregivers. They aren't so interested in talking about feelings. They want something tangible done.

Yolanda's girl friend moved in with her, bringing four children, a bed and a few kitchen chairs. They were more crowded, but now they each had a baby sitter and there was another welfare check. Both women were happy with an arrangement that would have driven me wild.

The last day I saw Yolanda, I told her that I was a psychiatric nursing student. Both she and her new roommate were suddenly interested in my specialty. Yolanda had questions about her husband's prognosis and medicines. The roommate wanted to discuss problems she was having with a boyfriend. Gosh, they were ready to talk a little about feelings.

Yolanda had a more complete answer to my usual question about her coming hysterectomy. She said she was tired of having kids and would be glad to know that she would have no more. Her husband was a good Catholic and wouldn't let her use birth control, but now she wouldn't need to. "Hell, no, I don't have any bad feelings about it. I'm happy."

I wrote my final paper citing all the research about the culture of poverty, mental health work among the poor, etc. When I went in for my final conference, June slid my paper across the desk and I looked at it with happy surprise. There was a large red A written across the top.

I looked up at June, with a question on my face. "Yes, Florence," she said, "you convinced me. I've been trying to get you to use a strictly psychotherapeutic approach. It was inappropriate in this situation. You have done a wonderful job with this family."

Chapter 16
The Thesis

A requirement of the psychiatric nursing program was completing a thesis which meant doing a satisfactory piece of independent research, describing it in clear, scholarly language, and defending it before a group of fellow professionals. My classmates were dreaming of doing research that would bring important knowledge to all psychiatric nurses. I was praying that I could come up with a problem, study the literature, gather the data and finish the program in the proscribed two years. I wanted to gain something from all that work besides a diploma, but I had no illusions about the value of master's level research.

When I was teaching at Saint-What's-His-Name. I had taken my students to the long-term state hospital for tours. During the program, I had also spent time practicing there. The psychotropic drugs that had been developed in the fifties had made a difference in the acute nature of the patients' psychosis. But the people who had been in the hospital for years, totally dependent on the staff, restricted by locked doors and rules, were not mentally well. They were not equipped to manage their lives outside the hospital. The efforts of the more enlightened staff were directed toward helping them relearn the skills of living they had lost years before. Enlightened staff were few in those days. Dr. Ishiama, the psychologist at the hospital was one, perhaps the only one, who believed that many of the patients could live elsewhere.

When I visited the back wards, and one women's ward in particular, I was surprised there was so little interaction between the patients. They spent their days in a large square room, with heavy oak chairs lined up against the walls. Some paced, others sat, and a few, who had not been helped by the drugs, hallucinated. The television blared high above in a wire cage, but no one paid attention to it, any more than to their raving ward mates. The patients were unkempt and poorly dressed in the mismatched clothes issued each week. Since the state-issued dresses all went into the laundry at the end of the week without any individual marking, nothing fit. Personal shoes and bras were frequently stolen. The staff, usually one or two untrained aides, spent the day in the locked office, venturing out only to give medications, line up patients march them through the shower or to the dining hall, and herd them to bed at night.

As I looked at these wards, I had the impression that I was looking at strangers in a railroad station, so little happened between them. Some of these women had been here for twenty years, and yet they behaved as though they had never met. They spent their days waiting. Were they waiting to get well or to die?

I had always been interested in how space affects interaction. My first husband had worked for a contractor and I was fascinated by the house plans he brought home. I planned my parties carefully, arranging the space so that my guests would move about and meet each other. My doodling was always of house plans and furniture arrangements.

When I looked at the arrangement of the ward, I thought, the chairs were arranged in a way that discouraged interaction. I wondered what would happen if I could change that.

I was aware of some of the research that looked at how space affected what happened between people. I began to search the literature for more. The conclusion of most of the researchers was that people talked more if they faced each other or were at right angles to each other. But the subjects had been normal people. Would the mentally ill women on the ward react the same?

I talked with Dr. Ishiama and he thought I might have an interesting study. When I discussed it with my advisor, Dr. Fay Spring, she said, "So what?" I said that I was aware that nurses managed space instinctively. Shouldn't they be doing it more knowledgeably?

The next day she called me to say she'd been thinking about my idea, and thought that maybe I had a question.

I got permission from Dr. Abdul*, the physician in charge of the ward, to use it for a study. On the break between semesters I did a literature search and talked at length with Dr. Ishiama about a design for the study. Then I wrote a proposal, which was actually the first two chapters of my thesis.

I was on my way. I would finish on time, I told myself. Holly had a proposal but my other classmates had decided that they would not do a thesis at the same time they were finishing class work. They teased me a bit about my "concrete research, " and some of them were put off by my aggressive determination to finish. I refused to join in gripe sessions about the difficulties of doing a thesis because I didn't dare dwell on the negatives.

The day before I was to start collecting data, the doctor in charge of the ward changed his mind and said that I could not do research there. I made an appointment with him to discuss his refusal. I dressed carefully for this meeting, just few touches of femininity on a business-like tweed suit. I slipped the heavy chain of my grandmother's 18K gold watch over my head. (Old money impresses some people.) I wore heels to give me two extra inches of height and I carried a leather briefcase. I also said a prayer, and asked my dead father, if or wherever he existed, to put words in my mouth.

Dr. Abdul was a Turk. Many of the state hospitals at that time were staffed by physicians from other countries. The pay was poor and the conditions were depressing. Only a few dedicated or incompetent physicians from this country were willing to work in those conditions. Administrators hired doctors from other countries, some of whom spoke little English and did not understand our culture.

Dr. Abdul did speak English. He had been doing pharmacological research on the ward although he wasn't doing it at the time. I entered his office, and reached across his desk to give him a business-like hand shake—the greeting of an equal. He looked surprised. Then I sat in the only chair available, an easy chair across the desk from him, the patient's chair. I quickly slid the brief case under me, so that I was sitting at the same level as my opponent.

I don't remember his objections to my research but I do remember that I countered each of them, coolly and logically. Then I talked about the advantages of having research going on in a ward for which he was responsible. When my arguments were finished, I stayed in the chair, not willing to end the interview, and not willing to give up.

Finally he breathed a resigned sigh, stood up, reached across the desk and shook my hand. "All right, go ahead."

The data collection period covered more than a month. I divided the ward's waking hours into time periods and randomly selected times when I would be there. The ward was also divided into sections and I drew lots to decide which sections I would observe and when. I defined interaction and then observed for it. Then after a week, I moved the chairs in circles and recorded what happened. I did this twice, using the subjects as their own controls.

I finished data collection on May first. The thesis had to be finished, approved, defended and typed by May seventeenth. I had no calculator to analyze my data—they were expensive then—but I had two willing, capable daughters. Susan, Shevawn and I counted, added, multiplied, checked the data and ran the statistical tests.

The patients had talked twice as much when the chairs were arranged in circles. Several began to form friendships. They liked the ward arranged that way so much that I had to be firm about keeping the chairs against the wall during the control period. The staff liked the chairs against the wall because it was easier to sweep the ward. When I showed them my results they decided that keeping them in circles was worth the extra effort. I hoped that other staffs would make the same decision.

It was time to write. I got up every morning at six, put on my robe and made a pot of coffee. Then I wrote until noon, when Shevawn came home from school for lunch. She made me lunch and brought it to me on a tray. At one, I showered, dressed, and took my work to Faye. Then I went to my other classes. In the evening I studied.

My marriage had continued to deteriorate during the two years I had been in the program. My husband refused to go for counseling with me and unless he did, there was little hope for us. I concentrated on helping Susan through her teenage years, keeping the bills paid and finishing the program. My husband moved out three times during this period. I don't remember why. I hardly noticed. Nothing was going to stop me—I kept on writing. I was certain that a master's degree would contribute more to the happiness of my daughters and myself than hanging on to a relationship that was doomed to fail.

I graduated in June 1966. The National Institutes of Mental Health, Western Reserve University, Dorothy Greg, Dr. Fay Spring, Dr. Anita Werner, and June Watt, had all cooperated to give me a superb education. My mother, Floray Fisher and Susan and Shevawn Hardesty had supported me through a difficult but rewarding two years. A research journal published an article based on my thesis a few months later. Once again, I was moving on.

The Community College

1966-1969

Chapter 17
And So to Work

I was finished with school, for the time being and desperately needed a job. It was easy to pick up temporary work while I devoted myself to the search for a position which would use my new education. Saint-What's-His-Name wanted me back, and the school of the hospital where I had worked in Pennsylvania wrote and offered me a position. I was flattered by their offers, but I wanted new challenges.

I explored the possibility of being an instructor at Western Reserve. When I learned that they paid less than I had earned at Saint-What's-His-Name, before my Master's degree, I decided that I could not afford to spend so much money for status and prestige.

A community college, the first in the city, had opened a few years before. Classes were being held in abandoned warehouses in the industrial area of the city, while a modern campus was being built. The college had just opened an associate degree nursing program, the first of its kind in Ohio. There was much interest and controversy about these programs.

Up until this time, most nurses had been educated in schools run by hospitals. It was the hospitals' way of insuring an adequate and well-trained staff. Although the programs were increasingly education oriented, vestiges of the apprentice system clung to them. In addition to strictly educational experiences, the students were expected to do a portion of the work of the institution. The person who directed the staff of registered nurses usually also directed the school. It was difficult for the director to separate educational goals and staffing demands and few succeeded. These programs were three calendar years long.

Four and five-year nursing programs leading to bachelor's degrees had existed in universities for many years. It was felt by most nursing leaders that this was the best way for professional nurses to be educated, and the American Nurses Association agreed. But the rank and file of the profession who had gone to hospital schools felt that the way they had learned to be nurses was the only acceptable way. Their attitude reminded me of soldiers who had endured boot camp and now felt that everyone should undergo the same experience.

Dr. Mildred Montage at Columbia University had developed and demonstrated a new type of nursing program, a two-year, associate degree program which produced what she called a technical nurse. Everyone agreed that the graduates of a four-year program were professionally educated. However, most nurses who were educated in hospital schools also called themselves professionals. Dr. Montage called into question the term professional when it was applied to nurses who had been educated outside of systems of higher education. She believed that hospital school graduates were not professional.

Hospitals were finding that nursing programs were becoming expensive, especially since they could no longer insist that students staff the hospitals. Community college presidents were looking at nursing schools as a way to increase enrollment. Prospective students were no longer willing to endure the military or finishing school mentality of the three-year school. These schools had drawn young women, fresh out of high school. Now there were many older women, some married with children, and men who wanted to be nurses. Few three-year schools would admit this group and not many of the prospective students could afford a four-year university program.

I had gone to a three-year school and then on to a university to obtain a bachelor's degree. I spent almost seven years earning a degree which I might have obtained in four. Even though the hospital was a university hospital, the science and humanities courses I took did not carry college credit. When I was seventeen, no one told me the difference between nursing programs and I did what most nurses had done: enrolled in a hospital school.

I resented the lost time and the long hours of unpaid work in my basic program. Although I was grateful for the good education I had received, I had no emotional ties to three-year schools in general. I was ready to learn about a new type of program that produced nurses more efficiently. The chairman of the community college nursing program was scheduled to speak at a Nurses Association meeting, and I went to hear her. The auditorium was filled with interested nurses, many of whom were hostile.

A tall, poised woman was introduced. Her black, short hair was crisp and curly and her blue eyes were fringed with black lashes. She smiled at the audience, and speaking without notes, described the philosophy and structure of degree nursing programs.

Helen Burnside had obtained a master's degree in nursing education at Teachers College, Columbia University. She had been a student of Dr. Montage and had developed an associate degree program in New York State. What impressed me most was the logic of her presentation. Nothing was taught in the program because it was a tradition, she said. It was there only because it was needed by practicing nurses.

When Helen finished her presentation, she smiled at the audience again and asked for questions. She was barraged by them, and answered in the same logical friendly way she had made her presentation.

How could she produce a nurse in two years when it took other schools at least three? Her answer was that the program was not redundant, and each of the experiences was designed to teach a specific skill. Once that goal had been met, there was no need to repeat the skill again and again, as was the practice in hospital schools. I sat there thinking of the hundreds of enemas, thousands of bed baths and ten of thousands of meals I had served in my basic training. She added that hospitals expected newly graduated nurses to be experienced practitioners. This she said was unrealistic and not expected in any other occupation.

Someone had heard that her program had not taken the best students first. If that were true, wasn't it a waste? She replied that the students had been waiting for the program to begin and had met the prerequisite requirements. Of those students, they would be admitted in order of their enrollment in the college. She thought that this was the fair way to do this. Besides experience and research had shown that they had no reliable criteria to judge who among these students would be successful.

"I hear you aren't going to have caps. Is that true?" a voice from the back of the room asked.

Helen sighed and answered. "I'd like not to. They just get into the way when you are working and they are hard to keep clean. Patients are more interested in what is in the students head than on it. However, the student's want caps. So I suspect we may have them."

One woman rose, and asked a question, her voice filled with emotion. I don't remember the question, but I do remember the anger in it. Helen smiled and said, "I can see that you have strong feelings about this. I would like to talk with you. As soon as we are finished here, please come and let's discuss this."

The hostile woman was disarmed and flattered. I had witnessed the performance of a master speaker. That night I went home and wrote a letter applying for a position in the new nursing program at the community college.

Helen called me for an interview. A few days later I was hired as an assistant professor, at a salary twice as high as I had received from Saint-What's-His-Name. In two years I would earn back the salary I lost when I left my job to go to graduate school.

Helen invited me for dinner and I had a chance to learn more about my new boss. She was divorced and had a son, a small male replica of herself. Curt was a few years younger than Shevawn. Helen had been raised in an exclusive suburb of New York City and her parents were wealthy. Most nurses were products of middle-class backgrounds, few upper class women choose nursing. After a year at Hunter College, she entered a hospital school. She did well academically and with the patients, but she did have trouble with some of the rules.

She was an excellent tennis player and had even considered a pro career. She played as often as she could. One day she was called to the director's office and threatened with expulsion. Helen had been seen wearing shorts on the tennis court, instead of the required tennis dress. She was not expelled, but she was told never to use the name of the hospital in her resume. She never has.

She worked as a school nurse in Harlem and did a tour of duty as a Navy nurse before she became a teacher. Her marriage was brief, but she was happy when after the divorce she discovered she was pregnant. Helen and I became close friends, almost as soon as she hired me.

There was another psychiatric nursing instructor at the school. I hoped that I would be able to work easily with her, but we had very different approaches to education. For a day or so I worried that I might have made an unfortunate decision when I had accepted the position. But, Helen said we could manage the course any way we chose, as long as we had the same course outline and the same final exam. Connie* and I split the student group, each taking thirty-five. We lectured to our own class every week. Each class was divided into three groups and we spent a day a week with each group in the clinical area. We prepared questions for the final and then together chose which ones would be on the test.

I was very grateful that I had my own group of students, to teach in my own way. Because I spent time with the students in small groups and conferred with them individually on the ward, I knew them all well. If they had trouble with a portion of the class work, I would take a little of the clinical time to help them. Helen's wisdom had permitted this, and she obtained the best that each of her psychiatric nursing teachers had to give.

I had a good paying job with congenial people. I happily began three years of satisfying teaching.

Chapter 18
The Students

School didn't begin until September. Until then, I worked as a staff nurse at the state hospital and happily prepared my lectures. I spent 40 hours reviewing the literature and writing my lecture on schizophrenia. When it was finished it wasn't much different than what I would have said if I hadn't prepared. But I was satisfied that I knew all there was to know, at that time, about helping these patients.

Fall came and, with an mixture of elation and fear, I met my students. Of the thirty-six students, seventeen were black, four were male, and most had worked as aides or licensed practical nurses. Their ages ranged from eighteen to fifty. I delivered my well-rehearsed introductory lecture and got acquainted with them.

I got to know them even better when, in groups of twelve, we spent a day at the short-term state hospital. One innovation of the associate degree program was the pre-conference. The students and I met for a brief time before we went to the ward and outlined the things they hoped to learn that day. Some of the objectives would be mine, but each student discussed her/his individual learning goals. At the end of the day we met again for an hour and discussed how well the objectives had been met and anything else about the day that had interested, puzzled or enlightened us. So while the students spent only one day a week with psychiatric patients, the day was focused, and they learned not only from their own experience but from the experiences of their fellows.

The hospital was adjacent to a city hospital. When I think of it, the color gray, dark gray, is what I remember. That was the color of the cement floor, worn smooth by the feet of thousands of troubled people and a few staff. The walls were dark green to shoulder height and then a dirty light green. In each ward there was the inevitable day room with its rows of chairs and screened television set, sleeping rooms that held six cots, isolation rooms for the most disturbed patients, bathrooms without doors, a sun porch with heavy steel screening, and the locked office, a glass cage with scarred desks and a chart rack. The doors leading outside were battered metal, and always locked.

The staff was poorly educated. There were one or two aides on each ward. They kept the patients and ward clean. Medications were given as prescribed and the sickest patients were prevented from hurting themselves and others. The ward routine was well established and they followed it. Therapy was something the doctors did, if they chose. The staff were not interested or prepared to do it.

It was a far different setting than the ward at Saint What's-His-Name or the psychiatric hospital that was part of a university. There were no role models available among this staff. On the other hand, we were free to do what we thought would help the patients. Their needs were so overwhelming that even the most inept student made a difference.

The first week passed and I was delighted with the students. When we went to the hospital they showed a remarkable amount of common sense. I suspect that having older students in the group helped spread this rare trait.

I decided that I would give them a short essay test at the beginning of each three-hour lecture class. Part of my rational was coercion. I wanted to be sure they studied psychiatric nursing every week. They were also in another nursing class, and it was possible that the demands of that class might be more imperative. A weekly quiz would insure that they would devote time to my class. I had another reason. I wanted to know how they were progressing and how I was doing. If I weren't clear, or if there were something they didn't understand, I would know and could remedy it.

When I read the first essay test I, was shocked. Many of the black students did not understand the words I had used. These were relatively simple words, such as facility and resource. Unlike many of my colleagues, I had managed to keep my vocabulary free of medical jargon and prided myself on speaking simple English. Yet the very students who had performed so well in the clinical area the week before did not understand me.

The next week, I handed back the tests, liberally marked with red. I had written in all the right answers and defined the words they hadn't understood. Then I discussed the problem with the class. I told them that I could simplify the terms I used, but I was concerned that they would not to be familiar with the language they would hear in the hospital.

A middle-aged practical nurse raised her hand. "Don't do that. We've already been cheated enough. Use the words you want us to know. We can learn them."

"All right," I answered, "but you must stop me if I use a word you don't understand and give me a chance to define it."

Heads nodded in vigorous affirmatives. Then another voice, "A lot of us are in remedial English. We're getting better."

I was awed by their determination. I knew that many had made As in chemistry, anatomy and physiology, and in their other nursing classes. Yet they dealt with handicaps because of their poor education. This was 1966 and the civil rights movement was beginning to make an impact. My students convinced me that these changes were long overdue.

The students kept their promise and I kept mine.

My students could draw on knowledge that could never be learned in books. Yvonne* was a black woman in her thirties, as was her patient. The patient was depressed and complained constantly that no one could manage financially on a welfare check. The more she complained the more depressed she became. Yvonne kept reassuring her that it could be done, but the woman didn't hear her.

I had told the students that they should focus on their patients and not talk about their own personal lives unless they were sure that doing this would help their patients. The books and the text did not include the last exception and Yvonne was following the book.

After a day of trying to break through the hopelessness of her patient's statements, Yvonne made a decision. "Look, I know it is tough. I have four kids and I was on welfare for six years. But you can manage to feed the kids and keep them clean. And have a little fun now and then, too."

The patient was silent for a moment. Then she said, "Oh. When you come next week will you help me learn how?"

Julie* was eighteen. She took a bus into the school from her home in an affluent suburb. Her patient was a woman in her forties, a widow with eight children. The medicine had removed her psychotic thinking, but as her discharge neared she was concerned about how she could manage the problems that faced her.

In conference, Julie said, "I'm just overwhelmed thinking about this lady's problems. Here I am, eighteen, no kids, living at home. How do I know what it is like to have eight kids and no one to help with them?"

I offered the usual formula. Let her tell you how she feels. Learn all you can about her life. Your interest and concern are supportive. Help her explore and solve her own problems. All the time I was thinking, what would it be like if I had six more kids to cope with? The other students were having similar thoughts.

But not every student. La Donna* was a large Black woman about forty. She listened to us flounder around for a while and then said, "Listen, don't go down the drain with this patient. She took care of her kids before she was sick. She managed then. Remember babies come one at a time, usually, and you get used to them. I got ten. The oldest is thirteen. They all have their jobs and we manage fine."

Ten children, working weekends and in school! Again we were awed. Now, how would we use our expert mother?

We decided that Julie would keep the patient and use the formula I offered. However, she would introduce La Donna as a resource who would spend some time with the patient. Julie would listen as La Donna offered help and pass it all on to us in conference. I felt as though I were gathering knowledge from my books and experience and funneling it to the students, and at the same time, I was gathering wisdom from them.

One student in particular taught us all something. Helga* was an attractive woman in her forties with a German accent. She was late to the hospital one day and in pre-conference she explained why. She and her fourteen-year-old son had taken a small decorated Christmas tree and placed it on the grave of her daughter, who had died at three, the year before. When I asked more she said her daughter was a mongoloid who had inoperable heart problems. When the baby had been born, her husband sought refuge from sorrow with a younger woman and now she was alone.

Helga's classmates had questions and we learned more. Her married daughter had had a stroke during childbirth and was partially paralyzed. Six months before, her brother in West Germany had killed himself because of the pressure put on him to return to East Germany and help with weapon development.

Helga had faced all this pain and sorrow, and yet she was not a bitter or unhappy woman. She was excited about school and the prospect of being a nurse. She viewed her retarded child's birth as a blessing in spite of the pain it brought. She talked about how sweet the baby was, and how loving her had brought her a special closeness with her teenage son. This wasn't denial; it was an affirmation of the richness that life can offer even in the midst of sorrows.

The next week she told us that the Christmas tree had been stolen from the grave. "Oh, I am sorry," I said.

"No, Willie and I had fun doing it, and if the baby exists somewhere she knows we remembered her. We have been imagining all week who the child is that is enjoying it now. It served a purpose for us. Now let someone else enjoy it."

The quarter was ending and I was saying good-by to my first group of students. They did well on the final. It turned out that Connie liked my questions so well, the test was really my test. I felt enriched because of the ten weeks spent with this class.

But things were not so good at home. My husband insisted that the family go to Florida for the Christmas holidays. He was still a doctoral student and I was supporting the family. We only had seventy-five dollars after we paid the bills so I refused to go. He continued to insist that we make the trip. Finally I told him to go if he liked but that I was going to file for divorce. I don't think he believed me because he went happily off to visit his aunt in Miami. He drove his red MG convertible, a most unreliable vehicle. I saw a lawyer and the girls and I spent a relieved Christmas, glad to be free of the tension we had dealt with for three years.

I was embarrassed that I was to have a second divorce. But my heart was not broken. I felt that I had made a real effort to make the best of an initially bad choice. To continue trying to reconcile our diverse personalities required more effort than I could summon. Susan was relieved with my decision. Shevawn was saddened, but not deeply. My daughters, my mother and I were a close family. This family and my students were enough to fill my life.

Chapter 19
Denise*, The Dancer

Denise blended into the student group so well that at first I hardly noticed her. She was small, blonde and in her late twenties. Aside from looking a little tired, she was attractive. I assigned her to a patient on the men's ward. Late that afternoon I walked into the day room that held the gift of a generous donor, a pool table, and watched Denise in action.

Her patient was teaching her to play pool. Denise leaned across the table, arms outstretched along the pool cue, her uniform skirt hiked up to expose muscled thighs. When she made the shot, she laughed—a tinkling sound— straightened and pirouetted gracefully on one foot. I watched, reluctant to interrupt the game. I was thinking, "Careful, Miss. He is going to get the wrong idea about you."

It got worse. Her patient wanted to show her how to make a difficult shot. She was leaning across the table again, and the man leaned over her, pressing his body close as he lined up her cue. My face must have shown alarm, because Cecil*, another student, winked at me reassuringly.

In post-conference that day, I talked about the folly of seductive behavior with psychiatric patients. No, this does not mean one is attempting to seduce the patient. So many of the behaviors that are perfectly acceptable between men and woman at a party, or in social situations, can be misconstrued by the patients. So caregivers have to be particularly careful in what they say and how they behave, so as not to promise the patients more than a professional relationship. Students who don't learn this can get themselves into situations that are dangerous for themselves and for their patients.

Then I tactfully talked about Denise's movements during the pool game. Denise *just didn't get it*. She didn't see how a simple pool game could be misconstrued by anyone. Maybe it was, she said, because she was a dancer and was graceful.

I didn't want to embarrass her, so I just told her to be conscious of her movements. I noticed that the two men in the group looked amused. Cecil was a compact Black man. Bill* was a tall red-headed man who was recently discharged from the service where he'd been a corpsman. We moved on to other topics.

The next week I was making rounds and walked into one of the sleeping rooms. Denise was sitting on her patient's bed and they were engaged in intense conversation. I had told students it was better to talk with their patients in places other than the sleeping rooms, however, this was only a suggestion. I had also said that generally it was better not to sit on patients' beds. However since there were no chairs in the rooms it might be necessary.

Denise was sitting on the foot of the bed, her feet tucked under her, her face resting on her hand, arm propped on her knee. I looked at her and thought, she looks like a sensuous kitten.

I asked her to come into the office for a moment and privately told her that the way she was sitting was "seductive behavior." She wasn't defensive. She just didn't see what she was doing that was upsetting me.

Once again I brought it up in conference. I hoped the other students could help me explain what I found objectionable in what she did. She had been in school and in small clinical groups with these students for more than a year. The knew each other well and liked each other. They talked to her and told her about times when they had seen her behave in ways that could be construed as provocative.

I had a hard time understanding how someone who had studied dance, with all its movements couldn't conceive of how she appeared to others. But Denise was firm. She heard what everyone was saying and she would try to be aware, but she just didn't understand.

Every week, I would see her doing something else. I hated the way I felt when I would tell her about it. I felt as though I were forced into acting out the role of a rigid puritan. It turned out that Denise's major patient was gay, so I did not need to worry about him making advances. But I did want her to understand what we were telling her before she moved on to her next class.

Several weeks later, in post-conference, Cecil and Bill brought up the subject of Denise's behavior. They began by describing an incident that had occurred the week before in the parking lot. It seems that Denise's car wouldn't start and she had to wait for help to arrive.

Suddenly Cecil adopted a falsetto, and offered a perfect, if exaggerated, impression of Denise's speech. Then he got out of his chair and began to move gracefully around the room, making distraught sounds about the car not starting. He perched on the conference table, as she had perched on the hood, one leg bent and the other straightened out. Looking at Cecil you could just imagine, a skirt pulled up a little with a lot of thigh showing.

Bill then got into the act. He played the role of a typical male when faced with a seductive Denise/Cecil. He panted, preened, leered, wiped his brow and tried to peek under her skirt. The other students were laughing and Denise had her hands over her blazing face, laughing an embarrassed laugh.

The men went on until she begged them to stop. "I get it. Now I see what you mean. Stop, please, stop!"

They continued. Bill talked about wanting to hear what she was saying but being so aroused that he couldn't concentrate on her words. They then pantomimed my arrival on the scene, even though I hadn't been there. Cecil did a perfect imitation of my voice, telling Denise she was being seductive. We laughed until we cried.

The performance and post-conference were over. Denise finally did get it, and began to behave like a professional nurse. I was relieved and very grateful to Cecil and Bill for their contribution to nursing education.

Chapter 20
Winners

I don't remember who, among the first class, had the highest grade point average, but I do remember two students who were real winners.

Lottie Crumpkin* was a practical nurse who had worked at Saint-What's-His-Name, when I taught there. At the time, the psychiatric staff was doing experimental work using sleep therapy to treat psychosomatic illnesses. Using drugs, the patient was put into a deep sleep for several days. He was totally dependent on the care of the nurses. Lottie was the nurse most frequently called to be the private nurse of these difficult patients. (The treatment has gone the way of many others—it was very expensive and its effectiveness was questionable—so it is no longer done.)

I was delighted at the first of the quarter when I met my new class to find an old acquaintance among the students. Lottie was an excellent practical nurse and I was pleased that she was studying to be a registered nurse.

When we went to the hospital to work with patients, Lottie chose as her patient a withdrawn woman who had been diagnosed schizophrenic. The student asked me what she should read so that she would know more about her patient's difficulties. I recommended Silvano Arieti's book, *The Interpretation of Schizophrenia*. At that time, it was the most authoritative book available. The author was a classically educated scholar, as well as an excellent psychiatrist and his prose reflected his background.

The following week at the beginning of the class, I gave the weekly essay test. That evening I settled at my desk, eager to read them because they told me so much about the students abilities. When I got to Lottie's my heart fell. Her sentences, her spelling and the words she used were what you would expect of a fourth grader, not a college student. How, I wondered, had she ever gotten so far when she wrote, and I suspected, read, so poorly. It seemed cruel that I had told her to read such a difficult book.

The next day, I looked at her record. She had taken one remedial reading class before she began the other classes in the program. For some reason the college had counted this class as an English class. She had scored high in the sciences and in the nursing classes. She hadn't yet taken the sociology and psychology classes.

Helen's office door was open and I went in to discuss Lottie's problem. Helen didn't seem as distressed as I did. She reminded me that this student had completed two thirds of the program and had very good grades. I expressed worry about the state board examination. Then, this was a two day long examination that nurses had to pass before they could be licensed to practice as a registered nurse. Helen reminded me that students were permitted to take the test three times.

Then she went on to tell me something I hadn't known. She had a form of dyslexia. Until she was twelve she couldn't comprehend anything she read. She could, however, remember everything she heard. Her teachers recognized her problem and made allowances for it. Her mother read all her assignments to her. The problem improved and she graduated from high school at sixteen. However, she continued to have more problems with reading and writing than would be expected of a college professor. She dictated letters and articles and her secretary typed them. She edited them and managed to have a respectable number of publications.

When Helen told me this I understood her mistrust of test scores as criteria for admission. I also had more hope for Lottie's success.

I talked with Lottie and she told me that she was aware of the problem. She had gone to a segregated school in the rural South. She said, "My teacher didn't write much better than me, and my folks didn't write much more than their names."

I thought, how well she has done with what was given to her. She went on to explain that one of her children and her pastor were tutoring her, and that she did understand the book I had recommended.

Lottie's answers on the essay tests were correct, even though her writing did not improve much. She was the last person to complete the final exam, but she did pass it. She finished the other courses and graduated from the program. Later, I heard that she had passed the state board examination on the second try and had become a registered nurse.

Five years passed during which I obtained a doctorate and left Cleveland. One year I was at the American Nurses Association convention in Atlantic City. When we nurses met, we engaged in the usual questions that one asks to get acquainted—"Where are you from? Where have you worked? What schools...."

I met a nurse from a small southern Ohio town. When she heard that I had lived in Cleveland, she said, "My husband went to the Cleveland Clinic to have heart surgery, a very complicated revision of a valve. He was very sick and I don't think either he or I would have survived without the help and support of a wonderful nurse. She was the head nurse on the coronary intensive care unit. She took such wonderful care of him and gave me endless support and information. She made me proud of my profession."

"It is always so nice to hear that about one of us," I said. "By the way, do you remember her name?"

"I'll never forget it. Her name is Lottie Crumpkin."

Arturo Brown* was a tall, light-skinned Black man, exceptionally handsome and polite. He had just completed a tour in the Army and I imagined that he looked better than a recruiting poster in his uniform. While it was nice to have such a decorative and pleasant student in the class, I worried that he would never make it through the program.

He made the same grade in all the essay tests, C-. Now if the truth were really known, some of the tests probably should have been D+. But I liked him so well, and he seemed to try so hard, that I gave him the benefit of the doubt.

I had met his wife at one of the open houses. She was small woman—very intense and extremely intelligent. She was a teacher but aspired to become a lawyer. I wondered what it was like for Arturo to be struggling through a community college program, married to such a bright ambitious woman.

I checked his record and he had been consistent. He had passed all the courses—with C's. He did the same with the final and surprised me when he got through the state boards on the first try—with scores one point above the cutoff point.

The next part of the story came from an acquaintance who was the director of nurses at the long-term state hospital. Arturo applied for a job, and was immediately hired. He requested the geriatric ward and was assigned to the back ward occupied by people who had spent their lives in the state hospital. Psychotic patients get old just like the rest of us.

When he was taken to the ward the first time, he walked through the corridor, breathing the air tainted with the smells of such places, the ammonia of old urine, the musty odor of unwashed bodies, and the strong smell of Lysol. His first question was, "Where are their clothes?" The patients were wearing hospital gowns.

Then he asked, "Why is it so gloomy in here? These walls haven't been painted in years."

Six months later the ward was a model geriatric unit. Arturo persuaded paint stores to donate paint. He and the staff painted the walls sunny yellow. A florist from his church supplied plants and his wife's students painted colorful posters for the walls. The patients were clothed because Arturo had found better ways to deal with their incontinence than to dress them in skimpy gowns with open backs. The ward was flooded with music from a stereo. On Sundays, various singing groups came to the ward to entertain. The occupational therapist, who years before, had given up trying to do anything on that unit, began again.

Arturo taught me that C-, marginally satisfactory, is sometimes an excellent grade.

One of the faculty at the school did a study in an attempt to isolate those variables which would predict success in our program. The only variable that consistently correlated with success was being married and having children. The researcher concluded that those factors probably indicated that the student was motivated and persistent. Later when I was in my doctoral program and doing a minor in educational psychology, I searched the literature and learned that there was no correlation between grades in college (assuming one had graduated) and success in a job. There was one exception and that was in college teaching.

Knowing Arturo and Lottie made me very aware of a bias many nursing teachers have. We like students who are like ourselves. We tend to see the achievement of high grades as the only predictor of success in the work place. There are other equally important predictors that we can not measure in a ten-week quarter, or in a sixteen-week semester.

I became a better teacher for having known Arturo and Lottie.

Chapter 21
Friends, Family and Mentors

N
o one teaches in a vacuum. What students learn and what teachers teach is affected by their personal environment. Even though my marriages had failed, my family and my friends sustained me through the rough periods and gave me joy. I had mentors who taught me how to offer my best to my students as well as such mundane, but necessary, skills as how to write behavioral objectives. My children taught me humility and wisdom, especially during their teenage years.

My most important friends were my daughters and my mother. When I left my first husband and the community where I had grown up, some acquaintances felt sorry that I had the responsibility for two small children. They thought that my life would be easier without them.

The opposite was true. I took my family and my home with me. The children served as an anchor in the rather stormy sea of adjustment. They gave me a purpose and reason to strive. The home I created for them was also a nest for me. As they grew, they returned my warmth and love. I attempted to keep generational boundaries intact— jargon for not burdening kids with adult concerns and prerogatives. I didn't succeed entirely, as most single mothers don't. But I managed to hold on to the best that families bring to people, even through the stress of two divorces. The children's teachers referred to our family as a broken home. I knew that this was a misnomer.

My mother, Floray Baird Fisher, was my most intimate friend. She had retired and moved to Cleveland two years after I arrived. We lived together and then, when I married again, she moved to a house about a mile away.

Mother had gone to college in the late teens of this century and been a young, single teacher in the early twenties. She and her friends were more liberated than my generation which reverted, during the World War II, to older ideas about the role of women. The only generational gap between us was that while she approved of everything I did, she thought I shouldn't be so open about it. Example: She encouraged me to go to Europe with my second husband before we were married, but she told everyone that we were with a group. I saw Mother almost every day and involved her and my girls in much of my social life.

My brother, John, was discharged, from the Army shortly after my second husband left. He moved into my mother's home. When he first was discharged, he had a problem with drinking but soon joined AA and stopped. He was and is a dear, close friend, the only person now alive who has known me since I was a baby. Shevawn, my youngest daughter, asked John to give her away at her wedding; she named one of her sons for him.

In that year after the second divorce, I recognized that what I had with my family was more important than any relationship I was likely to form with men. I didn't date for a year and when I began again it was different. I stopped looking for a husband. I no longer cast every man I was romantically involved with into that role. Men were important, but no more than my women friends. As it evolved, the men came and went, but my friendships with women endured. It was many years before I met Verl, my husband, and was able to combine friendship, romance and commitment.

Who were these women who were important to me during those years? When I first moved to Cleveland and began working at University Hospitals, I had not worked in psychiatric nursing since my student days. I was an experienced medical-surgical nurse but a novice in my new specialty. After a year and a half at University Hospitals, I returned to school to secure a bachelor's and then began to teach at Saint What's-His-Name's.

At University Hospitals, Mary Jane Timmer, now Sawyer, became my role model. Mary Jane had graduated from the hospital in Pennsylvania where I had worked as a staff and charge nurse. She remembered me, but to me she was just another of the many students in the hospital school. When I began at University Hospitals I read the books assigned to the baccalaureate students, trying to learn as much as possible. I had trouble agreeing with the prevailing attitude among the nurses, a point of view more Freudian than Freud. Mary Jane was now an assistant head nurse. As I watched her work with patients I was impressed by her honesty and warmth. She was intelligent but even more she was endowed with common sense. She presented a model I tried to emulate.

The acceptance Mary Jane radiated to patients also touched staff. I was alone in a strange city with two small children dealing with the heartbreak of divorce. Most of the staff nurses were younger and single. I was sometimes the object of suspicion and jealousy. I felt that Mary Jane knew me and accepted me.

Mary Jane's roommate, Elinor, was also a nurse from Pennsylvania. Their apartment became a haven during those early lonely months. Sunday evenings I would take three-year-old Shevawn and seven-year-old Susan and drop by for conversation, popcorn and a chance to play with their cats. Our friendship continued through the years. Later when I was more established my home was home for Mary Jane and Elinor, especially during the holidays.

Helen Bramlette was a tall, attractive blonde, a former Miss Student Nurse of Mississippi who moved north and began working at University Hospital shortly after I did. She was interested in an attorney from Rochester, New York. She had met him when he was in the Army. She wasn't sure that he was the man she wanted to spend her life with. While she made a decision about David, she moved closer to him, but not too close. We spent a great deal of time together. When Helen finally decided that David was the one, Shevawn was her flower-girl and I was a bridesmaid. Helen and David's home in Canandaigua, New York, was a favorite weekend trip for my daughters and me. From Helen I learned that it was possible to be the most feminine of women, and at the same time be tough, strong and independent.

Ann Russell was a close friend. She was a teacher and psychologist, and had been voted the best-dressed Black woman in Cleveland by *Ebony* magazine. She was beautiful and had modeled when she studied at Columbia. I enjoyed going to restaurants with her and having the host rush forward to greet us when they saw Ann. She and my daughter Susan went to Europe together. Each was looking for a reliable traveling companion, and even though Susan was eighteen and Ann was thirty-six, they were compatible.

Elizabeth Warner, my walking encyclopedia friend who had been a classmate in both the master's and baccalaureate programs, was always available for advice and good conversation. Cecelia Schlosser, another classmate, lived at my house while her apartment was being renovated. It was wonderful to have another adult to share the space. I had adult conversation at dinner and someone who would go to Shevawn's swim meets when I had a schedule conflict. And best of all, I did not have to bend, adjust and compromise in order to have that. I remember thinking how much easier it was to live with a woman than with either of my husbands. Happily, years later, I found a man, my husband Verl, who is also easy to live with—and who possesses many other attributes as well.

Francise Bowman and Helen Burnside were not only professional colleagues at the community college but were friends and mentors. Francise Bowman helped me learn the theories of education and the practical application of them. When I began college, Francise was there, holding her last position before retirement. She had two master's degrees from Teachers College, Columbia University, and years of teaching experience. She was a fashionable woman with lustrous white hair and a very agreeable companion.

Francise lived in a lovely apartment close to the rapid transit line. She didn't drive to school. When we finished our work, I often would drive her home, and she would invite me in for coffee. In our conversations, I would talk about school, and casually, without lecturing, she would instruct me about writing objectives, test construction and teaching methods. She offered all she had learned from an excellent education and years of practical experience in such a palatable way that I hardly realized that I was being taught. I'd had only one education course, a curriculum course, when I started at the college. When I went into a doctoral program in education, I discovered that I already was familiar with most of the educational theory. It was then that I realized how much Francise had given me.

Francise was also fun. She had been an Army nurse in Europe and had many stories about the antics of famous generals, Allied and American. She liked men and when we went places together she engaged them easily. Her age was indeterminate (I never knew exactly what it was). Her white hair gave her the freedom to speak to people without seeming forward. An evening with Frances at the opera, an ice show or a sports event was always a delight.

Helen Burnside and I often combined our families for outings and entertainment. Her son Curt and Shevawn became good friends. Curt would occasionally sleep over, arriving with his rubber sheet and favorite pillow. In casual conversation with Helen about the school, I began to learn the principles of administration.

Five years later, when Helen and I had both finished our doctoral programs and were located in the same area of upstate New York, we were able to continue our friendship. Helen was an associate provost in the New York State University system at that time. She had contact with all the leaders in nursing education and the state officials in the health sciences. Every Sunday evening she would invite whoever was visiting in the area to her home for dinner. I was a regular guest on these occasions. I learned from the conversations and made valuable contacts—networking we call it now. Even more important, Helen and I were available to help each other with our children.

I lived in Cleveland for twelve years. Every Christmas, I invited all of my friends, married and single, for dinner and to spend the day. It became a wonderful tradition.

Now more than thirty years later, at Christmas time, cards and letters come from the old friends and we renew the ties that supported and sustained me during my Cleveland years, and gave me the strength to carry out my roles as mother and teacher.

Before my divorces, I had close supportive female friends and our relationships continued. What was different after the divorce was that I realized how valuable and helpful these relationships were.

Women have been and are still discriminated against in employment and career options. That is wrong and we must continue to fight it. But we must be careful to maintain the advantages we possess. We are able to form intimate trusting relationships with each other, relationships that most men can have only with women. We can teach and help each other to achieve our goals. It seems incredible that I learned this deep in my bones, only after my second divorce when I was almost forty. Some women never learn it.

Do we need some new fairy tales, ones in which sisters help each other? We have enough stories where the only goals are Prince Charming and happily ever after.

Chapter 22
The Winery

The community college had not waited until it had a building to open its doors. It rented old warehouses down along the railroad in the center of the city and set up classrooms. The nursing program was housed in a building that we called the winery. We shared the second floor with the art department.

Four desks were crowded into a tiny office with a sign on the door that said Psychiatric Nursing. There was hardly room between the desks to walk and that was accomplished only if the people seated at the desks got up and moved. There was one phone which was passed, dragging its cord, to the person who was wanted. We spent as little time as possible in the office.

Several rooms had been set up as classrooms and we had a nursing laboratory equipped with hospital beds and equipment. Mrs. Chase, the perpetual mannequin, occupied one of these. She was a hermaphrodite. You could screw off her female parts and screw in realistic looking male parts, should you wish to practice male catheterization. She was much better equipped than the Mrs. Chase I had practiced on as a student—the female parts on that mannequin were just two holes. In addition to realistic-looking genitalia, this Mrs. Chase had rubber arms so that the students could practice venipuncture, and a tracheotomy that could be suctioned.

Unfortunately there is nothing like learning from the real thing, a live, breathing nervous human being. No matter how much the students practiced on Mrs. C., the first real live patient was always traumatic. Every time I passed through the lab and saw Mrs. Chase lying there, her painted blue eyes staring at the ceiling, I thanked God that I was no longer teaching fundamentals of nursing.

The art department had learned something nursing had yet to learn—there is no use fooling around with simulations. Start with the real thing.

Helen's secretary was a prim woman in her fifties. She typed very well and had lovely phone manners. One day her phone rang. The call was for Dr. Art Teacher. The caller had tried to get him on his phone but had been told that he was in a drawing class, across the hall from Miss Prim. "Would you please ask him to come to the phone?"

Miss Prim crossed the hall, opened the door and looked for Dr. Teacher. It took her a moment to survey the room. The students were diligently sketching a large nude man, who reclined on a platform. Miss Prim saw the model, and shrieked, "Dr. Teacher, phone," and exited the room.

Our secretary was awash with girlish excitement by what she had seen. Did we know they drew naked people? We suspected as much, after all, it was a life drawing class. Since we were accustomed to viewing the naked bodies of our patients, this didn't hold much interest for us. But for Miss. Prim, it was rather sensational. She happily took messages and called Dr. Teacher from his life drawing class whenever necessary. You could ask her at any time who the model was and receive a mole-by-wrinkle description.

Some of the models may have had other professions—they were a pretty sleazy looking group. They undressed in the bathrooms, the ones shared by students, visitors and faculty, and marched out in thin robes or with towels draped strategically across their parts. We were careful to lock our purses in our desks and eyed the toilet seats with suspicion when the art department had models in.

One time I came up the stairs and was startled to see a pile of junk arranged at the top with a banner stuck in the top. There were tires, carburetors, the head of a rake, a beer. It somehow reminded me of the picture of the Marines planting the flag on Iwo Jima. It was an art exhibit, of course. The artist, a pimply student, was thrilled with my impression of his masterpiece.

The walls in the hall were covered with paintings and drawings. We could walk along and recognize the models we had seen. The students had made those sleazy people into objects of beauty. Miss Prim was so pleased by several of the pieces that she bought them.

Although the art department brought spice to our days the winery building was not conductive to counseling.

One of my students, Jennifer*, had avoided me all quarter. If I came into the office at the hospital, she dropped her chart and fled. The few times I had cornered her, she told me she had something urgent to do and left.

Jennifer was a small woman with lank blond hair and a pinched expression around her pale blue eyes. She was doing well with her patient and in class. I decided that I would not pursue her, although I did write on one of her essay tests that I felt she was avoiding me, and if she ever decided to tell me why, I'd be glad to listen.

The quarter was over and the grades were in. My elusive student, Jennifer, appeared at the corner of my desk, in the room with three other faculty and said, "I want to talk to you."

We left the office, searching for a place that was private, and ended up in the ladies bathroom with the door locked. We leaned against the sink and she told me that her father, a cardiac invalid, had been sexually abusing her for the last five years. She was now in therapy and had moved out from home, so the problem was being handled. She just wanted me to know why she had fled. She didn't think she could handle school and her own tumultuous emotions, so she had kept them locked in separate compartments of her life. My openness for confidences threatened that separation.

One thing that she expressed is something I've noted since in incest survivors and is not emphasized much in the literature; she really loved her father, and the bond between them was very deep. Breaking away and protecting herself was doubly difficult because she was not leaving a monster; she was leaving someone she loved.

One day one of the students, May Belle*, came into class when the lecture was well under way. She looked upset, but I didn't do anything to call attention to that. At break time she approached me with a strange tale.

Her girlfriend had been depressed lately, but May Belle had had no idea how sick she was until that morning. May Belle had received a call from her friend who was trying to decide which of two outfits she should be buried in. She wanted to be a pretty corpse, she said. She had a gun, and she had pulled the trigger when she was on the phone. The gun misfired.

My student was a mass of anxiety. We left the class and called the police. They hurried to the address. May Belle stayed outside near the phone, while I returned to the class room and began teaching. A few minutes later, a relieved-looking May Belle slipped into her seat. I interrupted class to ask what had happened. Her friend had been admitted to the psychiatric hospital. I dropped the topic of my lecture and we had a lively discussion of the signs of impending suicide.

Mary O'Donnal* did very well in class. She was quick, to the point and always had the right answer to any question I asked and she did well on her multiple choice final. But her essay tests were rambling, almost incoherent. I knew she was working part time while she was in school and taking some upper division psychology courses at the university. I thought that she was just tired.

She finished the course with an A and moved on. After she graduated she appeared one day and asked to talk. Again, I selected the only sure private place, the bathroom.

She told me she had been taking 125 milligrams of amphetamine while she was in school. She was in therapy and had been free of drugs for six months. "I knew you suspected that something was wrong and were concerned about me. I thought I owed it to you to tell you. I'm sure you'll have other students like me, and maybe you can get them help."

She went on to tell me that she, too, had been a victim of incest. Again I was struck by the conflict between the love she felt for her father and her anger because he had exploited that love. I thanked her for her frankness and wished her luck.

I never did find another student with the same signs of trouble. But years later when I was chair of a department, I questioned a faculty member who showed the same pattern. She confessed that she was using amphetamines.

The new building was being built and we all were looking forward to having privacy and space. Then I learned that my office would have no window. In class, I was teaching about phobias, and I mentioned that I had a slight touch of claustrophobia. I was worried that I might find my new office uncomfortable. I said, "I guess I'll have to find a picture that looks like a window, and hang that on the wall."

We had a small party the last day of class after the final—Kool-Aide and donuts. Then the students brought out a large package, a gift for me. When I unwrapped it, I found a large painting of a serene landscape. One of the students had an uncle who was an artist and the class had commissioned him to make me a window. I was very touched.

I had my painting framed. Then I learned there were rumblings through the faculty. It seemed that some of the people thought that students shouldn't give valuable gifts to faculty. It seemed like bribery, they said. I thought that this was a petty, sour grapes reaction, but I didn't object, since I already had my window.

We moved to our nice modern building and I hung my painting with pride. It is a picture of a blue lake that reflects the sky and the green hills surrounding the water. It has hung in every office I have had since, and today as I look up from my computer, I see my own special window and fondly remember that group of students.

Chapter 23
Party Girl

Shirley Jean* was the group's social butterfly. She flitted around the state hospital ward, smiling and happy. Her patient, a severely depressed old woman, was actually observed returning that smile when Shirley entered the room. Her grades averaged B which was good, considering that she was the single mother of two teenagers and worked part time. But she was not a *brilliant student*.

When she told me that she wanted to become a psychiatric nurse, I was surprised. Most psychiatric nurses are thinkers, intellectual types who enjoy observing the intricacies of the patient's psychodynamics and the puzzles presented when we try to change them. Many of us are shy and some have struggled with and conquered problems of our own.

Shirley didn't look beyond the surface; at least she didn't mention it if she did. She was willing to take life as it presented itself. Most nurses with personalities like this find their way into a more active specialty, such as surgical nursing.

I didn't discourage her. There are never enough psychiatric nurses. And I did remember Arturo, my C- student who was making such a difference on the geriatric ward at the long-term state hospital.

The end of the spring quarter was approaching and most of the group would be graduating. I would also be leaving and moving on into my doctoral studies. When Shirley came to me and asked if she could plan a party for the patients, as a goodby gesture, it seemed like a wonderful idea.

"Fine, you can plan it if you like. If you need my help let me know," I said.

"Oh, the group has been talking about it and we have already set up committees."

"You are in charge then?"

She laughed. "Yes, it always seems that I end up being the boss."

As the day approached, I asked, "Do you want me to bring cookies or anything?"

Sunny Shirley replied, "Don't you worry none. The food is all taken care of."

When I came back from lunch, I almost didn't recognize the gloomy women's ward. There were balloons and crepe paper strung across the day room. On a long side table, which had been covered with a sheet, was an elaborate display of party foods. Shirley, it turned out, had asked several caterers if they wouldn't like to help the mentally ill.

The patients, most of whom were depressed and usually dressed in drab shapeless clothes, were wearing their Sunday best. The students, too, had changed into party clothes—satins and sequins—the works.

Pinned to each woman's shoulder was a small corsage. Yes, Shirley knew some florists and had tickled their altruistic sense.

Then the music started. A three-piece band—the leader was a friend of another student—had arrived. They didn't mind having an afternoon gig, even for free. They owed the student a favor, they said.

Just as the music began, other guests arrived. Some family members had been able to leave work and had even taken the time to dress appropriately. The head of the hospital and the psychiatrists, a group that resembled a United Nations committee, drifted in.

The ward doctor was a middle-aged man from Spain. He was so painfully dignified and aloof that for the entire quarter we had hesitated to approach him. But this day we almost didn't recognize him. He was not wearing his usual rumpled suit and black tie. He was neatly dressed and had a rose on his lapel.

Shirley had selected a queen to preside over the party. Longevity on the ward was the criteria and a Hungarian woman in her sixties, who was very depressed, was chosen. Funny, she no longer looked depressed. She had a pretty blue dress on and when Shirley gave her a bouquet of roses she actually laughed. Then Dr. Garcia* led her to the center of the room and the band struck up a waltz. The most mismatched couple in the world, they danced a graceful waltz. Then the rest of the group joined in. There weren't enough men, but the female students asked the ladies to dance and soon the floor was filled with bright clothes and chatter.

The party was still in progress when the evening staff arrived. I thought, I bet they will be mad about the mess we've made. But they joined in the party, gobbling up the last of the food and providing partners for the patients. They weren't mad, because Shirley had organized a clean-up crew of students and patients.

By four o'clock the ward looked the way it had that morning, gray and forbidding, except that the patients moved more quickly and there were smiles here and there.

I caught up with Shirley in the parking lot and told her what a fantastic job she had done. She laughed and said that it was a lot of fun. Then she added that the party was a goodby present for me as well as for the patients.

Through the nursing grapevine, I learned that Shirley had passed her state boards and was hired by the Jewish Hospital to work on the psychiatric floor. I was familiar with the floor, and in my mind I called it the oy, oy ward, although I didn't say such things out loud. It was almost as though a thick black cloud hung from the ceiling, enveloping everyone in gloom. The only sounds that were heard were "Oy, mein Gott," of the less-depressed patients. Days on that ward were so monotonously depressing that when they admitted a young schizophrenic man—someone who might insist that he was Jesus or John the Baptist—staff and patients were glad for the excitement. What would it be like for bubbly Shirley to spend her days in such a depressed setting?

I needn't have worried. Shirley started bridge tournaments and dancing classes. She blew the dark cloud away with her activity. The only complaints voiced were about the aching backs of the shuffleboard players. Oh, and a few people asked to be discharged so they could get some rest.

The last I heard, Shirley was the head nurse. I suspect she did more for her patients that ten of the usual psychodynamically oriented nurses. And once again, I learned the folly of thinking one kind of nurse is better than another.

Chapter 24
Black Summer

Teaching in the summer is easier. My contract was for nine months, but my pay was divided into twelve sections and arrived monthly. When I worked in the summer, and I always did, the pay was extra, outside the usual budget and carried with it the illusion of a special award. The college had moved into the new modern buildings, out of the old winery, and in the summer the halls were deserted and my office was a peaceful sanctuary.

I met the class the first Monday and gave my introductory lecture. I also counted heads. There were twenty students instead of the usual thirty-six. The composition of the class was the same as always—a few men, a few just out of high school, a few more in their forties, the rest in the thirties, and of various hues. Great. I would have only two clinical sections, which meant I'd be with students only three days a week. It was going to be a nice summer.

The next day I met the ten students that would be in the day's clinical group at the short-term state hospital. The gray old building and the palpable misery of the patients hadn't changed but it seemed easier to manage. We had our pre-conference and the students went to meet the patients and choose which special patient they would work with.

At the end of the day we met for post-conference. I must have been more alert than I had been that morning. I began by inviting the students to tell me about their day. Suddenly I looked around, shocked. Ten dark faces looked back at me.

"My God! They segregated you. That's against the law. Who did this? "

There was general laughter. "It's OK, Florence. We planned it this way. We all signed up for Tuesday."

"Why?"

"It's summer. We're tired of minding our Ps and Qs. We want to relax and just be ourselves. We like to be together sometimes."

"I guess since you decided it, it isn't illegal. Of course, I'm the wrong shade."

"That's OK. We'll teach you."

And they did. I learned colorful descriptive expressions and was immersed in Black English. There was more laughter and teasing in the conferences, and I suspect more real learning.

They told each other and me about their lives. Mildred* arrived one day, badly shaken. Her ten-year-old daughter had been dragged into an empty building and raped. The group formed a protective circle around her, comforting her and offering suggestions for help. As I watched, I noted that I had seldom seen such effective and compassionate crisis management. They had learned that lesson well. Perhaps they already had known it.

Fredrick*, the lone man, was teased unmercifully by my standards. When I mentioned to the women that they were being a little hard on the poor guy, they all protested that they were very fond of him and were just expressing it.

He talked about how tough his mother had been on him and his two brothers. His father was gone and his mother raised six children on what she earned by cleaning houses in Shaker Heights. Desperately afraid that her sons would join the bad boys who roamed the streets, she set up a schedule that would have made a marine drill sergeant seem easy. The boys followed it, accounting to her for their every waking minute. It had worked, in that they all had turned out well. They were sober, had steady jobs, and had ambitions for better lives.

"But you know, we didn't learn how to have much fun. This group is fun. I don't mind the teasing. I'm eating up the attention."

Another student told about a gunshot that pierced the floor of her apartment and lodged in the ceiling. I learned just how dangerous life was in their neighborhoods and how frustrating it was to be trapped there.

At lunch time, I heard similar stories, but from the perspective of someone who was already a professional. May Wykle and I had gotted our bachelor's degrees from Western Reserve at the same time. She was now working for the hospital, teaching students that the three-year-programs sent to her for their psychiatric affiliation. It was good to relax for half an hour and be with an old friend. She was younger than me and her children were also younger, but we had a great deal in common.

One day May was concerned about one of her daughters. The little girl had come home from kindergarten, opened her mouth and poured out the accent of the ghetto. May was horrified. She and Bill were trying to buy a house in another neighborhood, where the schools would be integrated, but were meeting with barriers.

"I've even been thinking of sending the girls to my dad's in southern Ohio, so they can go to a good school. So much of being accepted as an educated person depends on how you speak. But darn, how I would miss them."

A few weeks later the problem was solved. May and Bill were able to buy a home in a racially integrated area of Shaker Heights. It was one of the few places in the country that have managed to maintain racial balance among homeowners.

During another lunch May told me her grandmother's story. Her mother, May's great grandmother, had been sold and sent away. The memory of that separation had reverberated through the generations, touching everyone who came after. My family has its own stories of the Irish potato famine, which have shaped my politics and thinking a century and a half later. I wondered what stories my students could tell and how they were affected by what had happened to their great grandparents.

May told me that she was the first black student in her basic nursing school. On the first day of school, the registrar had been waiting for her to arrive.

"Oh, here you are," she said. She assigned May to a room at the back of the nurses' residence.

May had also integrated the obstetrics department at Saint What's-His-Name. Black women who had babies were assigned to six bed wards, regardless of their ability to pay or whether they had a private physician. May's doctor wanted to challenge this. After all, a hospital named for one of the authors of the New Testament and affiliated with a church, should not treat any of its patients as lesser people. The doctor was waiting for a tough, intelligent professional who could not possibly be shunted to a ward on some pretext. When May consulted him early in her pregnancy, he had his integrator.

No mention was made of race on the admission form. May gave birth to a baby girl. Then she was admitted to a private room. The nurse on duty thought there was some mistake and tried to move her. May refused to be moved.

"Some people treated me like dirt. Others were fine. But I would never again try to integrate a hospital and have a baby the same week. It was too hard."

May was eager to return to school for her master's, but with the new house, money was a problem. I just happened to mention the amount of the stipend NIMH was giving to graduate students in psychiatric nursing.

"Stipend? They give you money to live on?" Somehow this information hadn't reached May.

She enrolled immediately and I lost my lunch-time companion and black studies educator. But we have maintained our friendship and I am very proud to say that Dr. May Hinton Wykle, who is chair of Gerontological Nursing and Director of the Center on Aging and Health at CWRU, is my friend.

It is impossible for a white person to know what it is like to be black in this society, but we can try to understand, and perhaps learn a little of what our black students, patients and friends experience. My summer with my black students and with my friend, May, was a fruitful one.

Chapter 25
Practice

Teaching brought me immense satisfaction and every day I learned something that made me a better teacher. Yet there was part of me that was frustrated. I could teach only a small part of what I knew about therapy to my students. In addition, I was a good therapist and I wanted to develop my skills further.

Then at a mental health conference I ran into Ernie, the psychiatrist I had admired so much when I was at Saint What's-His-Name. He invited me for a drink and we went into the lounge of the hotel where the meeting was being held. He asked all about my Master's program—what had I studied, how was the supervision done?

In the conversation I mentioned that I had verbatim recordings of the therapy I had done. I was surprised when he asked to see one of the transcripts. He went on to tell me that he was thinking of expanding his practice to offer his patients more options. He was particularly interested in offering group therapy.

I mailed him a transcription of a case. As I addressed the envelope, I thought about how much energy and time those pages represented.

A week later Ernie called and asked if I would come to his office suite. He showed me around the rooms. His private office looked like the library of an English manor house. Leather-bound books in walnut cases lined the wall. The chairs were rich leather and his desk, which he told me cost $1500 (a lot of money in 1967), was beautiful. The office also held the standard couch of a psychoanalyst, but he told me he hadn't done couch work in years.

The kitchen was packed with gourmet goodies and expensive wines; the refrigerator was filled with imported beer. One room was devoted to the electroencephalograph machine. Ernie was also a neurologist. A technician came in to perform the test when one was scheduled.

"I went out to Case and took courses in electronics so I could repair the machine myself," he said. "I'm pretty good at it. I can fix all the appliances and the televisions at home."

The waiting room was small. Psychiatrists don't keep people waiting.

"Would you look at what that kid did to this table?"

I looked. Initials had been carved into the leather top of one of the lamp tables.

"I was seeing his mother. He drove her down. I made her pay for it. He was too old be that destructive."

I met the very young bleache-blond secretary. She had startling green eyes.

"This is Molly*. She has been here for four years. I didn't know she was sixteen when I hired her—same age as my youngest daughter. She is excellent on the phone with the patients. That is absolutely essential in a psychiatrist's office."

Finally he showed me a room at the end of the hall, next to the door from which the patients exited his office suite. Psychiatrists' offices are arranged so no one meets in the waiting room. The room held a small desk, several chairs and a couch.

"If we can work out a satisfactory arrangement, this is where you will see patients," Ernie said. I wasn't suprised, but I certainly was pleased.

Back in the big office I sat in the patient's chair. We discussed our contract and arrived at an agreement.

Ernie would supply the patients, Molly would arrange the appointments, and Ernie's wife would do the billing. He would charge $25 an hour for my services and pay me $10. Remember, this was in 1967. At the college I was making $10,000 for nine months work and hoping to be hired to teach a summer course.

"I was impressed with your transcripts. You are just the kind of therapist I am looking for. I'll read your notes and if I have any suggestions, I'll leave them in the patients' charts. I have a special private line where you can get me at anytime, but I don't anticipate that you'll need it. Molly will give you the number. If you have any questions about medications, or think there needs to be a change, let Molly know. She'll tell me and call the change into the drugstore. Try to get a couple of groups started. We'll charge each patient $15 a session for them and you'll get $5. They should be good for patients and make us some money. Oh, I talked to my accountant. You'll be a private contractor so you'll pay your own taxes. Any questions?"

I had a few. When I left the office, Molly gave me a key and asked for my schedule. The office was only a few blocks from the school. At the end of my day there I could come to the office and see a patient or two before I went home.

I was delighted. I had an opportunity to develop as a therapist and to make extra money as well.

Soon I was seeing eight patients a week. I started several groups but the patients dropped out before the group members bonded enough with each other to be therapeutic. Those frank enough to tell me the reason said that for just a little more money they could have their own therapist and they preferred that. I tried to persuade Ernie that we should charge less for the groups, but he was firm.

Soon all the adolescent girls in Ernie's practice were assigned to me. Susan and I thought this was ironic. She had her own therapist, a social worker, who was helping her work out her own growing up problems. Now I was serving the same role for other young women.

Family therapy was new at that time and I wanted to develop my skills as a family therapist. I read all that was written. Ernie arranged for me to join a study group of therapists who were also interested. We studied and critiqued each others cases. Soon I was seeing couples. I also made it a point to meet at least once with the significant people in my patients' lives.

Ernie referred to me as his associate, and he treated me that way as far as my work with patients went. However, there was one unpleasant incident.

I came into the office ten minutes before I was to see a patient. Molly and Miss Jones*, as Ernie called his wife in the presence of patients, were there. Molly said that Ernie wanted to see me and I went happily into his office.

He sat in his leather chair across the desk and dumped a load of grievances on me. He didn't want me drinking in the office. I tried to explain that I had once had a beer after a tense group session and that was hardly drinking. He went on. I had been heard laughing and giggling with a patient. That wasn't therapy. And then there was the issue of my ring. Why was I wearing a band on the wrong finger? I shouldn't tell patients I was divorced. The mother of one of them had called and said a divorced woman shouldn't be doing family therapy.

I couldn't get in a word to defend myself. I had a patient waiting. When I left his office, Molly and Miss Jones were standing close to the door listening.

I was furious. I would have quit but I couldn't desert the patients with whom I had relationships. When I tried to find a time to discuss this with Ernie, he was too busy to see me. Finally I told Molly to make an emergency appointment for me and that I would pay for it if necessary.

I marched into the office, stood, and gave Ernie hell in the best tradition of my Irish fishwife ancestors. My invectives were all well reasoned and rehearsed, however. First I pointed out the folly of dumping that load of s_ _t on me just before I was to see a patient. Second, it was rotten to permit others to listen to our discussion. I told him that if he didn't want someone to take food from the kitchen, he shouldn't show it to them. I thought he was being hospitable; I didn't know he was bragging. The giggling patient was expressing anger, in the only way she could at the moment. She was giggling about wanting to do nasty things to her abusive husband. I told him I refused to lie about my marital status and besides that, talking about rings, he looked like a gambler with that big pinkie ring he wore.

I had been emphatic. (translation-loud) When I left Ernie's office, I saw Molly's shoulders shake. She tried to keep her laughter hidden, but I got the message. This time I didn't mind an audience.

It never happened again. Ernie exuded a great deal of power and that had helped him be an effective psychiatrist. But he could be difficult in ordinary relationships. Few people, and probably fewer women, had ever stood up to him. Molly told me that for weeks Ernie wondered if he should stop wearing his pinkie ring.

One day I went into the office and Molly met me with a long face. She motioned me back to my office and said, "What should we do? He has been in there crying all afternoon. When he went home last night, no one was there and the furniture was gone. She left him his chair, the bed and a television."

Then we heard the outside door close. Ernie had gone and we didn't need to wonder how to approach him in his grief.

Ernie's first wife had died of tuberculosis when he was in medical school. When he was in the army he had met an army nurse, a young widow, and they had married. They were devout Catholics and had been married twenty-five years and had four daughters.

Ernie never sexually harassed me but several months after his wife left, he let me know, that, if I were willing, he would like to see me socially. I was tempted, but good sense prevailed. I had heard him cry that day. I knew that I would be only a temporary distraction. I was glad I had made that choice when Ernie and his wife were reconciled a year later.

I was Ernie's associate for almost five years. I became a skilled therapist and earned money that made life more pleasant for my children and me. The last two years I was there, I was a full-time doctoral student. One of those years I was also paying Susan's college expenses.

In addition to the professional and monetary advantages, I gained a great deal from knowing this powerful and complex man. It turned out that those transcripts had been a very good investment.

Chapter 26
The Bickersons and the Angry Wife

I wish I could say that all the patients that I treated at Ernie's were helped by my superior therapeutic skills. The truth is that many improved because they decided to do something about their problems. The fact that they saw me was not as important as the decision to involve another person.

This was particularly true with the couples I saw.

The Bickersons* were a Yuppie couple who came in with the complaint that they weren't happy any more. Their complaints about the marriage were not specific; both were just disappointed in the way things were going. They were devout Catholics and separation was out of the question.

I tried to get them to tell each other what they were feeling. I was hoping that as they told each other I would learn what was going on between them.

They told each other, in loud angry voices. When I tried to get a word in edgewise to clarify what they meant, or to get details, I had to raise my voice.

Weeks went by. They came dutifully, paid their fee and fought for an hour, while I struggled to referee.

Ernie had created a small waiting room for me, so that when I saw patients in the evening, it was not necessary to open up the whole suite of offices. (I think he was afraid that someone would sneak in and steal something while I was distracted by a patient.) The soundproofing was not perfect in my office; anyone sitting in the waiting room could hear the sound of voices. It was impossible to hear what was being said, if the volume of the voice were normal. The Bickersons were not normal.

When I showed them out, the person in the waiting room would appear to be engrossed in his magazine. As the outer door closed, he would turn to me, his face twisted as he struggled to conceal his amusement. If a couple was waiting, they voiced thoughts such as, "Well, at least we aren't as bad off as that pair."

I felt bad that I wasn't helping this nice young couple, and I told them this. They responded with, "Oh no, Mrs. Hardesty. You are helping so much. This is the only place we can really talk. Things are great between us at home."

So I tried, between hurled accusations, to teach them how to fight fair—express their feelings without being destructive to their partner. I didn't feel as though they had learned much by the time I left the city. When I bid them goodby, she cried and he cleared his throat. They thanked me profusely.

A year later I got a birth announcement. They were the parents of twins. A note was included that told me how happy they were.

Daphne* and her police lieutenant husband had more serious problems. She was a lovely-looking young woman, a good Catholic, as most of Ernie's patients were. Her husband had a degree in journalism, but had been on the police force for ten years. They had two small children and lived in a home they were buying in a middle-class housing development.

Then one day, Daphne put her head in the oven and turned on the gas. She was found by the neighbor who had agreed to watch her children for the afternoon. Fortunately she survived. After three shock treatments and a week in the hospital, she was sent home. She was to see me twice a week.

I asked Daphne to tell me what had been going in the days before the suicide attempt. What follows are the facts that several hours of gentle probing produced.

The family desperately needed money for unexpected car repairs. She had found a job at a large drugstore, the kind that sold everything. She worked from ten in the evening until two in the morning, cleaning the store and restocking the shelves. Her husband was home to watch the children. She had begun a flirtation with a young black man who worked with her.

I asked what had happened between her and the man. It turned out to be a few long looks and one stolen kiss at the end of the cosmetic racks, after a few joking remarks about the flavor of lipstick.

That night, in a panic, she had quit her job and told her husband. He had very negative feelings about blacks and responded with rage. No, he hadn't hurt her, just yelled, but he had threatened to hurt the man.

"Nothing really happened. I'm puzzled about why you told your husband," I said.

She didn't have any idea. She knew how mad he would be, yet she told him.

"You must have been very angry at him," I interpreted.

She denied this and, as one does with an interpretation, I let it pass. Half an hour later, she almost shouted, "Yes, you are right. I was furious at him."

Every night he came home, ate dinner and sprawled in front of the television with a six-pack of beer. As the beer had its effect, he would become clumsily amorous, but, as Daphne said, "His thing would be soft."

In addition, their budget was so tight there was no money for entertainment or for her to have an allowance. "I can't even buy a barrette for my hair or an ice-cream for the kids, unless I can cheat and take it out of the grocery money."

When I saw him alone, he was obviously depressed. He hated his job. He said, "I spend my days with my head up the asshole of the world." He didn't see any way that he could change his career. He didn't think he drank too much, and, "...anyway, I'd go crazy if I didn't relax in the evening."

All my suggestions on ways he might consider to make his life better fell on deaf ears. He was deeply hurt by his wife's flirtation, correctly interpreting it as an angry act aimed at him.

When I saw them together, we didn't make much headway. I decided to see if we could negotiate an allowance for her, just a little mad money to help her feel less bound by the situation. It was a tough sell, but finally he agreed that she could have five dollars every two weeks.

The rest of my goals for the couple just didn't happen. But that five dollars started a whole string of events. It had to come out of his beer money. So he wasn't stuporous when his father-in-law suggested that they go fishing. He had a great time. Then he decided to buy some fishing equipment, and that also was paid for by cutting back on beer. The couple's sex life improved and her depression vanished. Finally she got a part-time job as a teaching assistant and he requested a transfer to a division that proved to be less depressing.

I often wonder what would have happened if I hadn't decided that they negotiate an allowance for her.

Sometimes a therapist is brilliant, but most of the time, you just try hard to help. And there are times when I've been lucky.

Chapter 27
Small Talk

Veronica Galanski* was like many of the patients I saw at Ernie's office. She was chronically mentally ill. Fortunately she had a supportive family and good mental health care, and because of that she was able to function and earn her own living about eleven months of the year.

Veronica was in her late thirties. When she was twenty-five her father died and shortly after the funeral she became delusional and confused. She spent six months in the hospital and was stabilized on anti-psychotic drugs. Her diagnosis was and is schizophrenic, paranoid type.

She lived with her mother and brother and did office work. Veronica's years followed the same pattern. She would get a job, usually at the lowest level in the office. Before long, the employers would discover her superior accounting and secretarial skills and she would be promoted. Then the office politics, the social demands of coffee breaks and the indecision about how to respond to office gossip, would assume massive importance. Her anxiety would build until she became psychotic. When her delusions became apparent, she would lose her job and be admitted to the hospital. In a few weeks she would be out, searching for a new job in which she would repeat the same scenario.

Ernie saw her for ten minutes every month and monitored her medications. He felt that if she had more therapy, she might be able to change the pattern of her life and he assigned her to me.

She sat across the desk from me with her hands clasped on her brown leather purse. She was dressed in browns and beiges, in excellent but subdued taste. I asked her to tell me in detail what had been happening just before she had had her last psychotic episode. She described the office situation. Then I asked about the previous times she had been ill. Over and over I heard stories about what happened in offices. She did not know how to handle the everyday give and take among the women with whom she worked, and this, combined with the underlying problem with her brain chemistry, caused her periodic psychoses.

We made the decision that I would see her every week. The focus of our time would be what happened at the office. I got to know Veronica's office as well as I knew Ernie's. We problem-solved, rehearsed and mastered the intricacies of coffee break gossip. I helped her select suitable topics for conversation with her peers, gleaned from the newspaper and the *Reader's Digest*. Soon she was the chief book-keeper for the small firm. That part of her work was easy; it was the relationships that caused the problem.

Christmas approached and Veronica was worried. There was to be a Christmas party and she would be seated next to the boss at dinner. What on earth would she say? We explored what she knew about the boss. He had recently taken a trip to Eastern Europe. Veronica had been to Poland several years before with her brother and mother. Wonderful! A common interest! I coached her on the opening phrases of a conversation designed to elicit lots of talk from her employer. "I understand that you have just returned from a trip to Eastern Europe. I was there several years ago. I would very much like to hear your impression of the situation now." Everyone likes to talk about his trips. All one needs is an invitation.

How sad it was that this intelligent woman, competent in so many ways, found the ordinary social interaction—the sort of activity that most of us do so easily—such an effort.

Veronica went to the party. At the last minute someone wanted to switch her seat so that she was not next to the boss. My patient objected, "After all," she told me, "I spent twenty-five dollars getting my conversation ready. I wasn't going to waste the money."

She gave the boss the lead and he poured forth about his trip. When he bade her good night, he told her how much he had enjoyed visiting with her.

As time passed, Veronica lengthened the time between visits to twice a month. She managed the grief of her mother's death without becoming ill and then helped arrange her younger brother's wedding. I saw her for the four years I worked at Ernie's. She was not psychotic during that time.

Knowing Veronica convinced me that most of us are blessed with our ability to access and respond appropriately to the usual social situations. Every ordinary contact was for her what it might be for us in Japan or Saudi Arabia. I have such respect for people like Veronica who struggle to support themselves and contribute to society when the struggle costs them so much.

Chapter 28
Madonna*

When I first began working in Ernie's office, I told him that I didn't want to see adolescents. My Susan was fifteen and was having a diffi-cult adolescence. She was seeing her social worker and that helped, but things in the house were not always like the family sitcoms of that time. I didn't think I could deal with one more teenager, even in the controlled environment of the office.

Ernie agreed. But then he would get a new patient, a teenaged girl who had trouble relating to a psychiatrist who exuded power, even when he was silent. So I would relent and agree to treat her. Soon I was carrying several teenagers in my treatment load and enjoying them.

I found that I was effective. I knew how precious these young women were because I was painfully aware of how much Susan meant to me. I also was able to help the parents, perhaps because there was no subtle hint of blame in my manner.

Madonna was a real challenge. She was a ward of the court and therapy had been ordered by the judge. Ma-donna wanted no part of therapy. She was a few months away from her eighteenth birthday and then, as she told me, she could do anything she wanted.

Madonna looked like a young Sophia Loren, with almond-shaped eyes, olive skin and black hair. She wore jeans and a fringed suede jacket. Mother was an older version of Madonna. Her father was blonde and had a Polish name. He had adopted two-year-old Madonna when he married her mother. The parents had been frantic about Madonna and had secured help from the courts to control her.

Madonna was attracted to motorcycle gangs. She had dated a fellow from a white gang, then left him, and was now involved with a man who belonged to a black gang. Another young woman had made the same switch, and she and her boyfriend had been murdered. Both gangs were using and dealing drugs. Madonna had gotten herself into a dangerous situation.

The first time I saw her, she was sullen and prepared to wait out the therapeutic hour in silence. I told her that she could talk about anything she liked; that I knew she was there under duress and was unlikely to talk about the situation. "However, since we will be spending an hour a week with each other, it would be foolish to just waste the time. I'm willing to help with any school problems, or we could talk about things at home. If I forget and ask any questions you don't want to answer, just tell me, and I'll back off."

So she began to talk about school. I listened and offered what Carl Rogers called "unconditional positive regard"—in fact, I've thought of it as great big gooey gobs of unconditional positive regard.

We moved on to talk about her family. Her stepfather was strict but she liked him. She also was very attached to her two younger half siblings. She had many questions about her real father, but her mother had been reluctant to talk about him.

When I saw her parents, I encouraged them to give Madonna more freedom and trust her, since she actually could see the boyfriend any time she liked, even with their restrictions. They agreed. I prayed that it wasn't a mistake.

I also asked about Madonna's father. The mother told me that he had been a Mafia soldier, the bodyguard of one of the bosses. He had been killed just after Madonna was born. She hadn't talked about it because she didn't want Madonna to know. (Oh, I thought, the mother also liked dangerous men.) I urged her to have a talk with Madonna since family secrets have a way of finding themselves repeated in action. She said that she would.

I was certain that clever Madonna was finding a way to see her motorcycle lover and I worried about an unwanted pregnancy. So I told Madonna that I wanted to give her some information. She didn't have to make a comment about it, I said, just bear me out. Then I launched into a long discussion of birth control—where to get it and the pros and cons of various methods. She sat across from me, laughing at my discourse. But I felt better. Weeks later she told me that she had known all about birth control and was using it.

Just a few weeks before her eighteenth birthday, she said that she was ready to talk seriously. "I know Death (his nickname) is bad for me and I want to give him up. But I do care for him and it is hard. Will you help me?"

I answered, "Of course." Inside I was shouting Hallelujah.

The eighteenth birthday came and went. Madonna accomplished her goal and learned a great deal about herself and her family in the process. When we finished therapy, she gave me a notebook of her poems, her deepest and most intimate feelings.

I heard from her mother a year later. Her stepfather had died suddenly but he and Madonna had had time to build a conflict-free relationship. The mother said that Madonna had been a pillar of strength for the whole family, helping her, and loving and supporting her younger half siblings. Madonna was working and attending college classes in the evening. She planned to become a high school English teacher. The mother thanked me for giving her back her daughter.

I've often thought about Madonna in the twenty-five years since I've seen her. I treasure her poems. I wonder what became of her fringed suede jacket, the symbol of her teenage rebellion. I hope she kept it to show her children.

Kent State University

1969-1971

Chapter 29
Back to School

I was comfortable at the community college. Helen had resigned to return to Columbia to study for a doctorate—the union card for teaching in higher education. The policies she had instituted were in place and my colleagues were congenial people. Each class of students brought me more challenges and more satisfaction. I had been tenured and was now an associate professor. I was able to teach every summer and earn more. And my work at Ernie's was satisfying and provided money for vacations and extras. I even had a savings account.

Why did I want that doctorate so badly? In part, it had to do with the wound my first divorce inflicted. During my first marriage, I had been a respected wife and community leader. Then, due to false, malicious stories and the divorce itself, I was perceived as a fallen woman. Irrationally, I suppose, I felt that being Dr. Hardesty would erase that.

In my previous positions, I had felt the lack of power. At times, I was at the mercy of people who weren't as knowledgeable as I was. For example, when the supervisor of the psychiatric division at the hospital had given me a bad evaluation—based partly on her outmoded theories and partly on hospital politics—I protested, but decided that it would cost me too much to fight it. (In retrospect, I should have. When references were opened by law, I learned that that evaluation had followed me all my career.) At Saint What's-His-Name when I had been used to terminate a student from the program, I felt I had no recourse but to accept. Knowing what I learned later from Frances and faculty senate meetings, I realized that I could have fought it. I also felt that the knowledge I would gain from earning my doctorate would give me the power to control my own teaching. Other people's perception that I had that knowledge would also give me power.

Now the questions were, how, where, and when could I go back to school. The most prestigious schools for doctorates in nursing were Columbia and New York University. I had met the deans of both schools, and was sure I could be admitted. But there was no way I could move my family to New York City. I would have to remain in Cleveland. Since none of the schools within driving distance offered a doctorate in nursing, I would have to get a doctorate in a related field.

Case Western was too expensive. Besides that ,I had two degrees from there. Kent State University was forty miles away and had a number of doctoral programs available. I signed up for a workshop in educational testing for nurses given by the education department at Kent and met Dr. Lawrence Litwack. His wife was a nurse and the two of them had written articles for nursing journals. I liked Larry's matter-of-fact approach to problems. I felt that he was someone who could help me learn what I needed. The road between Cleveland and Kent was a wide freeway and easily driven. Kent moved to the front of the schools I was considering.

Susan was a high school senior. Her adolescent turmoil was over and she would be graduating in a few months. When we talked about what had been happening with her, it became evident that the major problem had been her fears that she couldn't make it on her own. At times it seemed that she had been hacking the bonds that connected us with a dull hatchet. But that was over. Although her grades in school were low, her SAT scores were high enough for her to be recruited by colleges. Her education had a higher priority than mine and I decided that I could not go back to school full time. Shevawn was four years younger than Susan, and her college would come next.

There is a psychology parlor game that goes like this. Imagine you are going down a road to a desired destination, and suddenly are faced with a high smooth wall that extends as far as you can see in each direction. You have no tools, no ladder, and there are no toe-holds in the wall. What will you do?

The answer is supposed to give the therapist some idea of how you deal with problems. My answer has always been that I would walk along the wall in both directions, looking for an opportunity that would enable me to cross. "There has to be something—a stream, a tree close by or one blown down by the storm, a gap in the wall. Whatever it is, I'll use it and get through."

I found the gap.

One evening Susan said, "Mom, we need to talk." This kind of statement makes a mother's pulse race. "I don't want to go to college right now. I promise you, I'll go sometime, but right now I want to work."

Susan expected that I would object, but I surprised her. "Well, Honey, if you aren't going to go to school this year, I'll go. If I carry a very heavy load maybe I can get most of my course work finished."

Susan got a job as a bank teller and I began to look seriously at what Kent had to offer.

I interviewed at the psychology department at Kent. The professor with whom I talked was not very encouraging. He told me that they had never accepted a woman as old as I was in their doctoral program and they had never had an *older person* of either sex finish the program. I was in my early forties. This was the late nineteen sixties. Evidently they hadn't yet had any age discrimination suits.

The more I talked with the man, the more angry I became. Defiantly I trotted out my credentials—my master's program, my academic rank and tenure, my thesis, publications, my work as a psychotherapist, and finally, my Miller's Analogy test score. He was impressed. He leafed through my thesis and became excited. And he was floored by my high Miller's score. (I took the test on one of my *smart days*.)

He handed me an application and encouraged me to apply for admission. I told him that I would think about it, and left, knowing that I would never return.

When I talked with Larry Litwack in the counseling program at the school of education, he welcomed me. He said that I could plan my own program, in line with my educational goals, as long as I met the requirements of his program. I decided to do a major in counselor education. Since I was teaching nursing students how to counsel mentally healthy patients, and help the mentally ill, this program should help me do it more effectively.

I planned a double minor, thereby avoiding the necessity for a foreign language. I did this sadly because I always wanted to speak other languages, but my time was limited and languages demand a lot of time. My minors were psychology and educational psychology. I would take courses with the psychology department but beyond grading the course, they would have no control over my program. Larry urged me to take a cognate area in group since I already had expertise in group.

I asked for and received a year's leave of absence from the community college. I had five busy quarters ahead of me, and if I were lucky, I could crowd my course work into it.

It was too late to apply for an NIMH traineeship. Larry mentioned a job as a graduate assistant. If I worked twenty hours a week at Kent, I would get free tuition. I declined. My reasoning was that I would already be working at Ernie's, and If I wanted to work as a teacher, I could work at the community college and be paid much more than the amount of the tuition. My objective was to finish the course work as quickly as possible.

Larry called a few days later with great news. I had been granted a Kent State Fellowship. My tuition would be free. I would not be required to work at the school, and I would be granted two hundred dollars a month. That isn't much by today's standards, but then it was enough to make the house payment and buy the groceries.

Susan insisted that she pay board but I suggested that instead she pay the cleaning lady, Allie. Allie, who had spent ten years picking up Susan's toys, now gave her special service—she washed Susan's stockings for her. And I was free of most of the burdens of the household and able to concentrate on my studies.

At the end of spring term, I began my leave of absence from the community college. Every day for five quarters, I bounced down the road to Kent in my VW bug. I carried fifteen credit hours a quarter, much more than the usual load for a doctoral student. At home I studied, often as much as eighteen hours at a time. My grades were good and I was learning things that would be useful to me when I returned to teaching.

Susan advanced from being the most inexperienced teller in the bank to being the head teller. She dated the assistant manager who was a nice young man, the most stable and well educated man she had yet chosen. I began to worry a little that college might be forgotten.

One day Susan said, "Mom, I want to live the way we live. I'll never do it on a teller's salary. I think I'll be ready to go to school next fall."

I had applied for an NIMH scholarship for the next year—just in case. Susan's education had the highest priority, but maybe something would happen, another gap in the wall.

Then I learned that I had $1500 in my pension fund at the college, and it was possible to draw it out if one resigned. That was enough to pay for Susan's tuition, room and board at a state school.

I did resign and drew out the money. NIMH granted me the scholarship—tuition and $400 a month. Susan also enrolled in Kent State. I was determined to pass my comprehensives and finish my dissertation in the next year and complete a doctorate in the shortest time imaginable, two years.

Chapter 30
In School Again

I am one of those fortunate people who enjoys being in school. In spite of the drive, the exhausting hours of study and the frustration of not being quite as smart as I wanted (or thought that I was), it was a happy time.

The psychology department was focused on experimental psychology, which, I discovered, looks at behavior in an entirely different way than psychiatric nursing does. Nursing is always concerned about the broad context. We look at patients and what is happening with them, keeping in mind our own responses, the patient's interaction with the family, community and society. Now it seemed as though I was looking at behavior through a microscope, trying to isolate and test each little part. It took lots of hours on the porch that first summer, totally immersed in books, to change the way I thought—for psychology classes only. I wanted to add this new approach as an extra, a tool that I might find useful at times, while I maintained the broader perspective of nursing.

The educational psychology and counseling classes were fun. I was building on and refining knowledge I already possessed. With one exception, my teachers in that department respected and admired me. I felt as though I were with peers.

The counseling department ran a free counseling service for the college. Students who chose could be seen by students in the counseling program. A young woman I had seen at Ernie's office began school at Kent, and Ernie suggested that I continue to see her, since I could now offer her free counseling. This delighted me. Her therapy was proceeding nicely and I hated to see her end it before she had achieved her goals. She told all the people in her dorm, and soon I was seeing a number of young women in the center. We worked in pleasant rooms that had two-way mirrors. Other students and teachers were able to watch what happened in the sessions. (The clients had consented to this.)

One day when I finished with my clients, I came out of the door and saw about twenty master's students stream through the door leading from the viewing room. I learned that they had been advised by their teachers to observe me as I worked with clients.

I was flattered, but also a little worried. I was afraid that having an audience would make me self conscious and that the clients might be hesitant to be frank with me. I needn't have worried. I forgot the people behind the mirror as soon as I turned my attention to my client. The clients seemed to do the same.

It was strange, however, to have people I had never seen speak to me as though they had always known me. I would quickly search through my memory of my classes, trying to remember if that is where we met. Then I would realize that they had watched me work with clients.

The students I was with at Kent were different than my fellow classmates in my nursing programs. My adolescence and young adulthood had taken place during World War II. My basic nursing took place in a cloistered atmosphere.

I had returned to school in the early sixties, but most of my classmates were other nurses. Even though I had young students when I was the teacher, I was not a peer and much of their lives were not available to me.

Suddenly, in my forties, I was spending time with people in their late twenties and early thirties, who were unmarried, much more open about their sex lives, and who used words I had heard only from psychotic patients or seen scrawled in bathrooms. Now as a nurse and a therapist I had seen and heard everything, but that was in particular places where there was license to be open—not in college study rooms.

In addition to becoming accustomed to the F word, I had to accustom myself to seeing the prevailing dress code. I had always tried to dress to enhance my attractiveness. (My mother had made sure I was aware of what was unattractive.) Some of my fellow doctoral students seemed to run competition to see who could make themselves look the least attractive. Ragged tattered bell bottoms, gray grungy sweatshirts, long greasy hair, dirty feet and no deodorant or perfume was the accepted costume for some of my male and female fellows.

I insisted on maintaining my individual way of presenting myself. A few fellow students called me a conformist. I insisted—laughingly—that they were. I wore dresses and blouses that were pretty, shaved my legs, and smelled good. Perhaps that is one reason most of my professors treated me as a peer.

Some of the culture did rub off on me—just a little. When Susan began at Kent, I was invited to attend Parent's Day, an orientation day for the parents of new freshman. I arranged to be absent from my classes and gathered with the other parents in the lounge of the newest dorm. My, they looked old, much older than me. And they asked such dumb questions. I could hardly believe my ears. I didn't fit into the group at all.

There was a young man there, a fellow of about twenty who had driven his girlfriend down to Kent. She was registering and going to meetings and he had been advised to join the parents group. Our eyes met across the room and I recognized the *I can't believe it* look. We gravitated to each other and had lunch together. I had the strangest feeling that I had just slipped out of my generation into his.

There were a few rough spots that first year. I had followed Larry Litwack's suggestion that I take a cognate area—a series of classes—in groups. Now I had nine semester's credits in groups in my Master's program, and had been part of a psychoanalytic group designed to give us group experience. Then for three years, I had used group discussion as a teaching tool, six times a week. I knew the theory and had plenty of practice. I was aware of how effective groups could be, or if not handled properly, how destructive. I felt it was the teacher, or group leader's responsibility to see that no one was damaged by the group.

The group program at Kent at that time was based on the sensitivity group model. Learning and growth were supposed to occur in the individual members of the group if they were open and honest. Responsibility for what happened in the group resided in all the members. The leader's role was that of a catalyst or interpreter of behavior. The head of the group section was Millie* a woman in her fifties who was sort of a guru to many students.

In one of the group classes, a seminar, shortly after I began school, I remarked that I was thinking of doing my dissertation by testing a group teaching method. I was looking for feedback about my idea from the supposed experts. What I received was a virulent personal attack. Not only was my idea crazy, it was unethical, etc. I tried to defend myself, logically, and it got worse. So I quit speaking. They mistook my silence for hurt and sadness and ended up by consoling me and offering hugs. Millie watched it all with an amused look.

I was furious. When I stormed into Larry' office after the class, I learned that Millie had already been there to report that Florence didn't know as much about groups as Larry thought. My adviser consoled me. He said that he realized now that I was a threat to Millie. We talked, and I made the decision to continue the group cognate.

So I remained in the group, being careful to keep a low profile and not incur anyone's wrath. The norm was to be open and honest. I looked as though I were abiding by the rule. In truth, I was just appearing to conform, a talent I had learned well in my basic nursing program. I assisted at sensitivity weekends and even made some good individual friends. But I never became a convert to this type of group. They can be destructive and even trigger psychotic reactions or worse. But I know the jargon and can speak groupese if needed.

Incidentally, I did develop the idea and test it in my dissertation which was accepted two years from the time I began the doctoral program. None of the rest of the groupies even had an idea for a proposal when I graduated.

Susan, my daughter, had a parallel experience. She had been in a therapy group with her social worker. When she was a freshman, she signed up for a group class. The teacher was one of those touchy-feely group leaders that were so prominent in the sixties. Susan is very warm, but cautious when she first approaches strangers. It seemed that the teacher's method of building the group was by having everyone hug each other. Susan resisted and the teacher attacked, "Something must be wrong with you if you don't want to be touched."

Susan stood and said, "There is nothing wrong with not wanting to be mauled by strangers. This class is a bunch of shit." Then she left and dropped the class.

Good for my Sue.

One episode occurred within the psychology department that proves that Susan and I have a few traits in common. I had a class in theories of personality taught by Dr. Teller*, a young experimental psychologist. Our mid-term was an essay test and one question was about the Oedipal complex. Now I had psychoanalytic therapy at the time of my first divorce, worked in psychoanalytic settings and was working at an office with an analyst. I had read everything Freud, his followers, and his critics had written. I was amazed when my test was returned with a zero on that question and a C on the whole test.

So I made an appointment to discuss this with Dr. Teller. When I told him about my background, he said, "I wish I had known that." It appeared that he thought I was a school teacher, taking a course for her master's, who was out of her depth and trying to show off. But he wouldn't change my grade.

Then he said, "Something is wrong with you if you are upset about getting a C."

"Oh, Dr. Teller," I replied, with a smile, "Nothing is wrong with me. I'll call you a dirty bastard for a few days, and then I'll forget you."

He looked as though I had hit him. Funny, his research was in aggression.

Time passed, I finished my course work and studied for my comprehensives. Dr. Teller wrote the psychology portion. I spent two grueling days writing.

A week letter I received a letter telling me that I had passed. The letter went on to say that I had written the answers completely and clearly. The committee knew me as a fellow professional and felt that I was a peer in every way. Therefore they felt that it was not necessary to hold an oral examination and that they would not require me to do that. The letter was signed by the committee, with a small *Dr. Teller* at the bottom. This was the first time that a student had been excused from orals.

I must balance my typical student gripes about the program with gratitude for the learning I gained from the program. The minor in experimental psychology made the perfect background for the work in educational psychology. I was able to switch from a microscope to the total context. What I learned greatly enhanced my later teaching.

I was supervised by Dr. Wonderly, an experienced school psychologist, for a clinical experience with school children. This was missing from my earlier education. I found that I worked well with children older than eight and this enhanced my work with families at Ernie's office and later. Dr. Wonderly treated me as a peer. He offered me a few tactful suggestions and plenty of support and reinforcement. It was a very valuable experience.

I had been in school a month short of a year when a disaster occurred. On May 4th, the National Guard marched onto the Kent campus. The school was open with most of the 20, 000 students going to lunch or changing classes. On the green in the center of the campus, a group of students gathered to protest the war in Viet Nam. The Guard marched into the crowd, knelt, shot, and killed four of them.

Chapter 31
May 4, 1970

As I drove to Kent State just before noon that bright Monday in May, I turned on my car radio to see if there were any further developments at the university. It sounded as though all were well. The National Guard was still in Kent, but the school was open.

There had been trouble over the weekend. Richard Nixon had just moved troops into Cambodia and there had been a peaceful protest on Campus. Saturday night in the area where the bars are, someone had built a bonfire on the street. The kids who were celebrating the first warm days of Spring had wandered out to look, beers in hand. Then some motorcyclists rode in, the police arrived, and someone threw a beer bottle. Suddenly there was a student riot.

Later that weekend, the rickety old ROTC building, one of those portable World War II structures, had been burned. The governor, with a great deal of anti-Communist rhetoric, had ordered the National Guard into Kent.

I discounted the role of war protesters in the situation. I hadn't met any radical anti-war people on campus. In fact, the war was hardly talked about. When I was at the University of Pennsylvania, just after World War II, there had been a student riot after a pep rally. Kids ran through the streets and stopped traffic by disconnecting the electric lines from the street cars. A boy from my home town, a former navy ensign, had been arrested. I felt that what happened at Kent was just another student riot, the result of beer, warm weather and the excessive testosterone of youth.

I had supported the war. I was old enough to have remembered that British pacifists had allowed Hitler to swallow a great deal of Europe before they intervened. The general consensus was that World War II would have been shorter if we had stopped Hitler earlier. When politicians compared the situation in Viet Nam to the pre-war situation in Europe, it made sense to me. Although as time went on, I was beginning to have doubts.

I had an appointment at a garage down the street from the campus. Rather than parking in my usual space near Taylor Hall, I was going to leave my VW bug to be serviced and then go on to meet with my adviser and attend afternoon classes. It was mid-term time and I had spent the weekend studying.

I left the car, talked with the garage owners a little while and then walked down the street toward the campus. The street was empty and I heard the sound of voices—it sounded like a crowd of people moaning—coming from the direction of the campus.

Then an army truck came down the street. It slowed and a soldier stuck his head out of the cab and yelled, "Get off the streets! Take cover!"

"What is going on? What do you mean?"

"Get inside!"

"I'm going to the Education Building over there. Is that OK?"

"Right. Take cover."

I ran to the building and went inside. It seemed deserted. I went to the second floor and found a small group

of graduate students and faculty clustered around a portable radio.

"What is going on?"

Then they told me that the National Guard had come
onto the campus during a peace rally at noon. In the ensu-
ing confrontation, the Guard had killed four students and
wounded others. The kids were over on the green near Taylor Hall, waiting for ambulances. Many of the counseling
faculty were over there, trying to calm and control the students who were frightened and afraid to move for fear the
guard would kill them also. One of the women in the room,
who was a faculty member was crying. She had just heard
that one of the dead was Sandra Shorr, her student.

We listened to the radio and waited. Someone ran
by one of the outside doors and a tossed a blood-soaked
shirt inside. An hour later, word came that the campus was
to be cleared immediately. Buses were being brought in and
all students and faculty were to leave.

I headed down the street to the garage and picked
up my car. The garage man wore a stunned expression on
his face and we didn't talk about what had happened. By
three o'clock buses had arrived and 19,000 students were
taken to Akron or Cleveland and dumped. Some were without money. The phone lines to Kent were tied up with calls
from frantic parents, who were trying to find out how their
children were. Some of the parents of the dead students
learned the fate of their children from the media.

I felt as though I were in limbo. I was ready for my
mid-term exams, and suddenly there was no school. The
news commentators speculated that perhaps the university would be closed permanently. I had invested a great
deal in securing this degree. Would it all be lost?

The next day was Tuesday, election day. When I went to vote I felt like a person in a strange land. I was mourning the loss of four young people; my faith in my government was shaken; and my educational program was in jeopardy. Yet no one I met seemed to care. I heard remarks like, "They should have killed more", and "They asked for it."

I wondered if this were the way the men felt when they came home from Viet Nam. One day they were in a war and the next day they were in an indifferent society.

By Wednesday, the professors from four of the five classes I was taking had called. They had scheduled classes in their homes or in churches. School would go on. We would not lose the quarter.

We students got a letter from the professor of the fifth class. He told us to continue studying the text on statistical inference. There were rumors that he was spending his days on the golf course. When final time came he mailed us a take-home, closed-book test. We could choose if we wanted to take a pass as a grade, or if we wanted, try for a better grade. One of the ten class members decided he wanted to try for an A. The other nine met in my living room with every statistics book we had—open. We handed in identical tests and requested that we be passed. We were. We felt we had shown that lazy son-of-a-gun. In retrospect, he probably didn't care that we had cheated on the test. Maybe he hadn't even read them and didn't know that they were identical.

It was announced that graduate students could return to campus to pick up the books and papers they needed. I needed to get some books from the department's library and so I drove to Kent. I parked my car in the parking lot, in my usual place, close to the spot where Jeff Miller had died from a shot to his head. What if I had parked here that day? It might have been me.

As I approached the walk, I was met by a deputy sheriff. He looked at my identification and then frisked me. I began to cry. He was very polite and apologetic. I felt he was as distressed by the insanity of the situation as I was.

The campus was like a dead thing. I looked at the blank windows of the dorms. I had read that the police, armed with search warrants, had searched the rooms, looking for contraband. They had discovered the dead pets of students who had been forced to leave before they could free the animals. The grass was unmowed and untrampled. My footsteps echoed on the walk, the only sound in a place that usually teemed with life and youth.

Ugly rumors swept Kent and the surrounding rural towns. The story was that Allison Krause, the honor's student who had been killed, was crawling with lice and riddled with venereal disease. The dorm was full of drugs and sexual devices. Suddenly the young had become the enemy. They were all long-haired, immoral, drug-ridden communists. The war was turning us against our hope, the next generation.

The police displayed the contraband they had found in the dorms on long tables in the gym. They invited the media to come and view these dangerous objects.

There were a few guns—a shot gun, a deer rifle, BB gun and a starter's pistol. Then there were tire chains, baseball bats, ski poles and other such weapons. Confiscated drugs included vitamin pills, birth control pills, insulin, aspirin, and several marijuana cigarettes. One lonely dead marijuana plant and a few seeds of the weed were found. Kent students led very mundane lives. The reporters thought the display was a joke and the stories the police hoped for were not written.

The school opened in June for the summer term. The copying machines were in constant use by fit-looking men, sporting crew cuts and three-piece suits. Federal agents were copying lecture notes and other material.

The FBI concluded that the Ohio National Guard could be arrested for violating the students civil rights. Attorney General John Mitchell made the decision not to charge them.

Before Susan went to Kent, I made her swear that if there was a demonstration she would go to her room and crawl under the bed. Kent students had been disinterested in politics before May 4. Now they were cautious and afraid.

What did I learn? I learned that good people, with the best of motivation, can—particularly in a group—do terrible things. The students and Guard were the same age with many of the same motives. Somehow, through the blasphemy of prejudice and stereotyping, they became mortal enemies, and four students and a great deal of naiveté were lost on May 4, 1970.

Chapter 32
The Dissertation

At the end of the second summer, a year and a quarter after I had begun, I finished my class work. I studied during fall term and completed the comprehensive exams. The only hurdle left was the dissertation.

I had spent more than a year immersed in theories of education and teaching. Although experimental psychology was based on research, most of the teaching theories were not. I wanted to know how best to teach psychiatric nursing to my students.

One of the teaching methods in vogue was guided discovery, an idea Jerome Brunner wrote about in a very convincing manner. He wrote that if the student is guided through a problem, and then solves it himself, the joy of the solution reinforces the learning. Also it is more embedded in the knowledge he already possesses. I wondered if this idea could be used in a group setting to help students learn about human behavior. If they talked about their own experience and the experiences they observed and, with my guidance, came up with facts born out by research, wouldn't they really learn it?

This method of teaching attracted me. However when I searched the literature, I began to have doubts.

Jerome Brunner had written a book and many articles about his teaching method. However he had tested it using only four exceptionally bright students, each of whom was guided by a psychologist who sat at his elbow. No wonder they learned so well, I thought. It amazed me that so few people had challenged this method.

David Ausabel did, however. Dr. Ausabel was a cognitive psychologist and psychiatrist. His method of teaching was to present material, by lecture or reading, with the broad, overarching concepts first. Then he progressively differentiated these ideas and presented more and more detailed and specific material. This appealed to me because I learn more easily when material is presented that way. I like to be presented with the big picture first, told how it fits into general knowledge, and then learn the details.

Since nurses learn in the clinical area when they are with patients, I was also interested in how best to teach them in that situation. Since I began teaching, the students and I had been discussing what happened on the wards between them and their patients. How did this method measure up against the others?

I decided that I would teach three groups of students, using each one of the methods described above, and then test them on measures of empathy and knowledge. The material I would teach would be the theories of grief and mourning.

The next problem was to find a paper and pencil test which would measure empathy. I called Elizabeth Warner, my master's classmate who read everything. Bless Elizabeth's heart—maybe it should be her brain—she knew of a well-tested instrument that could be adapted to measure that. I wrote the test of knowledge myself.

I wrote up a proposal for the research and it was accepted. Now I had to find a place to do it.

Kent had just opened a baccalaureate school of nursing. Two three-year nursing programs—Saint What's His Name and another hospital had closed their programs. Kent had absorbed many of the teachers from these schools. A former teacher of mine, Dr. Linnea Henderson, was Dean. I presented my proposal to the faculty and asked if I could use their first-year students to do this research. They agreed but asked that I work as one of the fundamentals teaching staff so the students would know me. I agreed.

It seemed ironic that eight years after I had begun at Saint-What's-His-Name, now with far more knowledge and almost two more degrees, I was again teaching the Miss Know-it-alls and the Miss Faint-Hearts. The place where these students were taught was Saint-What's-His-Name. So I truly was back where I had begun.

The students were just as inept as my first students. However they were much less impressed with me. When I dropped a pearl of psychological information from my lips, they looked bored. They were interested only in the really important things—like taking temperatures and blood pressures and making beds.

That changed a little, however. One of the students had a male patient, on bed rest, who experienced explosive diarrhea. The bed pan had not arrived in time and the poor embarrassed gentleman was swimming in a pool of his own feces. His student was in tears. She couldn't get him out of bed and into a shower because he was to remain in bed. What could she do?

Nurse Hardesty came to the rescue. I got clean linen, a basin of water, etc. and began. Fifteen minutes later, the man was bathed, in a clean bed, and I was giving him a back rub. God, were the students impressed! Here I was brimming with education, loaded with theories, a skilled psychotherapist—and I impressed them with the skills I learned when a seventeen-year-old probationer.

The time came when I was to begin teaching the three groups of students using the methods I'd chosen. I was all ready with my tape recorder—to validate the method—and I began. I was just winding up the third group when one of the students said, "Oh, this is just what Mrs. Blank* taught us in class yesterday."

Now Mrs. Blank—now labeled Blankety Blank—had agreed not to teach this material until I finished. I called her. "Oh," she said, "I thought you were finished. Sorry."

I had worked for the school, free, for a month, and now my research was ruined. I had to find another group of nursing students who hadn't yet studied the material I was going to teach. I might be delayed a year. I felt too sick to be angry.

I called Larry Litwack from the hospital and told him. He said, "Come down to Kent and let's talk."

It was a blustery March day. I hadn't eaten and when I drove through Shaker Square, I thought I'd better stop and buy a candy bar, energy to power my quaking heart and shaking hands. I went into a gift shop and saw a ceramic robin. It seemed to be a sign. I bought that symbol of spring and hope and have kept it in my study ever since.

Larry comforted me and urged me to do what I had already determined to do—begin again. The next day, I began calling nursing schools. Since it was spring term, most of the students had already learned the material I wanted to teach.

But the community college had admitted a new class that quarter. And yes, they would be glad to have me teach.

No, it was not necessary that I become part of the faculty. After all, I was one of their own, anyway.

And so I went ahead with my experiment and then tested the students. Once again my daughters, particularly Shevawn who was in junior high, helped me with the statistics and calculations.

The results surprised me. When I had used the guided discovery method, the students had freely expressed their experience with loss. One talked about losing a tooth and another about the death of her ninety-year-old mother. All had experienced loss of one sort or another. We identified the feelings and phases of grief and I repeated them. But the tests indicated that although they had learned most of the material, their scores on the tests I gave them were lower than the other groups.

The group that learned the most about what their patients were feeling was the group that heard the well-organized lecture. The group that had read the material I had given them, discussed it, and then applied the ideas to a patient they had taken care of, scored highest in knowledge.

There were many limitations to my research as there are with most small studies. To really test which method was most effective, a number of teachers would have to teach many matched groups of students.

But I did learn something important. I learned to mistrust many of the educational and psychological theories that are based on very little or faulty research. That is, most of them. I hear teachers talk about the lecture method as though it were old fashioned and useless. (I've observed that these people are usually poor lecturers.) One wonders why it has persisted so long if that is the case. Teachers who have no knowledge of neurology go on about right brain as opposed to left brain teaching. (I wonder how they manage to separate the two sides of the learner's brain?) I have concluded that people learn in many different ways, and teachers should use the method that best suits the teacher, the student and the subject. Until there is more and better research they will have to rely on their own judgment and their student's feedback to decide this.

I missed the June graduation, but I did defend my dissertation in June. I dressed in a soft yellow summer dress and wore my jade earrings. My hair was long that year, and that day I wore it in a loose pony tail with a few loose tendrils brushing my cheeks. In other words, I dressed for a hanging. The examining committee was, with one exception, male. Several people were from the psychology department. I didn't care if I was violating my women's liberation beliefs. I had to pass. Just before I began, I pulled out my glasses, the sign of intellect, and perched them on my nose.

I sailed through the defense. The only challenging question was from the woman. The men even rose to my defense and answered her before I had a chance.

Two hours after I began, I was being kissed, hugged and congratulated. They called me Doctor Hardesty.

I graduated in August. The ceremony was held outside in the stadium. Mother was ill and could not attend but my brother, John, and Susan and Shevawn were there. The forty doctoral students who finished marched up to a platform, one by one, and had their hoods placed on their academic robes and were handed the precious diploma. I was the oldest person in the group.

Afterwards, my family came running to me. John said, "I'm proud of you, Sis."

Susan, who would start her second year at Kent in a few weeks, said, "Mom, we're so proud of you. We are going to do it too."

Shevawn was a five-foot-ten, 110-pound fifteen year old, an ugly duckling who would be beautiful in a year. She said, "You looked younger than the others."

Surprised, I said, "Thanks, Honey."

"But you walked like a duck. I was embarrassed!"

There is nothing like a teenager to keep one humble.

Chapter 33
Back to Work

As soon as my dissertation was approved, I had to return to work. My car had died, and the washer and dryer had breathed their last. Susan's tuition and the first payment for my new VW would be due in September. I had to find a position in line with my career goals, and I needed a temporary job, any kind of a job, to give me a paycheck.

The four years at Ernie's had sharpened my therapeutic skills and I wanted to teach graduate students what I had learned. I realized that I would probably have to teach in a baccalaureate program first, and I was willing to do that. The community college had been very satisfying as far as the teaching went, but I was bored with the repetition of the more basic concepts.

I interviewed at Kent and could have taught there. I was very fond of the dean, Dr. Linnea Henderson, and I had taught with many of the faculty. In retrospect, it might have been better if I had accepted that position. But we humans do respond to the needs of the moment, and when one makes decisions, it is difficult to predict the outcome.

I had grown up professionally and in some ways personally in Cleveland. When I began at University Hospitals, twelve years before, I had a three-year diploma, no psychiatric experience, was newly divorced and alone with my children in a strange city. I was vulnerable and needy. Now I was a self-assured professional with an excellent education and broad experience. But many of the people I would be in contact with still held their first impression of me. I was haunted by the old me.

Any faculty position I obtained would begin in September. The week my dissertation was finished, I was hired at the Veterans Hospital for the summer. The chief nurse was delighted to have me and assigned me to the psychiatric floor. Before I began, however, the psychiatrist in charge, who I had known when he was a resident when I first got to Cleveland, vetoed my position, saying it would be disruptive to have someone for such a short time.

I was sure that this was an excuse. I knew this fellow well. At one time he had considered dating me, but he hesitated and I began to date his friend. Later, he had been the therapist for a man I had dated and who had been conflicted and depressed when we broke up. I was certain I was being judged on old and distorted information. Rather than work on a medical floor at the V A, I withdrew my application and took a temporary job at the short-term state hospital.

This experience reinforced the feeling that I wanted to leave Cleveland and go to a position in which I would be known as Dr. Hardesty, not as Hardesty, the nurse, a divorcee, who worked on Ward 4 and had dated several residents.

My mother had followed me to Cleveland, and if I left, I would be leaving her. She and my brother lived together in a comfortable house and she had acquired a circle of supportive friends. John no longer drank and had a good job. She spent time in Florida and in California whenever she pleased. I felt as though I could leave the city and she would be fine without me. I had a few twinges of guilt, but not enough to stop me from looking for a position in other cities.

I interviewed at a small private women's college in upstate New York, near the state capital. Its campus is in the center of town and it has a quaint old fashioned feeling. Many of the buildings are renovated nineteenth century townhouses. The school had a well-respected baccalaureate nursing program as well as a small masters program with one major.

Shevawn and I drove from Cleveland for the interview. I wanted to include her in the decision since she would be moving with me, if that is what I chose to do. Besides, although she was young and still, on occasion, a bratty teenager, her general judgment about people was good. In fact she had an uncanny ability to assess social systems and families. She packed her most ragged jeans and a pair of sneakers that were worn through and exposed her toes. I mentioned that that was not appropriate dress for the occasion, but she insisted. I told her that this was my interview and I couldn't be bothered worrying about her, that when she was embarrassed by her outfit, she'd be embarrassed all by herself.

The faculty at the college wooed me. They were planning to add a psychiatric major to their graduate program in a few years. If I joined the faculty, I would be in charge of it. I would teach the psychiatric nursing portion of the undergraduate curriculum and have an assistant teacher. They had no doctoral-prepared faculty at the time, although they had recently hired several very experienced faculty and several more were engaged in doctoral study.

My parents had lived in nearby Schenectady when I was an infant. Daddy always spoke of the area with longing. I liked the atmosphere of the college. My student experience had all been in large universities. I had taught at nursing schools that were isolated from the rest of the establishment and I associated almost exclusively with other nurses or physicians. The idea of being a colleague with psychology, English and French professors appealed to me.

One of the fringe benefits offered by the college was free tuition for my children. If they chose not to attend the college, they would pay their tuition elsewhere, up to the level of the college's tuition. This was a welcome incentive.

Shevawn and I drove back to Cleveland, excited about the visit. We discussed the pros and cons of the position and of moving. By the time we got back home, I had decided to say "yes" to the offer.

Shevawn and I had paused on our trip to visit my friend Helen Retchless who lived in the Finger Lakes region. David, Helen's husband, invited Shevawn and his daughter to have lunch with him at the country club. Shevawn took me aside and asked, "What should I wear, Mom? I don't want to be embarrassed." I guess she had been embarrassed by the outfit she had worn to the Campus when I interviewed. Chalk one up for the older generation!

When I arrived in Cleveland, I called the New York school and said I would accept the position. Susan decided that she would continue at Kent and transfer later to my new school. Mother seemed to take the news well. Later I learned that she felt abandoned.

What a summer this had turned out to be! I had to sell the house I had lived in for eleven years, find a place to live near my new job, pack up and move. All the while I was working at the state hospital, in—as I soon learned—a hostile environment.

Chapter 34
Super Nurse

When I asked about a job at the state hospital where I had taken my community college students, they were delighted to hire me, even for three months. Once they had me, however, they didn't know what to do with me. They had several teachers who taught the nursing students from the three-year schools in the city. They were almost finished with the group that was there and didn't need another teacher. The supervisors were experienced and there was no need for another. So they made me head nurse on a men's ward.

Until I arrived, the ward had been staffed by attendants who made sure the patients were fed, reasonably clean and quiet. Quiet meant medicated. Any time they had left after they accomplished these goals was their own, to read, play cards or gossip with each other. You can imagine how welcome an eager new nurse was, especially one that the director proudly introduced as Dr. Hardesty.

The students who were assigned to the ward had been enjoying the freedom of being away from their schools and their instructor, with no head nurses to interfere. The hospital's instructors taught their classes and appeared on the floors for a short time each day, but basically the students had been on their own. These students had chosen three-year schools and were convinced that their choice would make them *real* nurses.

When I insisted that they report to me and tell me what they were doing with the patients, I met resistance. I was surprised, since this is standard procedure in any hospital. I was ultimately responsible for what happened; I needed the information.

One day I got on an elevator crowded with students. As I turned to face the door, someone one behind me whispered, "That's Super Nurse."

I knew that if I were going to be there permanently, I would move more slowly and bring the staff and students around to my philosophy. But with the short time, I had two choices: do nothing or do what I could and ignore the resistance. I chose the latter.

There were fifty men on the ward, two attendants and me. There was no time to do individual therapy. I did spend time with each patient every day and observed how they were doing. I began groups, and every patient could attend at least one group if he wished. I had a group for men who would soon be discharged, in which they discussed their hopes and fears about leaving the hospital. Some had had many hospitalizations and had experience with the adjustment. They helped and supported each other. The medication group helped the patients understand the effects of the drugs they were taking. They learned which side effects were to be expected and which were dangerous signs that should be reported to their doctors. The more experienced men told the others which drugstores were less expensive. We had a parenting group and the young men requested a group in which they discussed how to meet girls.

Most of the patients were happy with the activities. Even if they weren't interested in the topics, it was less boring to attend a group than to sit in front of the caged television.

However, there was one man who was openly hostile to me and the groups. Gerald* was an educated man, an engineer, who had been admitted many times for acute alcoholism. His chart also listed anti-social tendencies. Until I arrived he had been the unofficial ward leader. The staff sometimes encouraged him because he did help keep the ward quiet. I was certain he was exploiting some of the more passive men, demanding money and cigarettes. His first wife had been a nurse.

The attendants resisted in subtle ways. Instead of attending to the ward while I held a group, they managed to be busy, too busy to answer the phone. This forced me to suspend the group to do that chore. When I specifically assigned one of them to answer the phone, the problem was solved.

The ward doctor had arrived a week before me. Dr. Chow had completed two years of his psychiatric residency at St. Vincent's in New York. He had transferred here for family reasons. He was experiencing culture shock when I arrived. At least *he* was very glad to see me, and we had a comfortable collegial relationship.

Billy Martin*, a patient, was also grateful for my presence. Billy was a man in his twenties, three years away from his home in a Kentucky valley. He had been earning good money as an auto worker and was living with his sister and her family. He had been on vacation, fishing in Canada with some buddies. When he arrived back at the airport on Saturday, he was picked up by the police on a 72-hour emergency psychiatric hold and brought to the hospital.

I met him when I came to work on Monday. He was fit to be tied. He had no idea why he was there or who had put him there. Over the weekend he had gotten so upset that the attendant had called the doctor on call who had ordered thorazine. Thorazine really hits people hard when they first take it, especially normal people, and it often produces faintness and dizziness when the person rises from a prone to a standing position. (The blood vessels are so relaxed that the blood runs to the feet, leaving the brain.) Poor Billy had gotten up from praying on his knees, fainted, and hit his head on the metal frame of the bed. He had a black eye and several stitches. He was a member of a fundamentalist church and his speech was peppered with biblical quotations.

He kept saying, "Call my sister. My sister will get me out of here."

Now I had read the chart and I knew that his sister had been the one to sign the complaint. As delicately as I could, I told him that. Then I went on to explain the 72-hour hold. I told him there would be a hearing the next day, and if he wished, I could get a legal aide lawyer to represent him.

"I'll get my own lawyer," he insisted.

I went outside the locked ward, to the patients' phone with him, and he called his lawyer.

When we talked, aside from being very upset with this situation, he seemed normal. He had a good work record, was a union officer, and was involved with his church. After I gave him the news about his sister, he was depressed.

I gave him support and reassured him. I also coached him about the hearing and urged him not to lose his cool. I knew that in psychiatric settings, normal behavior, especially expressions of emotion, can be misconstrued as psychotic. Billy was very emotional about being unexpectedly locked up in a psychiatric hospital.

He went to the hearing the next day and that is the last I saw of Billy Martin. He was declared sane and he left immediately. A few days later I received a thank you card from him with ten dollars enclosed.

I re-addressed the envelope and sent the money to the ACLU, the organization that had worked to pass the laws that enabled Billy to be freed so quickly.

About a month later, in the staff cafeteria, I heard one of the staff talking about a patient who had delusions about her husband and brother. She thought that they had turned into devils. I asked a few questions and learned that the patient was Billy's sister.

One day I was conducting the discharge group. The ward was quiet, and all seemed well. Then the fire alarm went off.

"Oh," I said, "a fire drill." I suspended the group which was meeting on the porch and went inside to see what was happening. Then I heard the fire sirens. I got the patients all into the hall, counted them and began herding them down the fire escape. Then the fire chief came clumping in with his big boots and red hat. He told me the alarm outside my door had been pulled. He inspected the ward and found no fire. I called to the attendants and they brought the patients back.

Patients were milling around, some frightened, most excited. I heard my hostile patient, Gerald, say sarcastically. "She doesn't even know the procedure. She is supposed to put the charts in a metal waste basket and carry them out."

I asked a few questions and learned that he had been off the ward making a phone call in the hall near the fire alarm. I wondered how many false alarms he had started. I had no proof. I decided not to act on my suspicions. I did unearth the fire alarm procedure from an ancient manual and learn it, however.

The things that went on at work didn't affect me as deeply as they might have. I was leaving soon. Besides my personal life was extremely busy. My large old house in Cleveland Heights was for sale. I had tried to keep it up but had not had quite enough money. Every year, the ancient gas furnace needed fixing. Each time I had been told I needed a new one, butneach time settled for a new part. A wind storm had damaged a third floor dormer. The insurance fixed it, but, later, Susan slammed the bathroom door, and the plaster ceiling, weakened by the water that had come in, fell in a thousand little pieces. (Thank Heavens, she wasn't hurt.) I spent my evenings painting and weeding, hoping the prospective buyer would see what a wonderful house it was for a family and not notice details.

One weekend I drove to New York and looked for a house. I found one, a small house that had just been completed. Susan was in college and Shevawn would be away at school in three years. This small new house with its baseboard heat, new fireplace, and hardwood floors really appealed to me, after eleven years of struggle just to keep the Cleveland house livable. It was cozy and I could envision living in it alone. I bought it, contingent on my selling my house. When the girls first saw it, they cried. Home was a three story house with a basement and interesting nooks and crannies, not a new little box.

The last week that I was at the hospital, I made a presentation to the medical staff about the use of groups in a psychiatric setting. They were very impressed. They asked me where they could receive training to lead groups and several came to the ward to observe group sessions. Even the attendants expressed some interest.

My house sold, and I packed up eleven years of memories. It was hard to leave Mother. The logical part of her supported me, but emotionally she felt abandoned.

Shevawn and I tranquilized our two cats, put them in boxes, loaded the VW to the roof and sped down the freeway to our new home in upstate New York and my new job.

The Women's College

1971-1976

Chapter 35
A New Job

Shevawn and I drove down the interstate to our new home, accompanied by the yowls of Tom and Tinkerbell. If I drove faster than 70 m.p.h. the cats were quiet, but if I slowed, their protests filled the VW. Half way there they clawed their way our of the boxes where they were imprisoned. Shevawn and I tore up towels to make straps to secure the boxes and continued on.

We arrived at our new little home and settled in. It was a very pleasant time. Shevawn, Susan and I had been together since Shevawn was born. My text books told me that a triangle was a very unstable group and my experience with my daughters bore this out—until I found a solution. When I withdrew a little and let the girls pair closely, there was less fighting and sibling rivalry. Oh, they still fought, but they developed deep and permanent bonds of love and common experience. Knowing this made me happy.

But now, Susan was in Cleveland preparing to begin her second year at Kent. I enjoyed Shevawn's company as we settled into the house and landscaped the yard. She rapidly adopted the role of gardener and still enjoys yard work.

In early September we both began school. I taught psychiatric nursing to the senior students and had an inexperienced teacher to assist me. I also taught a course called Family Mental Health to registered nurses who had returned to school to earn a baccalaureate in nursing. This course contained the newer content of psychiatric nursing, and maternal and child health. I taught it with a faculty member who was an obstetrical nurse.

The basic nursing students were very different from the community college students I had taught in Cleveland. They were college seniors, virtually all white, from upper-middle-class families. They'd had good basic educations and were sophisticated about higher education. They were disciplined students in the class and dedicated and committed in the clinical area. I have few stories about them overcoming the barriers to success, stories like Arturo's and Lottie's. I expected these students to do well and they did.

Sometimes I wondered if they had been too well raised. Allison* came to my office one day to express concern about her advanced medical-surgical teacher. The student felt that the teacher was very stressed and might be on the verge of a nervous breakdown. She had been trying to help and be supportive but felt she was not successful.

As the story unfolded, it was apparent that the teacher was very angry and that she was being punitive in the way she made assignments. In order to meet her demands for preparation, before the students went into the clinical area they would have to stay up half the night. When they had complained the demands increased.

Strangely Allison was not angry at the teacher. Instead she felt that she herself was inadequate. She came to me because she wanted very much to help her teacher.

Now my response in such a situation would be to be angry at the unfair authority figure and to discount her evaluation of me. My daughters and former students, would have reacted the same way. My new students had so little experience with injustice and abuse that they didn't know how to deal with it.

On reflection, I realized that I had learned at age three to ignore some people. My Great-aunt Florrie, who was my mother's adopted mother, never did like me. She would forget my name, a feat of forgetfulness, since I was named for her, and call me Thelma. Thelma was my mother's younger sister who had remained with her parents. Then Aunt Florrie would go on to say how and why she disliked Thelma. I thought that my legal grandmother was a crazy old lady and I ignored her. My self esteem has remained intact ever since, immune to the attacks of unfair authority figures. I decided, after listening to my student, I had something else to thank Aunt Florrie for besides my name.

The situation at school placed me in a difficult position. I felt that I must protect the students. Yet as a new member of the faculty, I knew that it was unwise to intervene in another teacher's class. I went to the director and presented the facts. My boss said she would talk to Miss Smith* and asked me to counsel her—a delicate job, fraught with danger to my status as a new faculty.

I approached Miss Smith cautiously. To my surprise, she welcomed me. She was depressed and overwhelmed. She had just become aware that she was being punitive with the students. I supported her and she went into therapy. Her doctor prescribed anti-depressants, and she improved rapidly. She dropped in every week to show me her students' assignments and exams and to get feedback.

What could have been a quagmire for me, turned out well. I did talk to my students about developing healthy defenses. I don't think it did much good. I hope they learned how to protect themselves from the slings and arrows of the working world without getting too many wounds.

The students in the family nursing course were more familiar and more diverse. Their ages ranged from early twenties to forties, and there were men and people of other races in the class. The army sent its nursing personnel to the college for more education and many of the students were nuns.

I was more at home in this class, although there were more arguments and less note-taking. I felt as though I were with peers. A high percentage of these students went directly into graduate school. They were more like me than the basic students who had been nurtured so carefully.

I tried hard not to let my preferences and prejudices affect my teaching. Come to think of it, I was being careful with them also, just like their parents.

Chapter 36
Katie*

T he student teacher relationship between Katie* and me began in a strange way. But first I need to give you some background.

In the late sixties and early seventies, mini-skirts were in. They were really short and really tight. There was never enough material to dip down between the thighs of my seated female students. Instead the skirts tented across, affording anyone who stood or sat opposite these women a clear view of their panties.

I encouraged the students to wear longer skirts when they were in the clinical areas, but other than that I tried to ignore the sometimes colorful view of their underwear. My own skirts were longer but still too short to be flattering; it was hard to fight the prevailing styles.

Just about the time I went to the college, there was an abrupt change in the standard college student apparel. Minis were out, and ragged jeans were in. The bell bottoms were long, dragging on the ground if possible and patches were displayed in prominent colors. I thought it was ironic that my students, most of whom were from upper-middle-class homes and attended class at an expensive private school, were dressed in rags.

The first day of class, Katie caught my attention. How could she not? She was a tall red-headed young woman, who carried herself with poise and self assurance. Her white shirt was starched. Her jeans were in rags and the crotch had worn out. Katie's bottom was patched with flaming red silky material. The effect was startling.

She couldn't wear those to see patients, I thought. I sensed that I might have trouble enforcing my dress code. I talked in a general way about appearance and told the students they were to dress in good taste. "Clean unpatched jeans, are all right."

I thought I saw Katie's mouth twitch.

When the students filed in after their first break, Katie approached me to ask a question.

I looked at her crimson bottom and out came the words, "Miss Jones, those jeans remind me of a rhesus monkey in heat."

Katie was shocked, and I heard the other students titter. I felt a stab of guilt. I had embarrassed a student in front of her peers.

When Katie regained her ability to speak she said, "Dr. Hardesty, you did it. I'll burn them tonight. My mother has been after me for six months to get rid of them and in one sentence you convinced me!"

A relationship of respect grew out of our first exchange.

I took my students to a day treatment center which was well staffed and operated using the ideas of a therapeutic community. The basic premise is that everything in the community—the patients, the staff, the program and the physical setting—should be planned to help the patient regain his health. This noble idea is almost impossible to carry out. Yet the staff worked diligently and as far as they were able, they did this.

The only stumbling block was the severe mental illness of some of the patients. Therapeutic communities have been effective with adolescents and people with behavior and personality problems. They don't work as well with people whose disturbed brain chemistry is causing the problems.

The staff consisted of a psychiatrist, several social workers, nurses, and a psychologist. Several days a week I arrived with eight eager students. We observed or took part in the community meetings, group therapy sessions, family therapy, psychodrama, and any number of educational sessions. In a short time, I functioned as a quasi-staff member. In exchange, the staff spent time teaching students.

My own skills increased and I had an opportunity to observe a variety of therapeutic styles. The staff became close friends and the students learned. Even our most withdrawn schizophrenic patients learned to play the therapeutic games. I am certain, however, that few of them were able to transfer their new skills to settings other than the one in which they were learned. However, their families did gain the ability to manage the illness of their loved one with less stress.

Katie, in new clean jeans, fit right into the program. She was a natural. The staff entrusted her with a group in which she taught dating skills to the adolescent patients. It is difficult enough for a young man to ask a girl for a date. For some of our patients it was almost impossible. Yet Katie demonstrated, had the patients role play, and some of them achieved success in the real world outside the center. She taught the girls how to signal a young man that they liked him, without frightening him away with seductive behavior.

A student like Katie makes a teacher look good. Although she was the star, the other students fit into the community easily and also contributed a great deal.

Katie's final paper was about the beneficial effects of relationships among siblings. In the early seventies, this aspect of family life and child development was not given much attention. Freud and most of the theorists focused on the relationship between the child and the parents. He wrote only of the destructive elements of sibling rivalry. Katie's paper was well written and she noted all of the research that had been done to that date. It stimulated my interest in the topic, and the key ideas were incorporated into my later lectures.

Katie graduated and went off to a master's program in psychiatric nursing at Yale. I look for her name when I read my journals but haven't found her. Very likely she has married and changed her name.

I remember her fondly, especially when I see a young person dressed in an outrageous outfit, or one with a nose ring and green or purple hair. Before any stereotypical conclusions form in my mind, I remember Katie's rhesus monkey jeans and tell myself, wait, get to know them. They might have as much to offer the world as Katie.

Chapter 37
Two Good Men

T he two men in my family nursing class were as different in appearance and outlook as they could be. Yet they were alike in that they gave thoughtful, compassionate care to their patients.

Charles Chadwick*, Charley to all, looked like a movie caricature of a hippie—a handsome hippie. His straight brown hair was long and sometimes restrained by a headband. He wore an earring—a rare ornament for a man in 1972. His bell-bottom jeans were ragged but clean and he usually wore a fringed leather jacket and a broad-brimmed leather hat. When he was in the hospital, he wore a white tunic over white trousers, and his hair was pulled back into a netted pony tail. But since he was getting clinical experience for the course in a public health agency, the earlier picture is the one he presented to his patients.

Captain William Jones*, United States Army, was the other student. He had been sent to the college by the army. Since he displayed leadership ability, the service was anxious that he have the education that would enable him to advance. He came from a military family but had surprised his parents when he decided to model his career after his army nurse mother, rather than his West Point father. He was tall and good looking as he marched around the campus in perfectly pressed-khakis.

I thought the two men would help and support each other. But each was turned off by what the other represented. Charley referred to Captain Jones as Captain Straight Arrow and the other students adopted the name, behind the soldier's back.

Charley's mother was also a nurse. His father was a chemistry professor at a nearby university and Charley had begun higher education as a physics major. He had married while he was in school and his wife gave birth to a baby with an inoperable congenital heart defect. His wife, young and terrified by her baby's illness, fled back to her parents leaving Charley to cope with the baby.

He dropped out of school and cared for his child until it died. Then he disappeared for several years, roaming the country and visiting hippie territory. He returned to upstate New York, got a job in a nursing home and breezed through an associate degree nursing program. When I met him he was working nights on an obstetrical ward, and easily mastering the courses that would lead to a baccalaureate degree.

Charley was probably the most intelligent student I've ever taught. He could have succeeded in any occupation. For a final paper he compared several theories of family therapy to the third law of thermodynamics. Now, I have no way of knowing how valid the comparisons were, since I know nothing about thermodynamics. But the paper did show that he had mastered and critically analyzed the family therapy theories. The paper was beautifully written, perfectly typed and footnoted. When I discussed it with Charley, he said the idea had come to him on a slow night at work. He had gone home that morning and typed it up. The paper I had received was a first draft.

Charley's patients loved him and he did everything right. The other students, with the exception of Captain Straight Arrow, were very fond of him. They brought him food in their lunches and they spent time together talking about school.

Now, I was still a little naive, and I didn't suspect that the reason for their solicitude was anything other than his personality. Several years later, when Shevawn was in college, I began to suspect there was something more involved in the students' affection for Charley. I learned that students sometimes write papers for their peers. I also came to the conclusion that if I couldn't recognize a paper written by anyone other than the student whose name appeared on the title page, I deserved to be hoodwinked.

Charley graduated and I lost track of him. I often wonder where his career has taken him. I imagine him doing very sophisticated research. Then I remember how good he was with patients and hope that he is giving direct care. Maybe he even cut his hair.

Captain Jones followed several families during the course. One was particularly interesting and sad. The husband was a strong patriarchal sort of man, married to a very dependent younger woman. They had two children in junior high. They had no close relatives and the woman had never worked. The husband discouraged contact with people outside the family. They were a tight little circle of safety in a hostile world.

Then the husband developed pancreatic cancer and moved rapidly toward a terminal state. This is when Captain Jones met the family. He gave the wife emotional support. He talked with the husband, encouraging him to give his wife permission to learn all the things she would need to know when she was alone with the children. Then

Captain Jones referred her to agencies, or taught her himself, how to plan a budget, use the bank, and contact social service agencies. He talked with the children about what was happening with their father, contacted the schools, and took the kids out for a day—a welcome diversion from the pain and grief in the family.

The father died. Captain Jones missed class to attend the funeral. When the class met again, the other students were eager to know how the family was managing. Captain Jones told us the funeral had been attended by the wife, children and the family's nurse. It was winter and the four people stood in the cold wind and said their goodbys.

My first thought was, "Thank God, he was there."

It wasn't over. Captain Jones followed the family the rest of the time he was at the college. He wrote an excellent paper about the dangers of an isolated, excessively bonded family. By the time he graduated and went back to his base and his own wife and children, the results of his intervention were evident. The mother of his family was taking secretarial classes at the community college, preparing for a job, and the kids were involved in scouts and church activities. The grief over the father's death was fading and they were looking forward to the challenges ahead.

Sometimes I am accused of being overly optimistic. I guess I would have to plead guilty. But my judgment is skewed by the fact that I have known such people as Charley, the brilliant hippie, and Captain Jones, a straight arrow.

Chapter 38
Susan's First Injection

While I was settling into my new teaching position, my daughter Susan was settling into Kent State University. As with most college students, she wasn't clear about her major .The first year she thought she might major in math, or perhaps French.

Then at the end of her freshman year, we were enjoying a quiet Sunday at home in Cleveland when she said, "Mom, I have something important to tell you. I don't know how you'll feel about it."

Alarm bells rang in my head, as every disaster possible raced through my mind. "What is it, honey?"

"I've declared my major. I've been accepted in nursing."

I was relieved and surprised. "Where did that come from?"

She placed her hand on her heart—or was it her stomach—and said, "Right from here."

I shouldn't have been surprised. My photo albums were full of little Susan, playing nurse.

The college granted free tuition for the children of faculty and also agreed to pay tuition in another school, so long as it was not more than theirs. Susan decided to stay at Kent. Her friends were there, and she was afraid she might have too much pressure if she were in a school where her mother taught.

As it turned out, her teachers had either taught with me at Saint-What's-His-Name or been my classmates at Western Reserve. Susan had all the comparisons she could handle.

I need to give you some background so you can appreciate this incident. When Susan was six weeks old, we went to the physician who cared for both of us. He examined my darling baby, then said, "Florence, I don't want her to be afraid of me. So why don't you give her shots?" I agreed. He even gave me a vial of DPT so I could follow up without having to return for that specific purpose.

When the Salk vaccine became available, his office was deluged with calls. He called me and asked if I would give the vaccine to his patients in the small village where I lived. In return, all my daughter's injections were free. Soon I was giving weekly allergy injections to a friend's daughter. She reciprocated by teaching me to drive. A woman whose baby had chewed the lead paint off the crib brought me fresh vegetables when I gave her son injections to counteract the lead in his system. Medical care for my children was free, and the doctor called my house his Mt. Jackson outpost.

Susan protested loudly when I gave her an injection. I remember dragging her out from under the television and sitting on her while I gave her penicillin for a strep throat. But she did love the doctor.

When she was seven, we moved to Cleveland. A year and a half later, my mother retired from teaching and joined me. When the new pediatrician found it impossible to give Susan a shot, I was elected.

One day I was working on the psychiatric unit at

University Hospitals and I was paged. When I answered the phone, I was told to come to the emergency room immediately, that my daughter needed me. I turned my responsibilities over to a fellow nurse and rushed to the ER.

There in the hallway, cowering against the wall was my nine year old daughter, her blue eyes wide with fear. I went into the office, and found my mother, the intern and a nurse, discussing this out-of-control kid who refused to let them give her a shot. It seemed Susan had stepped on a nail and needed a booster for tetanus. I gave the injection to a grateful little girl who made no protest. I began to wonder if I had been wise when I followed the doctor's suggestion.

One weekend shortly after I had moved to New York, Susan unexpectedly drove the 550 miles to our home. I was delighted to see her but concerned that all was not well. Sue enlightened me.

"We had nursing lab last week. It was on injections. The dumb teacher decided to have the students practice by giving each other shots. When I found out about it, I arranged to be sick. There was no way, I was going to let them stick a needle in me. You have to show me how and let me practice."

At least, I thought, she hadn't come home to tell me she had dropped out of school. "O.K. I'll go to the drugstore and get disposable syringes and sterile saline."

When I got to the drugstore, I learned that New York had new strict laws. You needed a prescription to get syringes and normal saline. Even a vial of sterile water was unavailable without a prescription. I explained why I needed the equipment but the pharmacist held firm.

I returned home and searched for my old glass syringe. I had kept it for sentimental reasons. I boiled it up along with needles. I also boiled water for my own special student to inject.

Susan had memorized the procedure book. I didn't have to teach her that. She fixed a #25 needle on the syringe and drew up the sterile water. "I want to do both an intramuscular and subcutaneous. O. K? I am going to put this into your arm."

I had heard how sterile water stings. I pulled up my sleeve and bared my deltoid. She cleansed the spot with an alcohol sponge and prepared to inject.

"That's right, Sue, at a 45 degree angle." She hesitated. "Push it in, Honey." I gritted my teeth, but continued smiling. She pushed the needle in—Suzy is no Miss Faintheart—and injected the solution. It stung like h___ . "That's fine, dear." No fainting here. "Now let's try the intramuscular."

As I got my sterile water in the buttocks, I had a vivid memory of me sitting on five-year-old Susan and injecting penicillin. It is strange how life repeats itself.

Susan has been a coronary intensive care nurse, a public health nurse, a teacher and is currently a public health supervisor. I wonder if my granddaughter, Leslie, will be a nurse. Susan makes sure the pediatrician gives Leslie her shots.

Chapter 39
Campus Life

Before long I was involved in what the accrediting agencies call college governance. All faculty were considered members of the faculty senate, which advised the administration on policy matters. I served on a committee called the Community Council. Students, faculty and administrators were members and our task was to decide the policies that governed student life at the school. Community Council meetings were long and loud. I enjoyed the repartee and hope that we found satisfactory compromises between the opposing points of view.

Remember, this was the early seventies. As a society we were just emerging from the revolutions of the sixties and the college, being a little behind, was in the throes of questioning. The big debate centered on this dilemma: Were college administrators to serve in the role of parent in regard to campus life? Or were students adults who should make their own choices about how to behave?

The free-thinking liberal part of me said, they are adults. Certainly the nursing students, who were responsible for the lives and care of very sick patients, ought to be free to make decisions about how their dormitory was managed.

The other part of me was the mother. I knew that well-meaning young people could find themselves in situations they could not control, particularly when their peers were involved. That is why I stayed around when my daughters entertained a group of friends in our home. I felt that it was sometimes helpful for the young people to be able to say, "You can't do that. The dorm counselor (or Mother) does not permit it."

Life in a dormitory can be very distracting. It is sometimes hard to study or sleep. My daughter, Susan, had been in a coed dorm, and left it as soon as she could live off campus. Her descriptions of life there reminded me of Animal House or a zoo.

One of my students fell asleep in class. I considered calling on her but decided not to embarrass her. At break, she woke up long enough to apologize and explain.

It seemed that her roommate's boyfriend had arrived two weeks before to visit. Since her dorm was "open", he was permitted to visit his sweetheart in her room. He was supposed to leave at eleven. Instead, he hid in the closet and when all was quiet, slipped into bed with his girl. Evidently they were noisy love-makers. My student escaped from these sounds by taking her blanket and trying to sleep on a love seat in the lounge.

I was appalled by this situation and encouraged the student to insist that the boyfriend leave. She felt she couldn't do that, and she vetoed my suggestion that she tell the house mother. She also asked that I not intervene.

My fellow students in the 1940s would have insisted that the man leave. My daughters would have been able to insure that only the designated students occupy the room. The well-bred young women at this school, in an era when liberal attitudes toward sex were politically correct, seemed too passive to protect their own space. And yet when the faculty and administrators tried to institute rules to help them, the students objected vehemently.

The college president was a young man who liked ceremony and tradition. He instituted college convocations. Several times a year, we donned our academic robes (I bought my own set of second-hand robes to save the cost of renting them) and marched to the auditorium for a program that always included a long talk by our leader.

Now truthfully, I liked wearing my robes with the velvet on the sleeves that announced I finally was a doctor of philosophy. I had struggled long to attain that privilege. However the president demanded that we march in according to our rank. Even worse, within the ranks we were lined up according to how long we had been at the school. I was right behind Dr. Snooty*, a philosophy professor who had spent two years in England a decade before and had acquired an English accent and a supercilious manner. Most of the nursing faculty were far back in the line, and my teaching partner, Cindy Taylor, as an instructor, was at the tail end.

I objected to our being paraded according to our "worth." It seemed undemocratic and divisive. My senate colleagues cheered me when I mentioned it, but we continued to have convocations and march according to rank.

One convocation, when we were seated in the auditorium, sweating in our robes and hoods and bored by the speeches, I made a list of what my fellow faculty were doing. A fellow associate professor of nursing was reading a paperback mystery that she had hidden in the sleeve of her gown. The art teacher was sketching the French teacher who sat next to her. The model was reading a volume of poetry, in French, of course. The music teacher was beating out a rhythm on the arm of the seat with his fingers, while swaying with closed eyes, listening to the sounds in his head. The rest were sleeping or in a trance.

I had an inspiration. I leaned toward the philosophy professor and whispered, "Wouldn't it be fun, if when Dr. President asks us to rise, we stood, opened our gowns and were naked underneath? Pass it on."

He did. Maybe he wasn't such a stuffy fellow after all. The message passed down the row to the hundred or so scholars; and left a smile in passing.

When the president asked us to rise, he looked down into the smiling faces of his faculty. It was such a change, he looked shocked.

This was the era of streaking. As graduation approached, everyone had wondered (hoped?) if one of the students would shock us all (and provide a little diverson). Other schools had streakers at graduation, but our college maintained its decorum.

However, we did have a streaker.

One morning, just a few days before graduation, as I drove to the day treatment center, I heard on my car radio that a naked woman had been seen running down First Street. Police had been called but were unable to find the streaker.

When I met with my group of students to plan the day, I repeated what I had heard. It wasn't news to them. In fact, Elsa* said casually, "It was me."

Elsa was a plump young woman from a rural community in eastern Pennsylvania. Her ethnic background was German, and her parents were farmers. She had a matter-of-fact-it-can-be-handled attitude that was very helpful to patients in crisis. She was also very bright, but too relaxed to get the As she was capable of.

I was surprised—O K, shocked—when Elsa said this. She went on, "The first time I went out, I wore my nurse's cap. After the police left, I did it again with my mortarboard. I live in German House. As I was running out the door wearing my cap, two guys were coming in to pick up their dates. The look on their faces made the whole thing worthwhile."

"Weren't you afraid of getting caught?"

"No, the other girls distracted the police. I slipped into one of the houses down the street and got dressed and walked back."

"Were you drinking?"

"Of course. Just enough to take the dare. But if you could have seen those guys' faces...."

So I had met a streaker. She is now the director of nursing of a large hospital, and the mother of teenagers. I'll never tell her real name. I suspect that it has been a long time since she told anyone about her naked dashes down First Street. ·

Chapter 40
Sisters

Many of my students were nuns. Their convents had sent them back to school to increase their skills and to obtain a baccalaureate degree in nursing. They lived in a convent in the town while they attended school.

I hadn't had nuns in my classes at the community college. I was a little nervous about how they would react to some of the things I would say in class, particularly when I talked about sexuality. I needn't have worried; they were more matter of fact about the whole topic than most of my other students.

One year I had three nuns in my class for registered nurses, Family Mental Health.

Sister Flaming Red* had hair that color and pale Irish skin that flushed readily when she was mad, embarrassed or emotionally moved. I often wondered how she had survived in the convent when her feelings were so evident. She was in her thirties and had made the decision to become a nun when she was a child. She moved quickly and had a no-nonsense manner. When I lectured, I would look back at her and notice that she seemed to be telling me by her body language to hurry up and get to the point.

Sister Ribbons*, in her early twenties, was a bundle of contradictions. She dressed in street clothes, drab conservative outfits, and wore no jewelry or make-up. She pulled her long dark hair back into a pony tail which fell in loose curls to her shoulders. The pony tail was tied with narrow brightly-colored velvet ribbons that flowed into her hair.

Carol, a nurse at the day treatment center, had attended high school in a suburb of New York with Sister Ribbons. She had a great deal of difficulty understanding why her classmate had chosen the religious life. Carol said that Ribbons had been very popular with the boys and wore the most stylish clothes. Perhaps she had distilled all her individuality into one expression, her ribbons.

Sister Happy* was a small woman, who would have been called beautiful in the early 1920s. She had thick curly blonde hair, a peaches-and-cream complexion and a soft curving body. There was a happy radiance about her.

The nuns spent a great deal of time at the school library and lingered after class to ask questions. I attributed this to the fact that they were diligent students.

When each group finished the term, we had a party. When we discussed where it would be, they always chose my home as the setting. I was flattered that they wanted to be there, and I do like to entertain. The drinking age in New York was eighteen and the youngest of my senior students or graduate nurse students were in their early twenties. I served wine and beer as well as nonalcoholic drinks, and the students were always careful to drink intelligently.

The class that the sisters were in finished the program in June, and we scheduled the party half an hour after graduation rehearsal. I was at home, making potato salad and chilling the dip, when Shevawn came home. I said, "Clean your bathroom, honey. In an hour I'll have thirty-five students here and your bathroom is a mess."

My daughter dutifully replied, "They won't see a messy bathroom." She disappeared into that part of the house for a while and then went shopping with a friend.

The students and party time arrived. They poured into the house, complaining of a long rehearsal and full bladders. I directed them to my bathroom and Shevawn's.

But there was a problem. Shevawn had made sure her bathroom would not be seen in its disordered state by locking the door. Thirty-five people make a long line when you need to go.

"I'll fix it," announced Sister Happy, "there is no lock that I can't pick."

With implements gleaned from the purses of her classmates, she had the door open in a few minutes. She went on to say, "No one could survive convent life without the ability to pick locks."

Once the urgent physical needs of the group were met, and they had had some refreshments, they composed a poem for Shevawn, remarking on the various sights in her bathroom. This composition was lost, as so many things are, when I moved from that house so I can not reproduce it. But I do remember that it was very funny.

The nuns gathered in a circle in the family room and proceeded to have a hilarious time. Sister Flame was the designated driver, so she didn't drink, but she sure did laugh a lot. All three lit up cigarettes, given to them by the other students. This was in the early seventies and more people smoked then.

Shevawn came home from shopping and was mortified to learn that everyone had seen her bathroom. It had never occurred to her that that room would be so needed.

She was seventeen at the time, a tall beautiful girl who looked older. She disappeared into the kitchen and joined the group who had gathered there. Shevawn was always interested in these students who seemed to think her mother was so smart. (Maybe I should say puzzled by.)

The last students to leave the party were the sisters. They kissed me goodby and thanked me profusely.

The next week, they invited me to the convent where they were staying to have dinner with the nuns who were their hosts. I drove down the street and parked in front of a large plain house. When I rang the door bell, all three opened it. As they kissed me, they whispered, "Don't say anything about our smoking or drinking."

The dining room was painted dull gray and the large table had a cloth that was almost the same color. There were no curtains or decorations on the wall except the cross and a rather gruesome crucifixion painting. The dishes were heavy dull white and the food uninspiring.

Then I noticed that Sister Happy wasn't smiling and Sister Ribbons was not wearing her trademark. I was introduced to the hosts, who were all elderly women. They were still wearing their habits. The conversation was stilted with long periods of silence.

I escaped as soon after dinner as was polite. Then my three students, who were dedicated not only to nursing but to their church, kissed me goodby. They thanked me, and they said it was for more than the class.

I left, now understanding the ribbons, the smiles and the blushing. And I had a lot of questions. Why do some orders think that for a life to be dedicated, they have to remove all pleasure? I later learned it didn't have to be that way when I had had more experience with nuns and their lives.

A few years later Sister Flame left the order; she is now working in a psychiatric hospital. Sister Happy had moved up in her order. I wonder if she leaves the refrigerator unlocked at night. I lost track of Sister Ribbons. I do hope that as she serves God, there are some brightly colored strands in her life.

Chapter 41
Guyana

T he college had an agreement with the government of Guyana, that small nation on the northeastern coast of South America. The World Health Organization (WHO) financed a program to send a group of the college's nursing faculty to Guyana for seven weeks to conduct classes and upgrade the education of the nurses. At the end of my first year at the college, I was asked to go.

My contract with the college was for nine months, but my pay was divided into twelve segments. The money WHO would pay me would be enough to bring Susan and Shevawn to Guyana for a few weeks and on the way home to give all of us a short vacation in Barbados at the Paradise Beach Resort. A free overseas vacation for the whole family and the chance to have an adventure! I said, "yes," even before the chairman had finished her sentence.

Susan decided to stay in Ohio and work for the summer, coming home only to accompany Shevawn to Guyana. Susan's boyfriend was the main attraction there. I did not want to leave Shevawn alone while I was gone. My good friend and former boss, Helen Burnside, was now Associate Provost for Health Sciences for the New York State University system. She lived about ten miles from me and she agreed to move into my house and be with Shevawn while I was away.

Three professors were scheduled to go: one from the college, who had been to Guyana a midwife who had been a teacher at the school several years before; and me. When I agreed to go, I did not know that the F B I would do a background investigation of me. Ernie called to tell me that an agent had interviewed him, asking if I were loose sexually or likely to drink too much. I had some fantasies about my former husbands being interviewed. Someday I'd like to request my file to find out what everyone had to say. It must have been good because I was approved.

For some reason, at the last minute the other person from the college decided not to go. Pat, the chairperson of the nursing program at a local community college and a maternal/child health nurse was named the third person. Elise*, the other original member, and I had been briefed on what to expect in regard to the culture, the geography and the health situation in Guyana. Pat had not. When I asked directly who was in charge, I received a non-committal answer. And so we went off to the tropics—one midwife, one maternal/child health nurse, and me, the psychiatric nurse with a doctorate in education. Our mission: teach the latest material in midwifery, maternal/child health, and psychiatric nursing; teach the nurses how to teach; and then supervise them while they taught the other nurses of the country. All this was to be done in seven weeks.

We arrived and were greeted by the Minister of Health. We lived in a small house on a compound for foreign visitors administered by the Department of Hydraulics and engineering. Like Holland much of Guyana is below sea level, so this is an important department. The

Minister of Transportation supplied a car and Mr. Hanis, our driver. The Department of Safety supplied two guards, each armed with large sticks, who spent twelve-hour shifts sitting in front of our house. I'm not sure which department supplied us with Mary, our maid, who shopped, cooked and cleaned for us but the department of finance paid everyone. When I remarked that the arrangement seemed an inefficient way to take care of us, I was quietly told that this method allowed the various departments to keep an eye on each other.

We were ushered into meetings with the various dignitaries and they all gave flowery, beautifully constructed little speeches in archaic English. Guyana is a literate nation. Most of our hosts were Black, descendants of African slaves. There were also a few people whose ancestors had been indentured servants from India. The faces of many people bore traces of several races.

Pat was older than Elise and I, tall with a regal bearing. She was assumed to be the leader and Elise and I gladly let her take that role. However, since she hadn't been briefed, she asked embarrassing questions, such as, "Is it possible to take a tour to see the back country?" Elise and I groaned inside. We knew that the only way into the bush was to go up a piranha-filled river in a canoe or to fly to a tiny airstrip in the jungle. Poor Pat was a truly gracious lady, and Elise and I, until we knew her better, behaved a little like adolescents who are ashamed of their mother.

Elise was a small woman, less than five feet tall, who was extremely knowledgeable in her field. She was going through a difficult time, however. We later learned, she was considering becoming a member of a religious community. She found it difficult to live with two strange women and adjust to the spicy food that Mary prepared. She got up early in the morning to take the first shower. The water was warmed directly by the sun's rays in a tank on the roof. There was only one warm shower in the tank. I was the last one to shower. By then the water was always room temperature.

Pat and I adjusted quickly to the flora and fauna that lived with us. There were cute little transparent frogs in the shower, and the walls were frequently decorated with lizards. We chose to live and let live, but Elise screamed and demanded that we attack the critters. I hated to do this, because, when threatened, the lizards abandoned their tails which kept on twitching. Elise's screams were more annoying than the twitching, so I became the lizard exterminator.

The light in the bathroom was above the sink, too high for Elise to reach. At night she would go into the bathroom, call, "Florence," and I would go in and turn on the light. I wanted to leave it on, but the others felt the light attracted more creepy crawlies.

It took more than a day for we three strange women to adjust to living together in a strange bug-filled country. We fit more easily into our nursing and teaching roles.

We had twenty students, nineteen female midwives and one male psychiatric nurse. Most had been educated in England. A few had gone to a university in the West Indies. Some were from other parts of the Caribbean; they had been recruited by the government and offered bonuses to move to Guyana.

They were all thirsty for new knowledge and soaked up every word we said. We had taken a number of textbooks with us and they treated them as precious possessions. (When we went home, we left the books.)

If you were a nurse in Guyana, you worked for the government and went where you were assigned. The fact that you had a husband and young children in Georgetown did not prevent you from serving a year in the bush. Knowing these Guyanese nurses made me even more proud to be a member of their profession.

What they had done in nursing was impressive. One told about stitching up the back of a man who had been in a machete fight when she was assigned to an outpost in the bush. He had slashes about an inch apart that extended across his back from his neck to his buttocks. Some went as deep as his spine. She gave him plasma and, as quickly as possible, sewed his wounds together. Then she and a helper brought him down the river in a canoe to the hospital in Georgetown. He lived, and when he was healed, returned to the bush.

Another delivered a baby in a jungle outpost to which the government had assigned her. The placenta would not separate from the wall of the uterus and it was holding the blood vessels open. The woman would bleed to death if it stayed in that position. She consulted with an obstetrician in Georgetown by radio. He told her to don a glove, reach up into the woman's uterus and pull out the placenta. She did, and the woman lived to see her baby grow up.

The first day our students became teachers was a memorable one. They were dressed in their best, and carried neatly written notes. Their students filed in respectfully to hear the latest information—and we listened as our students gave exact imitations of the lectures we had given a few weeks before. They were exact even to our gestures and our jokes.

Elise, Pat and I didn't say anything until the day was over. We were afraid our responses would demoralize our students and undermine their ability to teach the rest of the day.

When they had finished, however, we did tell them, "That's not the way it is done. You tailor the material you present to fit your own personality and experience and to fit your students' needs."

They weren't upset. Their response was, "Oh, fine. That would be much more satisfying." The next day they carried on in their own voices, with their own examples and Guyanese humor—all without missing a beat.

I had taught them about the use of role-playing as a teaching tool. They then demonstrated the method for their students. They decided to illustrate the public health nurse's role in a common family problem.

In generations past in Guyana, a young woman in her teens, unmarried, would give birth to a baby or two. There was no stigma associated with out of wedlock births. Her mother, who was in her thirties, would raise the children while the girl finished her education. Once the girl was in her twenties, she would marry. She was a more valuable wife since she had already demonstrated her fertility.

Now, however, things had changed. The grandmother often had a job and was not available to care for her daughter's children. Young men who were ambitious were not so impressed with a ready-made family. The unmarried mother was faced with all the problems that single mothers face in the United States.

The students entered to present their role play with signs around their necks. One was Helpful Home Health Nurse. Another was Nosey Neighbor. They played out a typical scenario in exaggerated comedy, emphasizing in the

midst of it all, the nursing behaviors that would help the family. When the nurse asked to examine the baby, the child was brought. Dark-skinned hands unwrapped the child. It was a white doll with long blond hair.

The students and supervising teachers exploded in laughter. I have never seen such a funny, or instructive demonstration of role playing.

Susan and Shevawn arrived three weeks after we did. At the airport, they kissed me, then immediately began voicing their complaints about each other. I hushed them, as mothers are prone to do in public and said we would discuss it all when we got to the house.

Once in the house, they met my roommates and then exploded into a loud sisterly argument. It seemed that Susan who was twenty-one had insisted on carrying seventeen-year-old Shevawn's passport and plane tickets. "She treated me like a little kid," shrieked my younger daughter.

The guard, hearing loud, voices rushed in. I explained. He said, "Oh, yes, sisters!"

Pat had nieces and nephews and had witnessed such arguments before. She was slightly amused. Elise, however, was in a state of agitation. "I don't know how I can stand to live with this anger and hostility," she said, wringing her hands.

I told her it would pass, that they really loved each other. I don't think she believed me. Half an hour later, all was well. The only problem was who would get the single bed in the room assigned to the Hardesty family and who would have to sleep in the double bed with someone. We solved the problem by rotating the privilege of sleeping alone.

The girls accompanied us to class most days. We were still doing the teaching. One occurrence demonstrated the rapidity with which knowledge can be dispersed.

Elise had taught the midwives about the latest research into the production of female hormones and their influence on the menstrual cycle. Pat had read about it in a journal a few months before. Susan, a nursing student, had just studied it in her physiology class, and Shevawn, a junior in high school, had just had it in biology. (The moral of the story—If you don't read your journals, the high school students will know more than you.)

The minister of health, a nurse, and Enid, the WHO representative who was a nurse from Brooklyn, took the girls with them when they made trips around the country. One time, Susan thought she was in a nursing home, and only when they had left the place did she learn that the patients were lepers.

Other days, the girls lounged around the pool at the Pegasus Hotel where the international crowd spent time and drank fruit punch. Both girls had been trained as life guards, and were horrified at the indifference of some of the mothers who permitted their toddlers, buoyed only by water wings, into the deep end of the pool while the mothers sunned themselves and drank rum punch.

One night we were all crowded into Enid's car on our way to a UN party. We couldn't find the address, so Enid stopped to ask a man standing along the canal for directions, realizing too late what he had been doing. He stopped, slipped the evidence back into his pants, and answered her question. As we drove down the road, we looked back and saw a stream of urine arching over the canal, as he finished the job.

Guyana was an education for my girls.

We went to the hotel for dinner one evening. For the drive home, we all crowded into a taxi, the three consultants, and my two girls. This was quite a feat since the cab was a Volkswagen bug. Suddenly Susan screamed, "Stop! Get out!"

The driver stopped and we spilled out of the doors. "I just saw a humungus spider. It was this big." She gestured with her hands.

The driver inspected the vehicle, even taking out the seats. Finding nothing, we coaxed Sue, a true spider hater, back into the cab and we drove home. I thanked the stiff-faced driver and tipped him generously.

The next day, the guard told me that the driver had recounted the experience as soon as we had gone inside. He was so amused, and laughed so hard that he couldn't stand up. He rolled in the road, slapping himself with glee.

The Fourth of July was approaching and we decided to give a party. Mary, our maid, told us of a good band, her husband's, that we could hire for $50. When we began to inquire about food we learned we could have it catered for $50. We found a man who would supply two waiters and all the drinks we needed for another $50. We invited our students, all the people from the various departments, our neighbors, Mr. Hanis, our guards and Mary. We invited the Chinese rice experts who were staying in a house nearby, but they didn't come to our capitalistic celebration. One of our guards told us it was customary to invite the other guards in the compound to come for a drink, so we gave him permission to do that.

It was a wonderful party. We danced the jump-up until we were exhausted. We formed a ring and danced to the calypso rhythms. Each person, one by one, got into the center and did an original dance. Mary looked beautiful and her husband's band was great. The food was good, and the drinks were weak, so no one became inebriated.

The next morning, our party, along with pictures made the front page of the Georgetown paper. It was the least expensive and best party I've ever hosted.

Several weeks before we left, I bid goodby to my girls and put them on the plane for Barbados. They didn't fight on the way home. Susan discouraged the young men who approached them because she thought Shevawn was too young to handle the young New York executives who were on vacation at the Paradise Beach Hotel. The dining room served French food and the girls devoted themselves to eating, the beach and shopping. After they were back home they sent me a card telling me to go to a china shop in Bridgetown, when I got to Barbados, and pick up a Royal Copenhagen plate for Susan. "You'll know which one to get," they wrote. And I did. It was one depicting a favorite fairy tale.

When we said goodby to Mary, she begged us to take her with us. Her husband had agreed to take care of her three small children while she made a start in the land of opportunity. Stoic Mr. Hanis said that if we ever needed a driver or handyman, he'd be happy to come to the states. We left our Guyanese friends at the airport with wet cheeks and sad hearts.

I was only in Barbados a few days but I managed to meet a government agent who was a good dancer. I made good use of the beach and the tropic moon. The food was also very good.

At the airport in Bridgeport, the handle of my suitcase came off. I took the belt off my dress and tied it around the suitcase to make a new handle. I was carrying an

Amerindian bow and spear I had bought for my brother and a carry-on full of china. Somehow, I made it to upstate New York and home.

At the airport, Shevawn, who was managing my checkbook and bills, informed me that I owed Helen money. She'd had to borrow from Helen to pay the fire insurance which I had forgotten to budget for. Helen gave me a friendly lecture about not budgeting my finances so tightly.

On the way home from the airport, in Helen's car, Shevawn told me that she had wrecked my car. I was so relieved that she wasn't hurt that nothing else mattered. The car was in the shop. Shevawn was the driver at fault. As it turned out, I was saved an increase in my insurance premium by an archaic law that said if the parent were overseas, the insurance company could not consider the accident the child's fault.

When I arrived home, tired and discouraged, I discovered that Helen had moved my bed. It was trivial, but almost the final straw. I was ready to get on the plane and go back to Guyana.

By the next morning, the world was bright again and I was able to look back on the time in Guyana as one of the most instructive and pleasurable summers of my life.

Chapter 42
Practice

T he year after I began to work at the college, the New York State Legislature passed a bill that described nursing as the profession that treats human responses to actual or potential health threats. This broad definition enabled nurses to practice without the supervision of physicians or institutions.

Nursing is not medicine any more than medicine is nursing. They are separate professions with separate bodies of knowledge. There is overlap, but not nearly so much as the public and lawmakers believe. Each occupation has something to offer the patient and while we should collaborate, one does not supervise the other. Finally the law codified this.

This new development meant that I could go into practice for myself. I was grateful to Ernie for the experience and opportunity working in his office gave me. But now I could do it on my own—and keep the fee.

Separately, I invited two psychiatrists I had met at the day treatment center to go to lunch. I asked each of them what they thought about a nurse in private practice. Both thought it was a good idea and said they would refer patients to me. Then I asked about the mechanics of beginning a practice.

The advice was the same. Do look professional. Do not see patients in your living room. Have a comfortable well-furnished office. Get announcements, stationery and cards printed. Charge enough so that the patients realize your value. If you charge much less than other practitioners they will feel that you are undercutting them and that could limit referrals.

I had a daylight basement in my house. It contained a laundry and the garage but there was also a large empty space in it, lit by several windows. I decided to have an office and waiting room made there.

My new office had a special meaning for me. I had always shared my home with someone—my husband, the girls, and my mother—and the rooms reflected the personality of all the inhabitants. This space would be truly my own.

The carpenters turned the space into a large and beautiful room, paneled in cherry with a warm dark red carpet. I bought a school master's desk and a comfortable couch. When I did therapy, I sat in the Boston rocker that I had purchased when I was pregnant with Susan. Bookcases filled one wall. I finished it off with an oriental rug and an original oil painting.

When I went to hang my diplomas, I realized that my master's degree bore my second husband's surname. When we were divorced I had taken my first husband's name, the name of my children and the one I had used since I was twenty. I wrote to Western Reserve and asked if I could have a new diploma with the name I now bore. They said they couldn't do that. However, they could issue a certificate that would look just like a diploma, which would say that I had received the degree on the same date. I sent the fee, and the certificate arrived. I had it framed and hung it proudly, vowing never to change my name again. I haven't.

Shevawn observed all this and decided that she would not change her name either. She hasn't.

Even before my new office was finished, I began to receive referrals. I did see my first patients in my living room. Each week at the end of the hour they would ask to see the progress of my office. They were almost as excited as I was when it was finally finished.

My students referred their family and friends to me. The people at the day treatment center sent me patients. Soon I was seeing the children of fellow faculty and the faculty themselves. I was active in the New York State Nurses Association (NYSNA) and the people I met there referred other people to me.

In a short time, my patients were sending me more patients. I began to see whole networks of people. I saw a group of former Rensselaer Polytechnic Institute students and their wives and girlfriends. Even now, at Christmas, I receive cards from them with little notes telling me about the others.

I met Frances Crane at a NYSNA convention, and we became close friends. She had entered nursing school in her mid-thirties after having been a dancer and licensed practical nurse. She worked a few years as a staff nurse and then opened her own business, a nurse's registry. She later expanded to include all sorts of health care professionals. A feisty, brilliant business woman, aggressive and deeply committed to the patients—that was Fran. She hired me to consult with her home health aides and nurses whose patients had emotional problems. I also did in-service training for the nurses on her registry. Each time I made a contact, I opened the way for more referrals.

I did an in-service program for the health service that treated the state employees. The staff later referred patients to me and even provided an office at their agency so I could see clients who didn't have transportation to my office.

My patients were middle and upper middle class. Many were health professionals. I devoted two evenings a week to my practice and would see two patients each evening. I charged $25 an hour. Considering today's salaries, that doesn't seem like much, but at that time I was making $14,000 a year. The money I earned helped send Shevawn to college and provided vacations and extras we otherwise could not have afforded.

In addition to the money, the practice enhanced my teaching. I was not only teaching I was doing. Being a nurse in private practice at that time put me in the forefront of my profession. Later when I was teaching graduate school, it was a great help to have had the experience.

Beyond the practical advantages, I received a great deal from my patients. I watched them struggle with overwhelming problems and emerge stronger. I supported people whose physiology transformed the ordinary stress of every day life into an agonizing gauntlet that they were forced to run each day. I marveled at their courage and persistence. With the couples, I learned anew the strength of love and commitment. Knowing my patients enabled me carry my own burdens cheerfully, certain that I have been blessed with good fortune.

Chapter 43
A Bad Evaluation

The first three and a half years at the college passed quickly. I became more fully involved in college life. I served on the school's promotion and tenure committee one year and on the committee that reviewed that committee's decisions the next. I was active in the American Association of University Professors. I was granted tenure and each year received glowing evaluations and merit raises from Irene*, the chairman of the nursing department.

My job at the school was easier. Cindy Taylor had moved quickly from a novice teacher to an excellent instructor and she was able to carry more of the teaching load. I was disappointed that the promised graduate program in psychiatric nursing hadn't materialized but I had hope that it would before long.

I had made good friends of a number of faculty in the nursing department and in the school at large. There was a group within the nursing department who had been hired the year before I arrived. All were experienced teachers and all were associate professors. Two were nearing the end of their doctoral studies. Marion had reached an age when the idea of further education was not practical. However, she had co-authored a book on nursing administration which was a classic, and she was well known and respected.

This group had changed the nature of the department. Before we arrived it had consisted of the chairman, Irene, who was a strong leader, two trusted cohorts, and a group of inexperienced young teachers. Now there were people who were willing to offer new solutions rather than accept Irene's ideas blindly.

Shevawn was by now a student at Boston University. She was dating George, a young man whose home was a few miles from ours. Susan was engaged to Jim, whom she had met just before she graduated from Kent State. She was still in Ohio and working in Akron in coronary intensive care.

My personal life (translation—male company) was satisfactory—well, sort of. After dating a colonel who drank too much and operated under 1940s dating rules, and a physician who vacillated, I had given up finding a stable relationship. I met Chris*, a disabled veteran, who was good looking and, most of the time, fun. He had spent much of his adult life in Europe and had a certain superficial sophistication. He came over to mow my lawn and stayed to cook me supper. He also drank too much and sometimes embarrassed me by flirting with other women. I knew we had no future, but he filled the needs of the moment.

Mother had had a heart attack several years before, followed by a stroke. After a period of spending several weekends a month in Cleveland, I had moved her to a nursing home about twenty miles from my house. Brother John said there was nothing to hold him in Cleveland. He bought a house nearby and his two teenaged sons came to live with him. Shevawn visited my mother every Saturday and I did the same on Sunday. We brought her home for family occasions and took her on occasional outings.

Taking everything into account, my life was going well at the college and at home. The spring of the fourth year, I received my evaluation. It described my performance as unsatisfactory. Parts of it referred to situations in which I had not been involved. I was shocked.

I showed it to Marion and she showed me hers. They were identical. In fact, the erroneous situations on mine were ones that she had taken part in. We carefully questioned our colleagues. The five associate professors with tenure, the majority of the senior faculty, had received unsatisfactory evaluations.

We met at my house to discuss the situation. Why had we gone from receiving merit raises to being bad teachers? We concluded that Irene was eliminating any rivals who might be elected chairman. A few years before, the president of the college had instituted a rule that stated that department chairmen were to be elected by the department every three years.

None of us had considered the position. I did want to have charge of a graduate program in psychiatric nursing, but I felt my talent lay in teaching rather than administration. Besides, I had enjoyed Irene and thought that, all in all, she had done a good job for the school. I was perfectly content, until I got my evaluation, to have her continue to head the program.

The women who were in doctoral programs had no immediate ambitions. Both were eager to finish their dissertations and wanted no more responsibility until they did. Marion was struggling with serious health problems and her goal was to pace herself so that she could continue working. We were not a threat to Irene, and yet it was apparent that she wanted us to leave the faculty.

We each saw the dean for academic affairs and the president. I took my evaluation to the review committee of the college. They investigated and placed a letter in my file which said that the evaluation was erroneous and should be ignored. They could not have it removed, however.

Elections were held and Irene was named chairman. I hoped that would change things, but it didn't. Then I heard from a friend in Boston that a friend of Irene's, who taught there, had referred to me as a dangerous troublemaker and the ringleader of other rebellious faculty. I knew then that I would have to find another job. Staying would jeopardize my career.

Enrollments in schools of nursing were down and the state university in the nearby city had just closed its school. There were no other baccalaureate nursing schools within driving distance. I explored service jobs in the area. I was overqualified for most and did not have enough administrative experience for others.

I concluded that I would have to leave the area. I was sick, literally. I contracted hepatitis and was hospitalized.

When I recovered, I talked to Mother, John and the girls. I told Mother that I would not leave her again. If she was willing, I would take her with me wherever I moved. If she did not want to move, I would find some kind of a job and stay in the area.

Her response was, "Honey, I'll go where you go. I'm just glad you want to take me."

John was also supportive. His boys were with him and he enjoyed his job. "Sis, you have no obligation to stay around here for me."

Susan and Jim would be married in a few months and Jim was considering teaching jobs in Ohio and California. Shevawn would begin her junior year at BU in the Fall. She had reservations about the way I disrupted the family by my moves, but she felt that I "would do what I wanted, anyway." She was right, considering that she was the lone dissenting voice. (Shevawn was rather prickly at this age.)

A doctoral student from Boston, a psychiatric nurse, interviewed at the school for a possible faculty position. When I interviewed her, she confidentially told me that she had been promised a position as head of the graduate program which was to begin the next year. The department was looking for someone to replace me, even before I announced my resignation.

I began to pass the word along the psychiatric nursing grapevine that I was ready to leave the college. I heard from a college in South Carolina that they would like me to consider a job in their graduate program. When spring vacation came, I drove to the small college town and looked at the surroundings. I decided that as a single woman it would be hard to live in an isolated Southern village, and I did not to pursue the matter.

I answered an ad in the American Journal of Nursing. A state university in Oregon was looking for a person to head a rural community mental health graduate program. I heard from them and sent my curriculum vitae. Evidently they called the references I gave and I began to receive offers from all over the country.

I spent several months engaged in anticipatory mourning. I toured my yard, noting the new growth on the blue spruce tree, and the blossoms on the apple tree that was still a few scrawny sticks. Now I would never harvest the apples, and would decorate the tree only one more Christmas. I walked through the rooms of my new little house and said goodby.

But being wooed by other schools helped heal the pain of leaving. I began to go through possessions and sent things I did not want to move to Goodwill. I was getting ready to go.

Susan and Jim were married in the summer at a small friendly ceremony in Kent. I was pleased with her choice. Jim was the kind of man any mother would choose for her daughter. Chris went with me to the wedding. I was glad I had a good-looking man with me when I walked into the chapel and saw Susan's father and his family.

The college had instituted a six-week intercession between semesters. Special concentrated courses were taught then. Every fifth year, each faculty member was permitted to take that time off. My six weeks off was approaching and I decided to take a special trip during that time. Chris wanted me to go to Greece with him and so I decided to go. His parents had been born there and he spoke Greek. I would reward myself for the years at the college, and when I returned I would begin interviewing for another job.

I had some pangs about leaving the girls at Christmas. However, the year before, Susan had decided to stay in Kent with Jim, and on hearing this, Shevawn announced, "I'm going to spend Christmas with my sister." She took off in the rickety old car I had bought for her for $75. Chris was not the man of my dreams but that Christmas I was grateful for him. I decided that if Shevawn could leave me alone during the holidays, I could spend Christmas in Greece.

I left Cindy in charge and spent much of the spring term interviewing. That was an experience in itself. I learned that all is not as it seemed at some of the famous schools. A little careful questioning and I learned a great deal about the politics of a number of nursing schools. In one school, I learned that the administration hoped to use me to overthrow the person in charge of psychiatric nursing, a woman who was a good friend of mine. Since I was leaving one minefield, I was leery of stepping into another. I declined the position before I left the city.

I was offered administrative jobs for which I was not qualified, by deans eager to have another doctoral-prepared person on their faculty. The faculty of a school famous for combining practice and teaching into one job, told me privately that it amounted to two-full time jobs. Each school I visited contributed a little to my education about nursing school politics.

I flew to Oregon on St. Patrick's Day to interview for a position in which I would manage a rural community mental health grant. I left New York in a blinding snow storm. As I boarded the plane, I prayed that Shevawn would drive home from the airport without harm. I drank green champagne on the plane and when we landed, I was astonished to see white azaleas and daffodils blooming at the airport. I did carefully consider all the other aspects of the position, honest. In fact I interviewed at three other places after I had been in Oregon, before I said that I would accept the position they offered.

Once again I was moving on, this time a distance of 3000 miles, and with Mother at my side.

The University

1976—Present

Chapter 44
The Move to Oregon

I accepted the position offered by the school of nursing in Oregon and then went home to prepare to move. In late May, as soon as I had finished at the college, I drove 3000 miles to Oregon. One of my friends, who wanted to visit in Denver, rode with me as far as that city, and I continued on alone.

It was dark when I drove through southern Idaho and found a cheap motel room. In the early morning, I crossed the border into eastern Oregon. From a high pass through the mountains, I looked down on miles and miles of rolling land, dressed in blowing pink grass. Later I learned it was cheat grass; it looked like gold to me that day.

I followed the road through the pass and down into fertile wheat land and cattle range, aware that I was traveling the route of the pioneers, the Oregon Trail. In Pendleton, I stopped for gas and saw men in ten-gallon hats and scuffed cowboy boots. I was out West.

The road led down the Columbia Gorge, with its magnificent cliffs covered with towering fir. I stopped to admire Multnomah Falls. By the time I drove into Portland and found a motel, I was in love with the state.

The school had arranged an appointment with a real estate agent, Dee, who showed me houses. In general they were less expensive than the houses in New York, although, as I later discovered, they weren't as well built. I made an offer on one and it was accepted, contingent on the sale of my place in New York. Now I had a home to dream about, and walls on which to mentally place my paintings at two in the morning when I couldn't sleep.

I also found a nursing home for Mother. It was a home run by a Catholic order. The people at the university assured me that it was the best in the city. When I decided that it would be Mother's new home, they helped get her moved to the top of the waiting list.

I left my car with Dee and flew back to New York. Brother John met me at the airport with a truck he was loaning to me. My house sold quickly, with the help of a good agent. Mother was pleased when I described the new nursing home to her. She said, "Maybe I'll become a Catholic. I felt bad when your father left the church to marry me. He would be pleased to know that I converted."

I gave a big party to say goodby to all my friends. I also invited my favorite patients, many of whom were friends and colleagues. Mother also had a bon voyage party, given by her friends at the nursing home. She said that she was one of the few who left the home to begin an adventure—most left in a long gray box.

I watched the movers load my possessions into the van and spent the night in a sleeping bag in the empty house. I thought of my furniture, china, oriental rugs, paintings and books, going down the highway in the van, and realized that my home was my possessions, not the four walls that surrounded them.

Shevawn moved in with George and his mother where she would stay until school began. She and Chris drove Mother and me to the airport. The goodbys were excited rather than sad.

I had put an in-dwelling catheter in Mother and had a little bottle in my bag. She wore a full skirt and I planned to unobtrusively release the clamp periodically and empty her bladder. Mother was obsessed with having an accident, and since she only could take a few steps, I wanted to avoid taking her to the bathroom.

My plan worked very well. We changed planes in Chicago, but a helpful porter pushed her through the airport in a wheelchair and she was carried onto the plane to Oregon.

An hour from Portland, Mother anxiously whispered, "Honey, I have to move my bowels." We were seated about twenty feet from the lavatory—it might have been miles.

"Mom, we will be there in an hour. I don't think I can get you to the bathroom. You'll have to wait."

A few minutes passed. "Honey, I'm afraid I'll disgrace myself."

"O. K. Mom, I'll get you to the bathroom, somehow. But if you don't go after I get you there, I'll be ready to kill you." This was the daughter, not a psychiatric nurse, speaking.

I told the stewardess to stand by, and got mother's walker out of the overhead compartment. Then together we heaved her uncooperative body upright and began the long journey to the lavatory. She took three steps and rested. I prayed and she took three more. Down the narrow plane aisle and across to our destination, clump, clump, clump went the walker. The lavatory was in the middle of the plane so our progress was watched by all the passengers.

Finally we made it and opened the door. There wasn't room for Mom, the walker and me. She went straight in and then I passed the walker out over our heads to the waiting stewardess. Then I pivoted her around, raised her dress and slid down her panties, while the stewardess provided screening. Then we moved away and closed the door. After five minutes, Mother called me. "Don't be mad, Honey, it was a false alarm."

When we got her together and emerged from the lavatory, the other passengers cheered.

The stewardess had moved our seat to one next to the lavatory. I went and got some water, broke Mother's prescription Valium in two and we each took a piece.

Dee met us at the plane and we delivered Mother to her new home. I went to a nearby motel and fell asleep immediately. I was now an Oregonian.

The next day, with my sleeping bag, I moved into my empty house. I cleaned for several days before the moving van arrived with the furniture. Just behind it was a RV, with Shevawn and George. They were combining their vacation to the national parks—Shevawn had had a geology course that featured them—and the task of getting me settled in Oregon.

We got up early every morning, unpacked and put one room in order. Then we took off on a day trip to the coast or Mt. Hood to see my new state. When the house was finally finished, we went to Crater Lake. At night we built a fire, made s'mores—Shevawn's favorite Girl Scout treat—and drank red wine. I felt very blessed to have such a daughter and a friend like George. Eight years later, in a beautiful wedding, friend George became my son-in-law and he is now the father of my three darling—most of the time— grandsons.

Chapter 45
The New Job

T he school was undergoing transition. The former dean had held sway for many years, although the school offered bachelor's degrees, it was much like a hospital school. A new president arrived to head the university. He'd had experience with schools that were in the forefront of nursing education and was distressed with what he found in Oregon. The dean was encouraged to retire and the new dean was to arrive the day I began.

Dr. Carol Lindeman was a nurse researcher who had held academic positions but was primarily known for her research. Before I accepted the position, I had asked who the new dean would be and had made inquiries about her. All reports were glowing and this influenced my decision to come to Oregon.

I met Carol in the hallway a few days after I arrived. She is a small woman and that day was dressed in blue jeans and cowboy boots, relics of her tenure in Colorado. She seemed a little shy, but I liked her immediately. As I knew her better, I was impressed by her enormous talent and dedication to nursing. I continued to like and respect her for the twelve years that I was an active part of the faculty. We are still good friends.

There were three doctoral-prepared people on the faculty. One was a sociologist and another was a nurse who had a degree in psychology, and the last was a physiologist on loan from the medical school. Carol, of course, was doctoral prepared. The dean of the nursing school at the private Catholic college was studying for a doctorate. My credentials made me a celebrity in the nursing community. It was a little frightening. I hoped that I hadn't made a mistake in coming to Oregon.

The two faculty members I would be working with were on vacation when I began. I searched around for the course outlines for the graduate program in psychiatric nursing, the program I would eventually take to various parts of the state. I couldn't find any. The day before class began, Katherine*, the chair of psychiatric nursing, and Vera* arrived and I received my teaching assignment. I would be teaching an assessment course, and "No, there isn't a course outline,"I was told. "The program is still new and is being developed as we go."

That afternoon I sat down and wrote up a course outline and bibliography. It contained elements from my own graduate education, master's, and doctoral, and information that I had found helped me in my practice. This is not the way such things are done; curriculum decisions are supposed to be made by the whole department. But I felt that I couldn't greet the six graduate students without being able to let them know what I expected them to learn.

Before I left for the day, I apologetically asked the secretary to type up my work. She seemed delighted to have it and suggested that I send copies to the graduate committee, the other faculty who were teaching graduate students. (Secretaries know a great deal about what goes on in a school.)

Before class I visited the library. It contained few of the books on my bibliography. Thank heavens, I had spent the money to move my books to Oregon. I brought my books to the school for the students to use until the library could order those on the bibliography. Even before my first class, I was wondering what I had gotten myself into.

The students convinced me that I had made the right decision. They were wonderful. Six bright, highly motivated young women, all of whom had extensive experience in psychiatric nursing. They had been waiting for the master's program in psychiatric nursing program to begin and were the second group to enter it. Since the program had been so unstructured, they had each designed their own and sought out appropriate clinical experiences. One was interested in political science and she had spent time as a legislative aide to a state senator. Another was interested in administration and was spending time at the state hospital, critically examining the administrative problems inherent in that setting. A third was studying geriatric psychiatry and was practicing in a nursing home.

They were, in effect, engaged in self study with the support of the faculty. They expressed relief when I gave them a course outline which told how they would be graded and what I expected them to learn. Although they were learning, they had been worried that they were missing important information that they would someday be expected to know.

Katherine had some ideas that seemed very creative. She had successfully translated them into grants which had been funded. In seminar, she frequently listened to the discussion without comment and then, just as the class was ending, asked a provocative question. The question would be oblique and vague, yet tantalizing. Before it could be explored, class was finished. The students and I didn't know if we were hearing an important original concept, or if this was a game she played. I frequently heard, "When Katherine does that, I don't know if I'm dumb, or if she is confused."

Vera had spent a number of years in psychoanalysis and her ideas about psychiatric nursing education were a mixture of psychoanalytic theories and precepts gleaned from the training group movement. She felt that if you thoroughly understood your own unconscious and were open and honest, you'd just naturally do and say the right things to help patients. This was the same kind of thinking that I had objected to when I first became a psychiatric nurse, almost twenty years before. It was also similar to the ideas put forth by the people who taught group at Kent.

I questioned this approach. Each year there was more knowledge about mental illness based on research rather than unverified theory. Many of the old theories had been proven invalid. For example, we used to talk about the schizophrenogenic mother, the mother who placed her child in a double bind and caused him to become schizophrenic. The tragedy of this theory is that professionals blamed the mother for the patient's illness, and she was forced to suffer not only from grief for the loss of a healthy child and the need to care for her child, but from the stigma of having created the problem. Now we know that schizophrenia is a disease caused by chemical problems in the brain. Mental health people now focus on helping the patient and family deal with the results of this faulty chemistry—using medication and what we know about behavior.

I also felt that a student's personal life and personality were her own business. They were of concern to the teacher only if they interfered with her ability to deal constructively with patients. My former students had taught me well. I found myself protecting students who were different from Vera's attempts to change their personalities by battering them with her interpretations of the *real* causes of their behavior.

Vera was a large woman with a hearty laugh. She was liked by people outside the department and I found myself being careful how and where I opposed her. Actually, I found her to be good company and enjoyed the trips we made together to meetings.

As I look back, I wonder how I managed to have a fairly peaceful first year with Katherine and Vera. I think it was because I was willing to do the work associated with teaching. Katherine was busy running a large department. Carol's arrival had brought great change to the school and reorganization requires effort. Vera tolerated me because she didn't see me as having much power. Because I did the work, she could continue to philosophize in class and be an interesting character.

The graduate committee was a loose structure that set policy for the graduate programs. They were delighted when they received the course outlines I sent them. They were so pleased with me that they unanimously elected me chair of the committee shortly after I arrived. Now that I am older and wiser, I know that groups in trouble often dump jobs on new people.

In addition to teaching in Portland, I was supervising students in community mental health centers around the state. These centers were in rural areas and sometimes in places that could be described only as frontier. I traveled to all parts of Oregon and got to know the mental health people. This part of the job was what had attracted me to Oregon, and it did not disappoint me. I was having some real adventures.

I settled into life in Portland. I began a practice, seeing patients in a study in my home. However, it remained small, much smaller than my practice in New York. And I had difficulty collecting fees, something that had never happened in New York.

Mother's nursing home was close to where I lived, and I stopped often on my way home from work to visit. I brought her home for meals on Sundays, until she told me that the trip exhausted her. After that I visited her, often arranging to have Sunday dinner at the home.

My yard occupied much more time than I had anticipated. The growing season in Oregon is much longer than in New York. My grass continued to grow until November and began again in February. I had chosen a house rather than a condominium. I began to wonder if I had made a mistake.

My fiftieth birthday came and I was depressed. I had achieved my educational and career goals. Susan had finished school and was married and Shevawn was a junior in college. I had done what I wanted and I wondered what would come next. I was dating a teacher, but there was no strong attraction. Chris was calling from New York and had visited me once. I viewed him as a temporary distraction—entertaining but hardly worth the trouble.

The evening of the big day I came home to the empty house and devoted myself to being blue. Then the door bell rang and there was a man from the florist, with two dozen long stemmed red roses. They were from Shevawn's boyfriend, George. Dear, dear George! As I was admiring them, tearfully, gratefully, the phone rang and it was Shevawn. A short time later Susan called. Then my next door neighbors invited me over for a drink.

With expressions of love like that, I didn't mind being fifty. (Well, just a little.) I was not yet an Oregonian, but I was settling in to my life in the West.

Chapter 46
The State is a Classroom

T he grant I had been hired to administer required the placement of our graduate students in community mental health centers around the state.
The psychiatry department had a similar grant. We were also required to hold a joint seminar with the nursing students and the psychiatric residents. Later, social work students from a nearby university were also included.

The rationale for the grant was two fold. One was to insure that the disciplines worked together smoothly. This was to be accomplished through joint training. The other was to introduce the students to the excitement and challenge of work in rural settings, in the hope that, in addition to learning, they might remain there when they finished their programs.

When I first began at the university, Jim, the chairman of the department of psychiatry, was my counterpart in medicine. Shortly after I arrived, we interviewed Joe, a Harvard and Albert Einstein-trained psychiatrist, who had finished a tour in Alaska for the United States Public Health Service, and who had stayed on there for a time. His return to the lower forty-eight had been precipitated by his wife's desire to go to law school.

Joe's background was perfect for the position. He knew all about frontier society. In addition he was an outstanding clinician and teacher. When "Northern Exposure" began on TV, I wondered for a fleeting moment if Joe had been the model, especially since his brother was an entertainment lawyer whom Joe had visited in Hollywood. But I dismissed the idea quickly—Joe was too wise to make the mistakes that the show's character makes. Joe is now the dean of the medical school.

A little later, Dave was hired to assist Joe. Even though he was young (by my standards) Dave was a warm, wise teddy-bear of a man, the kind of a therapist we professionals all decide we will consult if we find ourselves in need of a psychiatrist. Dave was from Cleveland, and had been raised a few blocks from where I had raised Susan and Shevawn.

Our seminars were rich in learning, and it was a pleasure to expose my students to physicians such as Joe and Dave. Our students did learn to know and respect each other. Several did research projects together. When I became chairman, I assigned other faculty to the seminar. I did it reluctantly, because in giving the faculty the opportunity to take part, I was relinquishing a role I had treasured.

Our students traveled to their clinical sites by any means available. For a time, Janelle, a student who was beautiful as well as able, flew across the Cascades and Blue Mountains in a small commercial aircraft. She made the trip several times sitting next to a nice young man who said he was taking flying lessons. Imagine her surprise, a few weeks later, when she saw the same young man in the pilot seat.

Several weeks later, that young pilot was fueling the plane and loading the luggage. Then the airline went bankrupt and Janelle was forced to make the trip by train or bus.

Most of the mental health center directors in Oregon were social workers or psychologists. They had no experience with nurses who were specializing at the graduate level in psychiatric nursing. For them, a nurse was someone who delivered pills in a hospital. Once they were exposed to the depth and breath of the students skills, they were very impressed and tried their best to hire them. The nurses were able to move easily from the office, to the home and then to the hospital. They understood the relationship of the clients' physical needs and their emotional problems. They spoke knowledgeably with the health workers in other professions. In fact, as one director put it, "Your student is Ms. Super Mental Health Worker. She can do everything but prescribe medicines." (A few years later the legislature granted our especially trained master's graduates the right to do that.)

I went to the sites where our students were placed for supervision, becoming familiar with the towns and roads of rural Oregon. One time I went to La Grande to visit Janelle. Her on-site supervisor was a psychologist called Jake.*

Jake was a small man, a few inches over five feet. He had been raised in the Bronx. Evidently he acquired his love of things western from the movies and when he finished his doctorate he moved west to La Grande. He bought a horse and was taking riding and roping lessons. He wore worn Levis, high-heeled boots and a big cowboy hat. The natives snickered a little when he passed by, but it wasn't cruel laughter. After all, how can you be down on someone who wants so much to be like you?

Janelle, Jake and I finished our day at the clinic about five one winter day. My bus for Portland was to leave at seven and with luck, I would be home at midnight. Jake suggested that we go to the Woodshed and have dinner. "They have wonderful margaritas," he said.

So we went. I had one margarita, which went down quickly, and then we all ordered steak. Soon it was six and with another hour to kill before my bus, I ordered another margarita. That was a mistake.

The margaritas in Portland had a little tequila and a lot of juice and sugar. The La Grande margaritas were all tequila with a little lime flavor. When I realized I was under the influence, I sat up straight, said little and struggled to maintain my dignity. My companions seemed not to be affected and I hoped they wouldn't notice my state.

Finally it was time for the bus. We left the restaurant and went out to the street. Large wet snow flakess were falling. I hoped that the pass over the mountains would be open. It is almost a mile high and La Grande is frequently cut off from the world in the winter by snow in the pass.

The bus had originated in Salt Lake City. We waited until the tired passengers spilled out, visited the facilities, and then climbed back on to reclaim their seats. I said dignified goodbys to Janelle and Jake and then boarded the bus.

I was assaulted by the smell of feet. Evidently some of the passengers had worn the same socks since New Jersey and were riding with their shoes off.

I turned back to wave at my friends. Janelle and that strange little gnome of a cowboy were standing in the snow, waving white handkerchiefs and calling, "Goodby, Mom."

The other passengers craned their necks to see who was the recipient of such an energetic farewell. I found a seat at the very back of the bus and, in spite of being very thirsty, giggled most of the way across the mountains.

Dave, the clinic director in La Grande, offered Janelle a job when she was ready to leave. Janelle thanked him, but confessed that she hoped one day to meet a man, marry and have children. La Grande didn't seem to offer much in the way of prospective husbands. Dave even swore that he would find her a husband, if she would only take the job. But she again declined and returned to Portland.

Charlotte, the next student in La Grande, drove to the town. She stayed, as all our students did, in the Star-light Motel. They gave us special rates, and in spite of being old and noisy, it was reasonably comfortable. The next morning, Charlotte, who was only a few years younger than I, drove to the mental health center. Dave and a social worker were waiting for her in the parking lot.

"We need your help. We have this lady, an old lady, who the neighbors think has leprosy or something. She is very sick but she refuses to go to the hospital. We need you to take a look at her and see if you can get her to get help. If you can't we'll have to take her in on a police hold." Then a sheriff's patrol car drove in. Evidently they expected that the lady would have to be forced.

Charlotte said she would go to see the woman and asked the address. The whole group, including the deputy insisted that they go, too. The little caravan pulled out of the parking lot and headed on their mission.

The sheriff insisted that he accompany Charlotte to the door. She insisted that she go alone. Charlotte's husband is a former navy commander and I suspect she knew the psychology of commanding speech. The sheriff backed down.

Charlotte knocked and after a while called, "Hello, Mrs. Smith*, my name is Charlotte. I'm a nurse and I came to see how you are."

The door opened a crack and a frightened old woman peered out. She looked at Charlotte and then opened the door for her to enter.

The woman had a gangrenous leg. She limped to the sofa and sat. Charlotte explained that she was very ill and must have that leg attended.

"I know. I've been a diabetic for a long time. But I just can't leave Baby."

Baby soon entered, rubbed against Charlotte's leg and purred.

It seemed that the last time Mrs. Smith had been in the hospital, Baby, had been boarded at the vets. She had cried so long she had lost her meow. She was just skin and bones when she was released.

Charlotte explored options for Baby's care and there seemed to be none. Finally she said, "Look, I'm at the Starlight and I'll be there till Friday. I'll take Baby with me, and by Friday, I'll find a place for her. I won't do anything without your approval."

Mrs. Smith's hospital bag had been packed for a week. All that was needed was to hustle Baby into her carrier, turn down the thermostat and get Mrs. Smith into her coat. Then the two women made their way slowly to the car and drove to the hospital.

Charlotte told me later that the whole town treated her like a hero. The social worker took Baby and it turned out to be a permanent adoption. Mrs. Smith had her leg amputated and went to a nursing home. Baby and her new owner visited frequently.

Dave offered Charlotte a job. He even found one for her husband. But Charlotte's teenaged children liked their Portland school. Some time later, Dave was successful and our former students now attend to the mental health of Oregonians who live east of the mountains.

Chapter 47
The New Chairman

I had been at the Health Sciences University less than a year when I became chairman of the Mental Health Department. Katherine had announced that she had been accepted at a Ph.D. program in the East. There were twelve faculty in the department and it was responsible for both the undergraduate and graduate curriculum. We taught half the sophomore year and a third of the senior year, as well as the master's program. At first I said that I did not want to be considered. I wanted to teach and do research. Besides I didn't think I had the temperament for the administration of so large a department.

Ruth said that she would be willing. She had been acting dean in the time before Carol arrived. I suspect, like many new leaders, Carol wanted to distance herself from the previous leadership. I felt some pressure from her to reconsider my position. Then people in the faculty began to urge me to take the position. The term was for three years.

I told myself that it would be great experience. I had a vague notion that I would someday return to the East, to end my career in a small school. If I had administrative experience, I would have more choice as to positions. So I said, yes, I would like to be considered and I was elected unanimously.

Carol had dreams of transforming the school into one of the best in the country. She was able to articulate her ideas to the legislature, the board of higher education, the community and her faculty. We were all inspired by her vision, and willing to do what was needed to make the transformation.

However, the exact means to do this were somewhat vague. Carol was, at that time, an inexperienced administrator, assisted by even more inexperienced administrators—I was the most naive—and a faculty that was generally undereducated for the task ahead. But ahead we went, making mistakes, trying to undo them, and following the vision that Carol articulated.

Aside from Ruth and Vera, the people in my department were young in years and experience. We were hoping to attract Ph.D.s, and every time Carol made a keynote speech, we got applications, but the recruitment for the mental health department was slow. We did, however, have very bright, dedicated people among us. I decided that I would make faculty development my major objective. If we couldn't bring scholars in, we would try to create them from what was at hand.

Although I still taught graduate students, the major part of my effort was on developing younger faculty. In a sense it was teaching, but of a different kind. I was providing the support and opportunity, and the faculty was using both to attain their goals.

The state had just passed legislation that licensed Psychiatric Mental Health Nurse Practitioners. I made sure that as many of our faculty as possible were licensed. If they lacked the necessary classes, they attended class with our graduate students. If they needed supervision, I provided it.

One of the faculty, Mary Kay King, was an experienced therapist. However, her master's degree was in counseling rather than psychiatric nursing. I knew that the accrediting agencies frown on people teaching a subject for which they have no master's. So I invited Mary Kay to take classes with the master's students. She could have simply sat in on the classes and I would have given her the credit. However, she went far beyond the objectives of the course, writing papers that were presented at conferences and eventually published. She provided a wonderful role model for the graduate students and obtained credentials that would satisfy any accreditor.

I had two grants. The first was one that Katherine had written. It described a new role for psychiatric nurses, as primary caregivers. One of the faculty, Mandy*, was already practicing this role in the hospital's emergency room. She was the person who first saw and diagnosed psychiatric disorders in that setting. She was an excellent therapist but did not have time to do the research associated with the grant since she was employed half time by the psychiatry department of the medical school so she could not administer the grant.

No marvelous Ph.D. presented herself to take on that task, and I didn't have time. So I assigned the position to Mary Kay. There was some rumbling in the department and school, but Mary Kay performed so well, it soon turned to pleasantly surprised murmurs.

Just before Katherine left, she had hired Susan, a young master's graduate from Ohio, who had done research for the mental health department of that state. Her education had been somewhat different than that of other people on the faculty. Her focus was on systems and how to influence them, rather than on individual patients. She possessed a bright analytic mind and wrote well.

I had written a grant designed to produce master's-prepared psychiatric nurses in other parts of the state. There were virtually no nurses with this preparation outside of Portland. I assigned Susan to this grant. We offered a master's program in Eugene, a hundred and five miles south of Portland. Some of the students who were enrolled drove seventy miles to Eugene. Susan negotiated with agencies and arranged for the students' placement and on-site supervision. We all took turns driving to Eugene, presenting classes and doing supervision. The program was very successful; during the time the grant was in effect, we graduated as many students in Eugene as we did in Portland.

Both Mary Kay and Susan enrolled in doctoral study. Eventually Susan left the school, for a high-level position in another state. Mary Kay stayed on. Her doctoral dissertation which was done with the cooperation of the state department of corrections was a landmark study. Later she helped establish a clinic where faculty and students could practice.

We began to be able to hire young faculty with doctorates, and we had more experienced teachers who were working to achieve theirs. The school began to take on some of the characteristics that Carol had described in her vision.

There were plenty of rough spots though. There were problems created by overlapping lines of authority between the graduate department and the four clinical departments. Some of the ideas that appeared sound when they were being formulated in our meetings bumped up against the state rules and had to be abandoned when they were half implemented.

I enjoyed the relationships with my fellow department chairs. We met frequently with the dean to plan and make policy. Occasionally we were able to get away for a few days, at someone's cabin at Mt. Hood, or condominium at the coast, to engage in two days of intense work.

The pediatric and obstetric departments had been combined into the Family Department, and Dr. Joanne Hall was the new chair. She had superb administrative skills, and was a great help to the dean and became my friend and mentor.

When Katherine had been chair there was an us-against-them mentality in the department. This was common in all psychiatric nursing departments at one time. Psychiatric faculty were seen as different, and there were remarks such as, "They are crazy like their patients." NIMH had funded projects to integrate the mental health concepts into the entire nursing curriculum, and as this happened, the separation and mistrust between the people who were concerned about the mental health of their patients and the people who focused on their physical health lessened. However, Katherine and Vera had enjoyed the position of being different (translation—superior) to the other departments and had fostered the separation.

My nursing and teaching experience had included both the physical and psychological aspects of health care. The separation didn't exist for me. My focus was on the good of the department and the school. However, some in the department viewed my friendship with my fellow chairs, particularly with Joanne, as selling out. They felt that she had too much power and would be getting resources our department needed. Vera had a great deal to say about this, not only to the faculty, but to the students.

All in all, my first three years as chairperson were satisfying. I felt that I had helped faculty develop, and with the people we had recruited, the department was in a good position to do its share to make the school into the one that Carol had envisioned. There had been growing pains, in the school, department and in me. I was looking forward to having time to do research and writing. I wanted to teach graduate students, but I also longed to teach the seniors, a course I felt had been neglected. Soon someone else would take over the administrative tasks and I could do what I do best.

One memorable experience occurred during my tenure as chair. To explain it, I must give you the background. When I divorced my first husband and left my home in Pennsylvania, I took my children and went to Cleveland. I got a job at a psychiatric hospital and enrolled in Western Reserve's evening classes to begin work toward my bachelor's degree. At that time, the hospital was run based on Freudian concepts, not only for the staff physicians, but the nurses, as well. The hospital was run by a very bright woman, Laura*, a nurse, who was respected by the doctors and had a following among the nurses. Most of the staff of the hospital were new graduates who hung on the director's every word.

I didn't. I was an experienced nurse. I felt that the general attitude of the nurses demeaned the patients in subtle ways. It seemed to me that by following the strict Freudian idea that the therapist should remain a blank on which patients could project their transference, we placed distance between ourselves and the patients. While such distance may have been appropriate for the psychiatrists, I felt that the nurses should provide an atmosphere that was more comforting. I also found the Freudian interpretations of patients' behavior distasteful. It almost seemed as though staff was playing "got ya" instead of listening to the information in a compassionate way.

An assistant head nurse position became available and I applied for it. Laura accepted my application and I thought I might have a chance. I was working all three shifts, which was very difficult with the children. If I got the job, I would work only days.

But two days after my application Laura called me in and gave me a bad evaluation. She said that she had discussed me with the head nurse and was concerned about my care of psychiatric patients.

I felt that my career was in jeopardy even before it had begun. I tried a ploy. I told her what my ambitions were and that I had twelve years of excellent evaluations behind me. "It would be a shame, if I were lost to a profession that needs me. Help me learn to be a better psychiatric nurse."

Laura said that she didn't have time, but said she'd have the supervisor help me. She also moved me to another floor, away from the head nurse who didn't want me as an assistant. The supervisor could find nothing wrong with what I was doing and my new head nurse concluded that I had made remarkable improvement since I was now an exemplary staff nurse.

A year later, I resigned to go to school full time, and when I graduated, began teaching psychiatric nursing. At conferences I met other nurses, two nationally known, who'd had similar problems with Laura.

The American Nurses Association had a placement service and all of one's references could be kept on file there. It was convenient to use this service, since the people who gave you references had to write only one letter. We never saw the references, as was the custom in those days. Finally when I was in Oregon, the ANA discontinued the service and mailed our references to us.

I was shocked when I received the packet. There in the midst of all the glowing recommendations was a letter which quoted the evaluation the director had given me. Her words had followed me all of my professional career. Thank heavens, the people who hired me had discounted that letter. It did explain some of the strange questions I had been asked on various interviews.

Time passed. Then one day the dean sent me an application she had received in the mail. It was from Laura. She was applying for a faculty position.

I wrote her a letter thanking her for her application, saying that we had no positions available, but that we would keep her application on file. This was not true of course. I would not subject students for whom I was responsible to this woman. Then I added , "I worked at University Hospitals. I wonder if you remember me."

She wrote back that she did and thanked me for my response.

Revenge was sweet. I felt a little guilty about my pleasure in it. But I blamed it on my Irish and Scotch-Irish ancestors, who had very long memories.

My personal life went on, even when I struggled with a demanding job. I was lonely for male companionship. I made the rounds of the church-sponsored single's clubs and although I met many men, most of them used the clubs as substitutes for a relationship. (Frankly, they were losers.) I didn't have the time or energy to do the things I needed to meet men in the conventional way. Besides, Portland was a small town, and as a chairman at the university, I felt that I had to be careful of my reputation. Acting in a way that would let the men I met at the school know that I was available would be detrimental to my career.

I signed up for a dating service and was matched with three men. I discovered that I didn't like fat bald men, even if they were intelligent.

Then I was matched with Verl. When I opened the door for our first date, I thought, "He's handsome". And then, "He looks like Daddy." So much about him was familiar, even the few traits I didn't like. It was as though I had known him for years.

We were married a year later. Our courtship and marriage are described in my book, *Down on the Tree Farm*, which is a light hearted account of life on Verl's wholesale nursery, fifty miles south of Portland. We have been married more than sixteen years now, the happiest years of my life.

My three years as department chairperson were over and I was happily anticipating return to full-time teaching. As it turned out I was in the position another year and a half, a very lame duck leader.

I won't go into all the details about that period, except to say that my department was restless. Groups formed—those who felt I was doing a good job and those who wanted a powerful new chairperson. I received memos from one faculty member accusing me of favoring another and then the next day from the two of them criticizing me. People whom I had considered close personal friends were now writing critical memos to the dean. That was the most painful part of the whole process. In retrospect, I began to feel some sympathy for Irene, the department chair at the college, when the president decided the chairperson's role was to rotate.

I wanted out of the job and I was tempted to resign. On the other hand, I felt committed to stay in the position until a new chairperson was selected. Finally, the dean made plans for the administration of the department and I was able to resign. My administrative assistant typed my letter of resignation and then typed hers.

I happily returned to teaching. I was resolved to be what my mother had termed a lady. She was not describing a teacup-holding matron, but a gracious mature person, who spoke ill of no one. I also resolved not to show any of the hurt I felt about the behavior of the people who I had thought were my friends. I knew that some people were feeling guilty about what had happened and if I increased their guilt, they would need to justify their part in it by degrading me.

I became the utility teacher, able and willing to teach at any level, willing to substitute for anyone who was sick or wanted a break from their assignment, or take on any committee task the school might need. The new chairperson was a strong, experienced administrator, and after an initial period of testing was willing to accept any help I could offer.

There was time to do research and hold national office. I especially enjoyed serving as an accreditation visitor for the National League for Nursing.   And I had time to enjoy my first love, teaching.

In a short time, the turmoil in the department was over. One by one, people began to tell me how sorry they were that they had taken part in it or hadn't defended me more vigorously. Recognition was made of the role I had in building the department. Those whose ambitions had been frustrated moved on to other universities, where they had more opportunity to meet their goals.

It was over and I was wiser. I'd had one administration course and was poorly prepared for the role. But I am not sure that a whole curriculum would have prepared me. Perhaps we have to live it to learn, or perhaps some of us are better equipped to teach and care for patients than to lead a department.

Some years later, when the dean and I were having a quiet lunch, I spoke about a department party I had attended shortly after I left the chairperson's job. All the people who once had clustered around me were clustered around the new chairman.

"Carol, I had thought they did that because they liked me. Then I realized that they were there because they thought I could give them something they wanted."

Carol nodded and I noticed that her eyes were moist.

Then she went on to tell me about how high the school ranked among schools in the country, the generous new research grants and the outstanding new faculty members. She had truly accomplished her dreams, and I had done my part to help her.

Chapter 48
Fighting for Students

Throughout my career I have always identified with the patients in my care or the students I taught. This has made me a better nurse and teacher. However I must confess, it has often gotten me into trouble with the hospitals and schools that employed me.

Why am I that way? I suppose because of the values my parents instilled in me as a child. The family myths were always stories of my ancestors fighting for the rights of the individual against the establishment. I learned to mask my rebelliousness early, first, because I was quiet and shy, and later, because I had learned that one pays a high price for voicing such ideas.

You need to have a certain amount of power in an organization before you can implement policies that make a difference for the individual. At lunches with deans and nursing leaders, when talk turns to their own early education, I have learned that most were once rebellious students who hid it all under their white caps and starched aprons and promised themselves that, "Someday, I'll make it different."

I was aware of this trait even when I was interviewing for the job at the university. The interview process took two days and part of it included a meeting with the students.

Vera and Katherine were worried about one student, Martha*, and when I was to meet with the students they asked me to check her out. Martha was bright and eager. When she listened and understood, her response was a quick smile and a nod. Vera was concerned that she smiled too much and inappropriately. Frankly, I thought Vera was rather strange to be concerned about a response that was a little different, but not inappropriate or unpleasant. I told Vera and Katherine that I thought Martha was a good nurse and that I had been impressed by her intelligence and interest.

I should have been more concerned about the question itself. Martha's smile was a deeply ingrained habit, or possibly a tic. In either case, it seemed to be a waste of energy and time to be concerned about it.

When I joined the faculty, my colleagues were still worried about Martha's smile. By then, I knew the student better and knew that she was an excellent psychiatric nurse. I found my self defending her by pointing this out to the others.

Martha finished and went on to do some very creative work as a community mental health nurse, developing a program in a region that had no care of this sort. Later, she joined the faculty and was an excellent teacher, smile and all.

Years passed and when I told Martha that I was going to retire, her eyes welled with tears. She said, "Florence, when you go, who is going to worry about and fight for the students?"

I reassured her that she and others would fill that role. In my heart I was thanking her. Later, I thought that if I could see my epitaph, I hoped it would contain something similar to what Martha said that day.

Catlin* was another student in the group who interviewed me. She was interested in becoming part of state government. Although she was young, she was already an experienced child therapist. She wanted to move beyond working directly with patients to a position in which she would have the power to make more sweeping changes—system changes that would affect many children rather than one child.

She later told me that on the day of her first interview she decided that I would be her thesis adviser. At that time, a thesis was required for a master's degree. The students chose an original question and carried out the research to answer it. For many, it was an exercise that enabled them to learn the process rather than add to the body of knowledge in our speciality. Most students just didn't have the time and resources to do the sort of study required to generate such learning.

After I joined the faculty, I learned that Catlin wanted to do a joint study of emergency psychiatric services in Oregon. The state was very interested in this question and a teacher of social work and two social work students at a neighboring university were planning to do it. They asked Catlin to join them.

No one had done a joint project as a thesis, and no thesis had been a joint effort between the two schools. I read the policies about theses, and they were vague. They didn't preclude joint ventures, although I knew that what was written was intended to apply to one student.

We went ahead with Catlin's idea. The graduate committee was concerned, but we were already underway, and it would have created an embarrassment to stop us. (O K, so I manipulated.) Catlin traveled all over the state, to all the little towns, interviewing police, physicians, hospitals and what mental health workers there were.

The end result was a little loose. It certainly was not a tight experimental study, but it was loaded with information about the inadequacies of the current system. The Oregon Department of Mental Health received it eagerly and used it to ask for legislation to fill the needs it demonstrated. Catlin's thesis made a real difference.

The graduate committee was a little upset with me. They developed more explicit guidelines for theses, making it clear that it was to be the work of one student. Years passed and things changed, however. Now students may work together on a research project, or they may take one aspect of a faculty member's research as their study. Catlin and I were just a little ahead of our time.

Catlin is now a high-level state official. In this job, she still exhibits the same daring and drive to make things better that she possessed as a student, and, as the result, the world is a little better.

Jake* was a physiologist on loan from the medical school. He taught physiology to the graduate and undergraduate students. The graduate course was very demanding and an excellent course for medical and obstetric nurses. It didn't have much relevance to psychiatric nursing. We needed a neurophysiology course and one was not available. So our graduate students struggled through Jake's course, which had to be taken the first semester of the program. All of their energy went into passing this course and they frequently scraped through with a C.

I kept trying to persuade the committee to drop the requirement for our students and allow me to go outside the university to another school in the city to find a science course more suitable for us. Jake viewed this as my lowering standards.

I tried to explain that psychiatric nurses seldom needed expertise in measuring blood gases, but not being a nurse, he didn't understand. I agonized for some of our students, students like Jan.

Jan* was in her thirties, divorced, with two teen aged children. She quit her job and, using a small inheritance and loans, returned to school for her master's. Jake's course terrified her. She poured all her effort into it, and only earned a C. She also got a C in Statistics. Because she was so worried about these courses, she only got a B in her six-credit nursing course. So she entered her second quarter on probation. She had to get As if she were to remain in the school.

Her son was in an auto accident and she had to return to work part time. She was an excellent psychiatric nurse. Her patients loved her and she helped them. But her studies suffered and although she made some As, there were also Bs. She was out of the program.

I felt sick. We were losing a student who could make a real contribution. When I pleaded for an exception and an extension, Jake again accused me of lowering the standards. Jan was out of the school.

She went to a small town on the coast and opened a new mental health clinic for the state. She began all sorts of preventive mental health care in the community. She started a group in the school for unwed mothers. She began a group for the recently bereaved. She taught sexuality classes in the high school. She attended council meetings, school board meetings and became a member of the hospital board. She gave classes to the police.

She kept in touch and I reported this in the graduate committee. When she petitioned for reinstatement, Jake was the only one who voted against it.

Jan made all As during the remainder of the program and then went back to the community she had helped change. Her program became a model community mental health program and was used by the state as an exemplary program.

I was appointed to the graduate council for the university. When I first joined the faculty, this group was the one who passed on the admissions to all graduate programs in nursing and the basic sciences. The other members were molecular biologists, anatomists, biochemists. The medical and dental schools were not represented in this group.

The scores of the Graduate Record Examination were used as the main criteria for admission. The scores for the students, new college graduates who were applying for graduate programs in basic sciences, were truly impressive. And then there were the scores for the students applying to the nursing graduate programs. Those of newly graduated students were almost as high as the basic science applicants. But the older students, who had been out of school for a while, or perhaps had not had the benefit of superior education, were much lower.

Some were so low, that the council wanted to refuse them admission. I remember one applicant well. She was applying to the graduate program in administration. She did have low scores, but her work experience was impressive. She was a full colonel in the army, and had been the administrator of a large army hospital in the Philippines, and several in the states. Her record was loaded with commendations and she was slated for advancement when she completed her master's. She had successfully taken master's courses when she was posted near a university, but none of them were in nursing. The Army was willing to pay her way and give her leave to complete our program.

I pleaded her case eloquently, while I seethed inside. How dare these men, who had never worked outside of a laboratory or academia, see such a woman as deficient, all because of one test score. They relented and admitted her—and I forgave them. She sailed through the program and returned to her post.

After a few years, the School of Nursing withdrew from the graduate council and joined the medical and dental schools in making independent decisions about admissions.

I did change the standards. I hope I humanized and broadened them. Jake left the school, still convinced that I had lowered them.

Chapter 49
Death, Sex, and Other Sizzling Topics

T here are trends in research and in the interests of teachers just as there are trends in fashion and entertainment. The teachers who anticipate the trends, who do research and publish, can make a name for themselves—and make money putting on workshops and giving keynote addresses. The ones a little behind, as I always was, can become the faculty experts.

In the early sixties when I returned to school for a bachelor's degree there was a push to integrate the ideas developed in psychiatric settings into the general practice of nursing. Dr. Peplau's book, *Interpersonal Relationships in Nursing*, was a must for every nursing student. When I had been in school in the forties, we had been taught to treat the patient as a person. Dr. Peplau moved beyond that, showing us how to help the person deal with, and perhaps master his illness, using the relationship between the nurse and the patient as the tool.

I had been trying to do this, and sometimes succeeding, but my tool was my own intuition. Dr. Peplau gave me formulas so that should my intuition fail because of fatigue or lack of time to explore, I could still use responses that would help the patients.

I became an eager student, happily absorbing from reading and workshops all that this pioneer nurse had to offer. It was not long before I even had the audacity to criticize a few of my teachers' formulations and modify them to fit my own personality. I was criticized for this by some of the Peplau purists, but I was sure that this great lady herself would approve.

The National Institutes of Mental Health (NIMH) offered grants to nursing schools to integrate these ideas into curriculums, and I took part in teaching them. But in this trend, I was only an enthusiastic follower.

Death was in vogue in schools of nursing during the sixties. Physicians and nurses were often inept in dealing with the end of their patients' lives. Studies showed that doctors spent less time with dying patients than with the ones who would live. They fought death hard and when they lost the battle, they avoided all that reminded them of the failure. Nurses were less likely to avoid patients, but they were uncomfortable with discussing what was happening with patients and families.

Before I became a teacher, I spent twelve years as a staff and head nurse in a small hospital near my home in Pennsylvania. Most of the time I worked on a seventy-bed, medical-surgical ward. There were few nursing homes and hospitals were relatively inexpensive then. Some of our patients were with us for years. Others returned frequently during the course of their illnesses. We nurses knew these patients well, and some were close to being family. Because of the population, we lost about three people a week.

I had lots of experience being with dying patients, and the patients themselves had taught me how to help them. Even now, almost fifty years later, the names and memories of some of those patients are clear. There was

Mr. Kennedy, who graciously asked me to thank the day staff for the good care, since he would not be alive in the morning. I remember John Kyle, who sang the Lord's Prayer, in his rich, trained baritone, and then slipped into a final coma. Ila Fields Hoffman, who had been my high school classmate, fought death hard and lost to bulbar polio.

At the hospital school and community college, I was the expert on death and dying. My doctoral dissertation tested three methods of teaching this material, and I had been surprised to learn that students learned more about what patients felt about dying from a lecture, than they did from a group discussion of their own losses.

When I moved to the college, I learned they had a contract with a geriatric psychiatrist to teach the students about dying using an experiential workshop. I attended one of these sessions, which happened to be at the end of the psychiatrist's contract.

A dozen students were seated on the floor in a comfortable darkened room. Somber music filled the room while they sat in silence, anxious about what was going to happen. Then the leader placed a chair in the center of the room and asked the participants to imagine that the chair contained someone important to them who was no longer available. Most students imagined someone close to them who had died. There was more silence and music as the tension built. Then they were asked to think of what they would like to tell that person, if they could. Finally they were invited to approach the chair and voice these thoughts.

This was a very effective psychodrama, but I questioned the use of it as a teaching method. Students cried and were distraught during the workshop. They were instructed to see me later if they wanted to continue to discuss their reactions further.

Then the psychiatrist departed and I was left with twelve very upset students. Some went into therapy as the result of this class, and one considered suicide. I recommended that we not continue the workshops.

I believe that no student should be required to undergo therapy in the guise of a class, especially a required class. Only if a behavior problem interfered with her functioning and endangered the welfare of patients could we ethically require that she seek therapy. Just because we had the tools to uncover our students' deepest conflicts did not mean we should use them.

Incidentally, I did learn something from that first psychodrama on death. I had always enjoyed writing letters, and I wrote many. During World War II when I was in nursing school, I wrote to my boyfriend every day and to my brother, cousin and parents at least once a week. My father wrote to me every day, short sweet notes that made being away from home more bearable. When I was single, I corresponded with several men who had moved to other cities. I was always disappointed when we met, because I liked them better at a distance than in person. As the psychodrama unfolded, I realized that I really hadn't been writing to them, but to my dead father.

My colleague, Marion, had an experience with a similar experiential exercise. She had gone to a university in another state to take a summer program in geriatric nursing. One of the young faculty had the students, all mature women, take part in an exercise in which they wrote their own obituaries. This teacher committed the cardinal sin of teaching—she didn't know her students.

Marion had buried her mother a few years before, a mother who had neglected her as a child, and to whom she had given loving care the last years of her life. Marion was then recovering from two surgeries for cancer and had just finished a course of chemotherapy. She didn't need a class experience to help her understand what facing death was about. Two other women in the class had had similar experiences, and another had just lost a son.

They did write their obituaries, some in rhyme and all hilarious. The teacher was very upset that her students were making light of the exercise and denying their feelings about death. The students laughed at her and cried together in their dormitory rooms.

Theories about how to help dying patients and their families filled the journals and workshops for about five years. Then it was time for a new topic. In the early seventies, nursing faculties were discovering sex. Now obviously it had been around for a while, but nurses, except perhaps obstetrical, gynecological, and urological nurses, had acted as though it didn't exist. Oh, we all had stories about finding our patients in bed with each other or a visitor, but such behavior was forbidden—even when the participants had been married fifty years. Psychiatric nurses, however, were supposed to be able to understand and talk about sex.

The college had a close relationship with the nearby medical school, and faculty members were invited to take part in a sexuality class. The idea was that we would first undergo the classes as students; we would later teach portions of the class and be team leaders for mixed sex discussion groups. I was elected to attend.

One of the professors from the medical school was a psychologist who had taught with a famous sex researcher. He had used pornographic movies to desensitize students to sexual topics. The rationale was that if you watched *Deep Throat, The Devil and Miss Jones, Female Masturbating,* or any of the hundreds of such movies in his collection, you could talk about anything.

So we watched them. I wondered what my friend, Sister Graciala*, a good Catholic nun, thought of them all. She was a marital counselor and had joined the class to increase her knowledge of sexual topics and her ease in discussing them with her patients.

The first thing I discovered is that pornography is boring. I concluded that sex is to be enjoyed, not watched. Most of the movies were poorly made and just plain dull. I liked the funny ones best. But watching a seventy-year-old woman masturbate, even if she did have six orgasms, only made me wonder why any woman would permit such a film to be made of her private activity. Maybe she was bragging.

In spite of my reservations about pornography, I could more easily take the sexual histories of the patients I saw in my private practice. Before the class, I would wait— I told myself—until they were comfortable. Usually that was the second visit. After the class, I matter-of-factly brought up the subject during the first visit. So it had been my own discomfort, rather than the patients', that caused me to postpone the task. I was convinced that those boring movies had really desensitized me.

Soon it was time for the next class and I moved back into the teaching role. The first movie marathon took place in an amphitheater at the medical school. It began with *The Devil and Miss Jones*. The room was packed. Only the students enrolled in the class were to be there, but janitors, electricians and attendants had sneaked in. It was so crowded, I had to sit on the steps. Sister Graciala came in late and joined me.

She whispered, "Have they shown our favorite film?"

"No, I think it'll be next."

It was. Our favorite was a 1920s silent film. Five beauties in bathing suits are on the beach. A man, leering gleefully, sees them. He offers the women money for their sexual services. They agree and take the money, but impose certain conditions. The sexual contact is to take place through a hole in the fence. The women bring up a goat. Camera pans to the man's face, wreathed in ecstasy. The viewer knows, of course that he is fornicating with the goat. Months pass. Man arrives on the beach and sees the women. He is horrified. Their abdomens indicate that they are all very pregnant. The girls whip out the towels they have stuffed into their bathing suits and chase him down the beach. The End.

All in all, a movie hostile to men. Sister and I laughed until tears ran down our cheeks.

In the second class, the faculty shared responsibility for the lecture. Then each of us led a small discussion group. My group was composed of medical students and their wives and a few nursing students. We met in the evening after each class, supposedly to discuss the content of the lecture.

But it was hard to keep the group focused on the content. The medical students wanted to discuss the pressures of school, and their feelings of inadequacy. The wives had their own problems that they were bursting to share. I soon found that I had to let them ventilate and express their most pressing concerns. Once the pressure was relieved, I was able to bring up the sexual topics. It made me realize how far ahead nursing schools were. Our students met each day in a clinical group and were able to talk about their experiences and feelings as well as the class content. I discovered that these young men (they were all men) were forced into a difficult role. Every day they put on their white coats and introduced themselves as doctors, then tried to live up to that image. They didn't have a sympathetic instructor close at hand, as my students did to help them understand the emotional aspects of health care. I began to understand the defenses physicians develop to keep from feeling what their patients are feeling.

I learned that these doctors-to-be were quite sophisticated about sex in general. However, they thought sex was invented by their own generation. They couldn't imagine their parents engaging in such an activity—well, maybe once, when they were conceived. By the end of the class, their attitudes hadn't changed much as far as their parents having sex, but they did begin to acknowledge that perhaps other old people—dirty old men and women—engaged in such activities. I do hope that time and their patients completed the sexual education of these young men.

When I moved to Oregon, the faculty was glad to have someone who had experience in teaching human sexuality. Before long a class for the graduate students was scheduled. I wanted to use pornographic films to desensitize the students. I was certain that watching those boring films had made me a better therapist.

I was new to Oregon, and since it was a state with a small population, what happened at the university was often in the news. I had visions of conservative legislators learning that the new professor from New York was showing pornography to nursing students and that state funds had paid for these dirty movies.

I checked the theater section of the *Oregonian*, and saw that Deep Throat was playing at one of the movie houses. In fact, it was the only movie that had played there for years. The owners gave my students a discount, and I made attending the theater the first assignment of the class—an optional assignment. We were the only females in the theater, among the raincoated men who furtively slipped into seats. The legislature never found out. For years my colleagues on the faculty teased me about this field trip.

I had some fun with this topic socially. Sometimes when someone asked what I taught, I would reply, "I teach a class called Sexuality." Then I'd watch to see the reaction.

In the late seventies, there was an explosion of sexual information in the media. Students read books, watched soaps, and rented X-rated movies. Doctors, nurses, and to some extent, patients were no longer embarrassed to talk about sex. Nursing homes and psychiatric hospitals provided privacy for their patients should they want to have sexual contact with their partners. Sexual issues became integrated into the regular classes in the curriculum. And I needed a new area of expertise.

Ethics became the topic of the eighties, and I immediately geared up to become an expert. I applied for, and was awarded, a National Humanities Fellowship to study ethics, specifically informed consent, in a class taught by a faculty member of the Albert Einstein School of Medicine. The five-week course was located on a state university campus, north of New York City.

Was I that interested in informed consent? Well, to be honest, the main attraction to this particular workshop was that I could drive to Boston on the weekends and visit my daughter, Shevawn. However, I had always been interested in philosophy and the major teacher of the course, Dr. Ruth Maklin, was excellent. We also had classes at the Hastings Center, with the nation's most respected experts.

Verl drove to New York with me, as he said, "... to check out the place, and let your classmates know you are taken." Some of the females thought he was one of the class and fluttered around him. I had to let them know that he was taken. He stayed a few nights in the dorm with me, abandoning the upper bunk and crowding into the narrow lower one with me. Then he flew back to Oregon and left me to my studies.

There were twelve in the class, doctors, nurses, dentists and hospital administrators. We worked hard at our studies, but in the evenings we crowded into cars and drove to the city. We parked in a garage near Times Square and rushed to the ticket office that sold discount tickets to shows for that evening. Then we hurried off alone, or in pairs or groups to see the shows. When they were over, we met, split the parking fee, and drove back to campus. The next morning we would be back in class, well fortified with strong coffee.

One of my classmates fainted during a movie which showed a man with disfiguring burns. We were sitting in a dark room, intent on the screen, when there was a flurry and then a crash. The lights went on and there was Dr. Jones*, a young physician, stretched out on the floor, pale and clammy. When he recovered, he told us tales about being the fainting physician in the emergency room. He must have been related to my student, Miss Faintheart.

Finally the class was over and I packed up my car and headed west. I stopped in Cincinnati to see Susan and then it was on to Oregon. I drove twelve hours a day and three days after I left Cincinnati, I was back home at the nursery, with Verl.

When I went back to the university I was one of the experts on ethics. Although I'd had more intensive training from the people who were national experts, there was more competition for this role and I did not contribute as much as I might have. I did play a small role in formulating the categories for the Oregon Health Plan.

I did three studies that dealt with rural mental health. Rural health was not such a popular topic then as it is now. If I were still working, I would likely be the school's rural expert.

I attended a workshop at the university recently. At lunch I mentioned that I was writing this chapter, and I was informed that the really 'in' topic for the nineties is managed care.

Somehow that made me glad that I have retired.

Chapter 50
The Rodeo Queen

May* was from an old eastern Oregon family, a famous one. One of her ancestors had been a famous politician, as well known for his drinking and riding exploits as for his political views. At one time, the family had owned as much land as several Pennsylvania counties. I didn't know about such royalty when I arrived in Oregon, but when I went east of the Cascade mountain range, I learned that certain people are important. Their daughters are usually elected queen of the local rodeo.

May was a tall, dark-haired woman with striking blue eyes, whose jeans looked as though they had been tailor made. She wore silk shirts and on her left hand a very large diamond. I had seen women with the same air in the airport at Dallas-Fort Worth. They had the look of western class.

She had received her bachelor's degree at the university, and while there she had picked up a husband as well, a young psychiatrist. When he finished his residency, they moved east of the mountains to a small town where he established his practice. He was the only psychiatrist for a hundred miles.

May had a baby and helped her husband in the office, but she grew restless. She wanted more education. When Katherine wrote the community psychiatry grant, May saw her chance. If we could send the Portland-based students out to rural areas to get clinical experience, why couldn't she stay there and get a degree?

She convinced Katherine that it was possible. However, she did have to come to Portland for the basic classes. When I arrived, May was already enrolled. When the weather was warm and the snow was gone from the passes, she had only one hundred and fifty miles to drive to get to class. In the winter, however, she could not cross the mountains, so she had to drive much farther. She attended some classes by phone hook-up. We sent material back and forth by mail and when one of the faculty could, we went to May's home to teach and offer clinical supervision. Now, all this is made much easier because of the university's television system and there are students all over the state. May was our first attempt at educating a lone student at a distant site.

May was a bright student. In spite of not attending every class, she made a solid A in Jake's class. She had an original but very effective style of doing therapy. Our long-distance student did well, and in time she finished all of her class work. Only the thesis remained.

At that time, it was possible to obtain a nurse practitioner license without having completed the thesis and master's degree. May secured her license and joined her husband in his practice. It was a very lucrative partnership.

At regular intervals, I contacted May and reminded her that there was a limit on the time she could postpone finishing the program. Masters' degrees had to be finished

within seven years, the amount of time for course work to be considered obsolete.

May's little boy was still young and she was so busy with the practice that she kept putting off the chore of a thesis. It seemed redundant because she was doing what she wanted with patients. Her husband's license covered her as well as her own nurse practitioner license.

Then it appeared that the State Board of Nursing was going to require that nurse practitioners have a master's degree. Third party payment might be based on national certification and that credential was tied to the master's. Time was passing and it was more and more necessary to have the proper credentials.

May's life changed. Her husband wanted out of the marriage and community. They divorced and he moved to a city in another state. May continued the practice alone, now the only mental health professional in the area. Her practice was busy and profitable. An internist in the town suggested that he become her professional partner, but she declined.

She needed the master's and the end of the seven years was approaching. I was her thesis adviser. She found a committee, wrote an acceptable proposal and began collecting data. But her time was up.

I went to the graduate department and pleaded her case. There were rumblings—who did she think she was to wait until the last minute, and if we do it for one, won't all the students want more time? I pleaded, not only for May's sake, but for the hundreds of mentally ill people east of the mountains who relied on her care.

They gave her an extension. Then May's husband decided that he wanted to have custody of their son. A doctor, a psychiatrist as well, has lots of power. May had a fight on her hands but she won it. But time had passed and she had neglected her thesis.

She had managed to collect the data for her study, however, and she hired someone to do the statistical analysis. The other students analyzed their own data, but teachers frequently hire someone, so I approved. By now it was December and the final deadline was January first.

I called and gave her the news. There would be no more extensions. I had done all I could but the committee had decreed, "Enough." She had to have her thesis approved by her committee by that date, and she had to defend, early in January. I told her that I would be willing to devote Christmas vacation to the project and unless she wanted to lose all her past efforts, she'd better plan to do the same.

We set a date three days before Christmas, at my home. May arrived a day late, driving her four-wheel-drive station wagon. Snow had blocked the pass and she had had to drive the long way to get there. That meant staying all night in a motel. In the back, cuddled in a thick down sleeping bag was her nine-year-old son, his face blazing with measles.

I wanted to bring him in the house, but he insisted that he was comfortable in his cocoon and would blow the horn if he wanted any thing. We checked on him every half hour and he dozed contentedly while his mother and I labored.

She sat at her typewriter in the kitchen and I worked at the computer in the study. She did the first draft; then together, we edited and polished. Finally I typed the copy up on my computer. She went to a motel that night and was back again the next day. About two, we concluded that the prose was acceptable for all five chapters. She would draw the charts at home and she had a typist ready to put the final product in order. Federal Express would get it to the other people on the committee, and she could defend in early January.

Then May confessed that she had forgotten her credit card. She had used all her money for the motel. She was almost out of gas. Verl filled up her tank and I advanced some cash for any possible emergency. Then May and her sick little boy went back down the gorge and into eastern Oregon, which is still the frontier.

She defended her thesis brilliantly and the long-sought degree was awarded. May, former rodeo queen, may be a cliff-hanger—my term for people who do things at the last minute—but she is also a pioneer. Her practice has continued to grow and provides a good life for May and her son. And the worried well and mentally ill for a hundred miles around her small town have the very best care.

Chapter 51
Getting Students Through

After my experience with May, the rodeo queen, I was in demand as a thesis adviser—and it worried me a little.

I didn't find that the brilliant students with ideas for large, ambitious studies beat a path to my door. True, I was often asked to be one member of their three-person committee, but I was not the leader. I was chosen because I could help them write clear strong English. I made a point to return any manuscript within twenty-four hours and I soon learned that I got the chapters forty-eight hours before the other committee members and that their copies contained the revisions I had suggested.

The students who selected me to chair their thesis were the ones who needed to finish the program and return to work. They seldom were the ones that planned a scholarly career or were exploring doctoral programs. After a little reflection, I stopped worrying. These students were more like me than the others. I had not had the luxury of spending much time in school, and neither had my thesis advisees.

Joan* was one such student. She and her husband, Dick, were long-distance truck drivers. She traveled with him and helped drive their big rig. She worked as an agency nurse whenever they settled in one spot for a week or so. I never knew her exact age, but she did have a son from an earlier marriage who was a physician in Florida.

She and Dick had bought land in Montana and their dream was to save money, sell their truck and settle there. Joan decided that she would have more choice of jobs, and perhaps could work independently, if she had a masters degree. So she stopped driving with her husband, moved her RV into a nearby trailer park and enrolled in our program.

I especially enjoyed the surprised reactions of the psychiatric residents in our joint seminar when they learned Joan's history. The seminar was often informal and during discussion we might have to justify our arguments by citing our own experience. When the young men learned that Joan drove an eighteen-wheeler, and was also a doctor's mother, their stereotypes were blown away.

Joan finished the class work and went on the road again with Dick. I received some drafts of a proposal in the mail and mailed them back to her. Then she sent Dick on alone, moved into the RV and began to work in earnest. Her research was to develop a profile of the patients in a particular rural mental health program. The program was in a logging community much like the one she would be living in in Montana. In record time she collected data, did the analysis and wrote her thesis.

Dick came to Portland for the defense. He wore a large sombrero, cowboy boots and jeans. Instead of sitting along the wall, as the visitors to a defense usually do, he joined Joan and the committee at the table. When Joan had presented her study, and answered the examiners' questions, the visitors were invited to question her. Dick asked searching questions. Joan thought a while and then delivered very intelligent answers. I suspected it was rehearsed—but it was also impressive.

When it was over, we congratulated Joan, and she and Dick left to take a load to the east coast. Several years later, the Christmas cards began coming from Montana.

Dino* and Mary* were the only married couple I ever had in the same class. He was a supervisor at a state hospital and she worked in a private psychiatric hospital. They had been married about ten years and had a six year old son, Johnny*.

They did not behave as a pair in class. Most often they had differing opinions about treatment. On one occasion they had an in-class marital spat.

Mary came in late. She had been to the library. She sat beside Dino and asked, "How's Johnny?"

"He's better. I sent him to school."

"Dino, he had a fever!" said his outraged mother. Then she flounced out of the class to rescue her sick child.

We all sat speechless, not wanting to take sides in a family quarrel. Then we went on with our class.

Dino and Mary finished their class work and each prepared a proposal for a thesis. The graduate committee had now approved the submission of joint theses, but they wanted to do separate studies.

One day they came in with good news. Mary was pregnant. Johnny had been born when they were very young. Now they were financially secure, and had just moved into a large new home. They were very excited about the baby.

I was out of town for a few days, and when I returned, there was an ominous call from Dino on my answering machine. When I called back, I received the bad news. Mary had breast and ovarian cancer.

They agonized for a several days and then went ahead and allowed the doctor to abort the fetus. Then Mary had both breasts and her internal female organs removed. Months of chemotherapy stretched into years.

I saw Dino often, not as a teacher but as a friend. I urged him to go ahead and finish his thesis. He needed it to hold his job and without it he could not advance. He said that to go ahead without Mary would be to communicate to her that he expected her to die. She had no energy for a research project, and had a vague feeling that the stress of graduate school had precipitated her illness. Both recognized that their feelings were probably irrational, but they persisted nevertheless.

Mary returned to work a few days a week. She did this to keep the good hospital insurance that job offered. Dino arranged to give her the chemotherapy at home on her days off.

Time passed. Then a good friend and classmate of the couple was passed over for a dream job because he had not finished his thesis. This made an impression.

A fellow faculty member, Dr. Mary Kay King, had finished her dissertation. She had data she had not used and wondered if we could persuade Dino and Mary to use it, ask a different research question, and finish a joint thesis. She offered it to them and we held our breath.

They said, yes, but they wanted me to remain as their adviser. This was not the usual procedure. It was Mary Kay's data and she should have been the adviser. She graciously said, "Don't push it, Florence. They need you for moral support. Let's just get them through."

They worked hard and soon were ready to defend. That day the room was packed with fellow students and friends. They mounted a brilliant defense, with just a little disagreement between them over one interpretation. By this time, Mary Kay had slipped over into the chairman's role, without any psychological upset. I have never approved a thesis with such relief and pleasure as I felt when I signed my name to theirs.

Dino and Mary finished their master's degrees six years after they began. Johnny is a teenager now. Mary still has an occasional course of chemotherapy, but she works full time and Dino has moved up in his job.

You'll not find their study in *Nursing Research*, but it is the best study, I have ever had a part in.

Chapter 52
More Students

After I finished my tenure as chairperson, I became the department's utility teacher—the person who would teach any class, at any time, with little or no notice. I taught interpersonal techniques and interviewing skills to sophomores in class and in the clinical area. This also involved orienting the students to the profession, holding hands and giving support.

Most of the students had had another life before they entered nursing. I had men who were horticulturists, accountants and salesmen in my class, and women with degrees in psychology, art, music and sociology. Some were young and a few were almost my age. They were all dedicated and fun to be with.

Bill* had been a high school drop out. He was a long-distance truck driver and was doing quite well, but he told me, "Life didn't have much purpose". One day he drove past a school and saw a sign saying that high school equivalency exams were being given there that day. He parked the truck, went in, took the exam and passed. He had made the first step—anything was possible. He signed up for classes at the community college, taping the lectures to listen to on his cross-country trips. Other students taped lectures for him when he wasn't there. He finished with honors and entered our program.

I was teaching interviewing and interpersonal skills to the sophomores. I assigned Bill to a home-bound elderly man who was depressed. Bill not only talked with him, he fixed the patient's car so he could drive then went with him to regain his lapsed license. Afterward, Bill took the patient to the senior center. Bill not only learned the techniques of interviewing, he showed his patient that life could be worth living. Bill was a perfect example of my theory that in nursing you can use all the talents and skills you possess.

I taught the psychiatric nursing class to the senior students. The beginning of the fall term was an ordeal. The students' junior year is unbelievably demanding. I doubt that all this stress is necessary but my colleagues in med-surg insisted that it is, and the students certainly leave their classes well prepared.

They also leave mad. The next teacher who comes in contact with them becomes the focus of their anger. Especially if it is a nice reasonable psychiatric nurse. Reasonableness in a teacher was viewed as weakness. When I entered my first class in the fall, steeled to face thirty-five angry students, I felt like a lion tamer entering a cage.

After a week or so, they settled down and began to think that maybe there was something valuable that they could learn in the class, and maybe the teacher wasn't a foolish old woman who insisted in talking about the patient's perceptions and experience. In a month they were happily into the class and teaching was a pleasure.

During September, however, I would meet my friend, Dr. Wilma Peterson, a nurse physiologist, who taught the research class. She would be having the same difficulty and we would commiserate and support each other. Bless Wilma, she was a great help.

What would the students do to show their displeasure ?

I remember one student who objected to reading an article because it was foolish and not written in good English. The article, which I had written, described an interaction with a psychotic patient. It illustrated with dialogue the use of humor. I was in a bind. The student was from Europe and spoke broken English. Should I defend my English, and point out her errors? Instead I decided to listen and said something like, "That's an interesting perspective." In my mind I failed her in Tact 101. I hoped that her rudeness wouldn't sabotage her career after she graduated.

I like feisty students who raise questions and disagree with me. It enlivens the class. Sometimes they may just be right. But lively exchanges should always be done with courtesy. Students demand that teachers treat them with respect. Sometimes they forget that the same is expected of them.

Most foreign students were courteous but challenged my teaching skills. One year I had two students from China who had been sent by their government to learn about nursing education in this country. They were bright, hard-working students, but they had so much to learn: the language, customs, and such mundane things such as how to use an electric stove.

I gave take-home open-book tests that the students could do alone or in a small group. I would present a patient and a situation, then ask, "You are his nurse. What would you do, and why?" My Chinese students asked if they could answer as if the patient were Chinese and the setting was China. I readily agreed, hoping only that they would apply what they were taught. Their answers were not only theoretically correct but very interesting. I learned a great deal about China.

I learned that health care workers in China also deal with patients who have alcohol and drug problems. In spite of the cultural differences, a marriage counselor in China would see people with the same problems I saw in the United States. Perhaps I shouldn't have been surprised to learn that all people are much the same, even on the other side of the world.

One Chinese student was married and her husband was coming to visit. She was happily anticipating the visit. When he arrived, instead of a honeymoon, she received political lectures. The government had sent him to straighten out her thinking which had been tainted with American beliefs.

The other student stayed on to go to graduate school. She decided to major in mental health nursing and was in one of my graduate classes. During the first class, when we were getting acquainted and talking about our back-grounds, she told about hers. She had been a barefoot doc-tor in China. She went on to say that choosing her major was the first real decision she had ever make in her life. All the decisions that preceded that one had been made by her government.

Kevin* was one of the senior students I supervised in the clinical area, a community mental health center. Many of the clients of this agency were street people. Some of the students had a hard time in this setting but Kevin fit right in. When I remarked about this, he told me that he had been a musician, a fiddler in a bluegrass band. When he didn't have a gig, he earned his living as a street musician. He knew all the inside information about which shelters were best and where one could get the best meals. His pa-tients received teaching about their medicine, exploration of their feelings, problem-solving, and the benefit of his street experience—all the best that he had to offer.

When I think of the seniors, I remember dedicated people who made such differences in their patient's lives. I attended their weddings, and met their parents, spouses and children at graduation. Later I met them again in my graduate classes, or as clients, when their marriages or lives weren't going as well as they had hoped. Every few years on my birthday, Moynell, one of my favorites who was a student ten years ago, sends me flowers.

Chapter 53
The Fight for Equity

N ear the end of my time as chairperson, I was invited to a meeting of women who were employed by the state university system. They were concerned about what they saw as systematic discrimination against female faculty members. Several of the women had stories of blatant abuse by their administration. All of us who attended had stories of more subtle discrimination. Finally the group had data that showed that, when all variables, such as time in position, responsibilities, education, and publications were matched, and the women were compared with men, the men consistently made $2000 more a year than the women. They also were more likely to have tenure and higher academic rank.

One of the woman, Anna Penk, had a case that more easily defied dispute. She was a mathematics instructor who had taught for years on a fixed-term quarter-by-quarter contract. This meant that she would receive a contract to teach for ten weeks during the fall term, and not know if she would be hired to teach in winter and spring. The strange part of this is that she taught courses that were required of all students in the major. She was never on a tenure track and was not considered for promotion. During this time, she was publishing her work in scholarly journals. After years of such treatment, she received a letter which gave her tenure and promotion. Our explanation was that the administration had become worried that such treatment might become known. When Anna resigned, a young inexperienced man was hired to replace her. He was hired on a tenure track and received a salary higher than Anna's.

I had not been discriminated against within the School of Nursing. We were almost all women, and gender was not an issue. But the school within the university had the status of a poor younger sister. We had no building but were crowded into offices spread across the campus. We had far fewer secretaries. Finally, although we had more students, the school's budget and our salaries were much smaller than the other schools, medicine and dentistry.

The group of women formed itself into a group called Faculty Women for Equity. They accepted the services of a prominent activist attorney, on a contingency basis, and instituted a class action suit, Penk et. al. vs. Oregon State Board of Higher Education.

I wanted to join the suit as a named plaintive. However, I was the chairperson of a department and one of the dean's administrative team. I supported all Carol had been working for. She had moved the school from its backwater status into an emerging position with the possibility of becoming one of the best schools in the nation. If it appeared that she was supporting this rebellion of faculty women, her position would be in jeopardy.

I solved the problem by joining as a Jane Doe. Then when my time as chairperson was over, I became one of twenty-two named plaintiffs.

I was in a position where I could do this without the risk that a younger faculty would be taking. I was no longer an administrator and I was certain that I did not want another administrative position. I had tenure and could not be fired unless I became incompetent or guilty of moral turpitude. I had the support of my husband and a secure personal life. I had nothing to lose and perhaps I could gain a great deal for other women in academia.

I wasn't alone. Donna was an associate dean. She was a native Oregonian from a prominent family. When Carol first came to Oregon, Donna had educated her about the political and social system and helped smooth Carol's entry. She and Carol were also close personal friends.

When the suit began, the state and its lawyers came to Donna for information about faculty salaries, curriculum vitae, etc. Donna was in a doctoral program and moved out of the associate dean position—and became a named plaintive. My, the state's lawyers were surprised!

Our group operated with volunteers. A psychologist-statistician on our faculty spent weekend after weekend collecting data and running statistical tests to support our position. Others spent weekends at our lawyers' offices typing, copying and doing secretarial work. Law students joined the cause as volunteers.

The state had the entire staff of the attorney general's office. In addition, they hired an expensive law firm from Philadelphia to represent the State Board of Higher Education.

When I gave my deposition, I was surprised when the volunteer lawyer, a young red-headed woman, insisted that I compare myself to men in similar positions. This is not what Don, our attorney, had told me. The stance of the school of nursing was that the school as a whole was discriminated against. But the young lawyer persisted. Finally, under pressure I mentioned Joe, my teaching partner, who was now the chair of psychiatry, and the man who was chairman of the psychology department.

In the ladies room of the courthouse, when the case was being tried, I ran into Pamela. Pamela was an assistant attorney general who handled much of the courtroom work for the state—in other words the enemy. Except, I liked her, and felt in my bones that she was sympathetic to our cause. She mentioned that she was defending a psychiatric resident from the school in a malpractice suit and was spending time talking with Joe. In this matter she was an ally.

When I called Joe to tell him that I had named him as someone I should be compared with, he groaned—and so did his lawyer wife. Fortunately, he never had to appear in court. His curriculum vitae was submitted as evidence.

You would think that in court, in a serious suit, that people would be enemies. The young volunteer lawyer certainly was worried when I said I liked Pamela. She kept telling me to be careful. Yet I watched while Don, our lead attorney, fumbled and looked for a document—which the lawyers from the other side quickly supplied. First name thanks were exchanged. I wondered, if lawyers could be professional, why not plaintiffs?

Some of the testimony of the faculty women was compelling. One sociology professor had sent a memo to her chairman, a man, and told him she was going to do a study about the problems of working mothers. He sent back a memo that said women belong in the kitchen, laundry and bedroom. He didn't think her topic was worth studying. He testified that he had just been kidding. She never did the study.

Pamela cross-examined me. She said sarcastically, "How could you compare yourself to a surgeon?" She got a lecture about the latest research about the nursing behaviors that reduce post-operative mortality rates. I'm sure she regretted the question.

I liked her, but I had spent my adolescence verbally jousting with my father, who had studied law, and I loved a good argument. The volunteer attorney stopped worrying.

While I testified, I looked back into the audience and saw Verl, my husband, looking so very proud. It reminded me of when I graduated from high school and delivered the valedictorian address. My parents looked so proud, and it moved me so much that I skipped a paragraph of my speech. I made sure I didn't do that again.

Carol testified for the state, and, darn, she did very well—as she always did. Then she, Donna and I went out to lunch. As I said, it was all very strange.

I received letters of support and thanks from the American Nurses Association and the school's faculty organization. They thanked me for taking the risk that could help all women. It was very gratifying.

Anna and one other woman won their suit. However, a higher court had ruled that statistical evidence could not be used to prove discrimination and the judge ruled against the class action. We also lost on appeal.

We lost, but in a sense we won. Administrators in the state system became very careful that no evidence of discrimination against women was apparent in their dealings. And in doing this, much of the actual discrimination disappeared.

Discrimination does still exist, however. Women are still judged by men's standards. But it is no longer politically correct to voice such ideas as those expressed by the chairman of the sociology department, even disguised as jest. Freed of some of the barriers, women are proving themselves, and other barriers are falling.

The School of Nursing at Oregon Health Sciences University is now housed in a beautiful new building. The faculty have received grants and they are doing research that will improve the lives of our patients. Recently the graduate program was named one of the best in the country.

I'd like to think that my becoming a plaintiff in the suit contributed in a small way to the school's success.

Chapter 54
Other Expectations

University professors are expected to do more than teach. In order to secure tenure and maintain it, one must do research, maintain practice skills, and do community and professional service. When I negotiated with Katherine for the position at the university, I asked to be allowed to apply for early tenure. A year after I was hired, it was granted without question.

Had I waited the usual seven years, it would not have been so easy. With the hiring of more doctoral-prepared people, the standards became more difficult. Each year more research was being done and the competition was fierce. Those of us who were tenured were expected to maintain the standards, but we didn't have to face competition from our peers as the tenured positions filled and became less available.

I didn't like to do quantitative research. I had done two experimental studies to obtain my degrees and was praised for them by scholars. Both were quickly published. They were considered good research. But I knew how flawed they were, not because they were poorly done, but because of the very nature of human behavior. There are so many variables and they are almost impossible to control. Only if there had been many replications of the same research in a number of settings could I have been sure that my findings had really generated new knowledge.

But I did learn a great deal by doing them. I learned to question the validity of research in general and to read it skeptically.

Feeling the way I did, it was hard to make myself do the meticulous work necessary to do a study and write up papers. Instead of doing large studies, I chose to do small ones that satisfied my own curiosity and contributed to my practice and teaching. I published only enough to maintain my tenure.

The state mental health division generously let me use data from a large study they had done and pose a new question. I wanted to compare the quality of life of rural and urban residents. The results of the study showed they were very much the same except that rural people made less money and that influenced the other factors.

The press picked up the results of my study and reported the differences between rural and country life were large. It embarrassed me a little because, as reported, the results were distorted. I did enjoy the fact that *Family Weekly* published a note about it, and that the people from my home-town, a Pennsylvania farm community, read it. I hoped my first husband saw it.

I did three qualitative studies of questions that interested me. I didn't try to analyze the data using all the techniques that scholars use to turn qualitative data into quantitative. My research was more like what an investigative reporter does.

In one study, I interviewed rural women in the counties surrounding my home about their lives and problems. A picture emerged that was different than the stereotype of the farm woman and the rural community. The only institution that tied these women together was the school. Distances between houses, diversity in religion, and the fact that so many women worked meant that they had little or no contact with neighbors. In planning care for someone with mental health problems, it is important to know their community. I learned that rural living could be very lonely.

I wondered what it would be like in eastern Oregon, which could be described as frontier rather than rural. So I went to LaGrande one summer and stayed in an apartment in the men's dormitory at Eastern Oregon State College. (It was comfortable until the football team moved into the dorm.) I interviewed women randomly chosen from the phone book.

I went to the sheriff's department to tell them what I was doing, in case anyone called in to check about me. I asked a woman deputy if there were places I should not go.

"Don't go into the Gordon Creek area."

"What's in Gordon Creek?" I asked, thinking maybe there were animals there, or impassable roads.

"Did you see the movie, Deliverance?"

I nodded yes.

"Well, the people are like that. We always go in the daytime and with three people. They just might decide to keep you."

I thanked her and crossed the phone numbers from that area off my list.

I found that eastern Oregon is a man's world. The men love hunting, fishing and western life, but many women are very lonely. Husbands often work away from the ranches and the women are left with small children and livestock to care for. There is a very high divorce rate in the area I studied.

The results were important to me because I sometimes traveled to our branch campus in La Grande to teach in our program there. We developed it, hoping to increase the number of nurses in that area. I needed to give them a realistic view of what life was like for the people who were their patients. But my project was not of much interest to nurses in New York or Chicago.

I did another small study of young Methodist ministers who were assigned to churches in rural areas. I found that many of them were from cities and suburbs and that they and their families had a difficult time adjusting to the differences in the culture. Their values were different than the ones held by their congregations. The Bishop in Portland was interested in the results of my study. It was discussed at meetings whenever decisions about assignments were to be made.

I did not make my mark as a researcher. I did enough to be credible in my job, and I learned from what I did. You won't find me listed in the galaxy of people who contributed great knowledge to nursing.

However, there are nurses who have done landmark studies and who have made a lasting difference in the way nursing is done. Carol Lindeman's research, which showed the beneficial effect of teaching surgical patients, is one such study. Before surgery, patients were instructed about the value of deep-breathing and exercise during the immediate post-operative period. The group that received the instruction, recovered and were discharged more quickly, had fewer complications and fewer re-admissions to the hospital. Ann Burgess' studies of the effect of criminal violence on victims have not only changed nursing but law enforcement. I respect these nurse researchers and admire their work, while acknowledging that I just don't have the temperament to do research like theirs.

I do hope that the American Nurses Foundation and other organizations that fund nursing research will continue. We need solid data to back up our teaching and practice. Those nurses who have the education and inclination to become researchers should be freed of other expectations in order to add to our body of knowledge.

After I married Verl, I opened a practice in Silverton. At first I saw patients in my study. In order to get to my study, my patients came in the front door walked through the living room and breakfast room. The dinner dishes might still be on the table or Verl might be at the dishwasher. After a few years, I rented an office in Silverton. It was in a building owned by a real estate firm and my office had an outside entrance. The building sat in the corner of a parking lot, far from any other structures.

I decorated my office so it resembled a comfortable sitting room, but I never felt secure there. Since I saw people in the evenings, it was frequently dark and lonely. My practice increased but not enough to compensate for the rent and the high water and sewer bills. (Four flushes equaled fifteen dollars.) Then I began to receive strange phone calls inquiring about my skills as a sexual counselor. I decided to move back to the office in my home.

We made a doorway between my study and the front entry. We closed the door between the study and the breakfast room and soundproofed the wall. The patients could come directly into my study and no longer saw my spouse washing dishes or listened to him talking to his mother on the phone. Yet if I were frightened I could call for help. It never came to that, even though I had a few shady characters consulting me who had been referred by their probation officer. I was more comfortable in my own home.

I maintained my practice until a year after I retired. I never was able to build the steady, paying clientele that I'd had in New York. Although I had a few professional people, most of the people I saw were laborers, men who worked in the woods or on farms, and women with minimum wage jobs. Having the practice enhanced my teaching. When I was no longer teaching, one rationale disappeared, and I began longing to spend the evenings with my husband. So I closed the practice.

Shortly after I began working at the university, I became a part of the Region X Task Force on Manpower. This was a federally sponsored group of mental health professional educators and practitioners from the northwestern United States. It included people who taught psychiatric nursing, social work, psychology and psychiatry, and heads of agencies that employed those professionals. We met several times a year in some inexpensive motel and spent two days exchanging information. As the result of the meetings, we formed some very useful alliances. We planned joint research projects, negotiated placements for our students, and improved our curriculums. We also had a very good time. Roselyn Carter was very knowledgeable about the state of mental health services, and President Carter's administration was supportive. But when Reagan was elected, funds were cut and the task force was eliminated.

I was on the National League for Nursing board which accredits schools of nursing for three years. This is the group that examines a school's self-study and the report of a team of visitors who verify the study and then decides whether or not to accredit the school. Board membership involved a great deal of work and preparation but it was worth it. The meetings were held in New York. No matter how busy I was, there was always time to see one performance at the Metropolitan Opera and for a hurried tour of Bloomingdales.

I was an NLN accreditation visitor for ten years. I made at least one visit each year, spending a week with one or two other visitors at a school of nursing seeking initial or continuing accreditation. We interviewed presidents, deans, faculty, students and sometimes patients. We read committee minutes, student's papers, budgets, and patient's charts. We toured agencies, poked into closets, measured space, examined library books and attended classes. Then before we left, we wrote up and publicly read, a detailed report of our findings. This went to the board in New York to be used in their deliberations.

Of all the work I did, outside teaching, this was the most satisfying. It was very hard work, a grueling week, but I learned a great deal about education during these visits. I met the faculty of the schools we visited and got to know my fellow visitors well.

Visitors were frequently viewed with fear and hostility. I worked hard to dispel the negative perceptions and to be open and supportive. At the same time I reported compliance with the criteria honestly. I think I succeeded. After a few visits, schools began to request that I be the leader of the team that visited them. I still receive Christmas cards from some of the schools I visited.

Sometimes a negative report could have a beneficial effect on the school. I remember one Christian school—at least they constantly reminded us that it was Christian and therefore different, much to the dismay of my fellow visitor who was the dean of a Catholic school. The faculty in the nursing school was poorly paid, and they were crammed into inadequate offices with battered desks and minimal secretarial help. The enrollment in the school was large, and the classes required of the nursing students supported a great part of the liberal arts faculty. They filled the English, sociology and science classes.

When we met the president, we were ushered into a suite of offices by a young, beautifully dressed receptionist. The offices were spacious and lavishly furnished and the president wore an expensive tailored suit and sported a large diamond. He too reminded us that this was a Christian school.

There were objections to the section of our report that stated that the school of nursing was inadequately supported, but the budget and floor plan could not be denied. The board in New York decided that accreditation be granted provisionally, dependent on increases in financial and technical support and the allotment of more space for the school of nursing. When we left the school, we were the bad guys. I hope they realized that we had helped them get what they needed to do a good job.

I served on a national council for the American Nurses Association just as I was retiring and removing some of my investment from nursing. I enjoyed the experience and the stimulating company of the dynamic younger council members, but I was glad when I wasn't re-elected. It was relief to leave the tasks to my younger colleagues.

Teaching is an important role of an educator, and I always viewed it as the most important part of my job. However, research, practice and community service enhance teaching. Without them, teaching becomes rote and out of date very quickly. No one role is more important than another and they each compliment the other. The researchers may be the heroes, securing new knowledge, but the people who pass this information on to students, and help them apply it, are also important. It is the fortunate person who focuses on the role that she does best while performing the other roles as much or as little as she wishes.

I was very lucky the last years of my teaching career, after I left the chairperson's position, because I was able to do just that.

Chapter 55
Winding Down

One Christmas when I was in my late fifties, I received three letters in which friends, fellow faculty who were a few years older than I, wrote longingly about retiring in a few years. What was wrong with them? Then when I talked with my brother who was born twenty-two months before me, he echoed the same thoughts.

Then I had a year-long sabbatical, my seventh year in Oregon. I was surprised to discover that I could live without nursing and teaching. In fact I enjoyed myself thoroughly without those occupations. I traveled to New York and studied the issue of informed consent on a National Humanities Fellowship. When I returned to Oregon, I did research.

My study involved interviewing rural woman. I soon learned there were days when I could not make appointments. I filled the empty time by learning to type and I wrote my first novel. This epistle is now resting quietly on the shelf of my study, worn out from rejection. I learned a great deal from the effort, however.

When it was time to return to work, I wrote sad poems about the end of summer. I suspect that this was the beginning of my disengagement from work.

When I was back at work, I began to find the long committee meetings intolerable. It did help to have my needlepoint. I found that it helped me keep my mouth shut. When I was tempted to make a sharp retort, I just took another stitch and then responded rationally. No matter how much time we spent discussing and not arriving at a decision, I always accomplished something, a portion of a needlepoint pillow.

Troubling things also occurred. Katherine returned from her doctoral studies. She hadn't finished. A family member had become ill and Katherine had resigned from the school. She had been on an educational leave of absence. In order to draw out her pension to help her relative, she had to resign, and give up tenure. There was no position open in Portland when she returned to Oregon, and she was hired to teach on the La Grande campus. Eventually she did come to Portland. Time passed and she advanced no further toward the degree. She didn't publish. Then her probationary period was over and it was time to apply for tenure.

I was on the committee for our department. She applied the first year she was eligible and didn't make it. The committee, operating in an advisory capacity, felt that the best course was for her not to try a second time but to accept a fixed-term contract. She would be off the tenure track and could work year by year. There were people in her position in other departments who were working from year to year, and it was unthinkable that they would be asked to leave. If she chose to try again for tenure, and failed to meet the criteria, she would have to leave the school. Both the committee and the department chairperson told her this.

She had helped develop the department, secured the grants that financed our beginning programs, and had had tenure before she resigned. She had been at the school fifteen years. However, the school was a much different place than it had been when Katherine had been first awarded tenure.

She ignored our advice and decided to apply again. The departmental committee told her what she would need to do to gain it—publish. There was no need to publish in a prestigious journal, just get something into print. She finally prepared an article and sent it to *Nursing Research*, the most demanding nursing journal. Her paper was rejected. Tenure decisions are made by a number of people— the president, the dean, the school's committee—using explicit criteria as a guide. Katherine was not given tenure and she left the school.

She had hired me, recommended me for tenure and the chairperson's position. Yet the policies of academia dictated that I be one of the people who sent her away. At the same time, I understood that in order to achieve Carol's dream, which was also mine, we had to demand high standards from our faculty. Academia had stopped being fun.

I began to hate to leave the house each day, to leave the flowering bushes, my computer, the swimming pool, and drive the fifty miles to Portland. One of my fellow NLN visitors told me how much she enjoyed having the summers off. I'd had nine month appointments in the past, but had always found another job for the summer. I asked for a nine-month appointment.

After a few years, the letters my friends had written about retirement seemed perfectly natural, and I began to look forward to mine. It was time. I decided to retire at sixty-two.

The department gave me the mother of all retirement parties. The school had never had such an elaborate celebration. It was held in early December, close to my birthday. They hired a string quartet and instructed them to play Mozart. Verl supplied poinsettias and filled the room with them. The catered food was the finest available in Portland, and everyone from the school came to say "God speed".

A professional cameraman manned the television camera and the department gave the film to me. Dino was there snapping pictures. A book filled with cards and messages was presented to me. Carol presented me with a beautiful colonial enameled chair with a brass plate on it and the dates of my employment, 1976-1988, twelve years. People told funny stories about me, distorting the facts just a little, but they were told with warmth and affection. It was a wonderful end to a career.

When graduation came in June, the President appointed me Emeritus Professor. I've offered to teach if I am needed, and still do occasionally, but the calls have become less and less frequent.

How can it be that the career that gave me so much satisfaction could be abandoned so easily? Perhaps it was easy because it was satisfying and I accomplished what I set out to do.

I began late. Although I entered nursing school at seventeen, my goals were to marry my sweetheart, have children and live happily ever after. I believed the myths that said this was the only way for a woman to achieve happiness. When I was in my thirties, I learned the folly of this idea, and then a career became important.

I have always been persistent, but I never was possessed with driving ambition. My goals were realistic. I achieved them and managed to gain a great deal of pleasure in the process. I have been privileged to enter into the lives of thousands of nursing students and patients, and be with them, for short but crucial times. To be able to do this has been a wonderful gift.

Now is the time to explore other facets of my life that have been submerged by the demands of my career, my family and my own personal needs. When I was a child, I wanted to be a writer. Now I am writing. My book, ***Down on the Tree Farm*** was published, and I write a column for a farm newspaper. I am embarked on a new career, more confident because of the long years of pleasure and satisfaction that the careers I chose at seventeen and thirty-five—nursing and teaching—have given me.

ORDER FORM

Name _____

Address _____

City/State/Zip _____

Phone _____

Enclosed is my check/money order for **$17.95** (**$14.95** for

I Always Faint When I See a Syringe and **$3** for shipping/

handling).

Silver Tree Books
Box 707
Silverton, OR 97381

Phone **1-800-925-9979, Ext. #70** for orders
or **1-503-873-3707** for further information
or FAX to **1-503-873-8726**
or E-mail to **F3707@aol.com**

☐ Check here if you'd like the book signed by the author